TATTERED
ENSIGN

TATTERED ENSIGN

JOHN JENNINGS

NEW YORK

Thomas Y. Crowell Company

ESTABLISHED 1834

THIS
is not a book that can be
inscribed to any one man.

Therefore, I

DEDICATE
it to the men and officers of
the United States Navy of

YESTERDAY, TODAY,
and TOMORROW.

CONTENTS

1	THE SHIP	1
2	COME, BULLY BOYS!	14
3	SHAKEDOWN	26
4	AND MAIDEN VOYAGE	41
5	FLAGSHIP OF THE WEST INDIES STATION	55
6	HIGH BARBAREE	74
7	PREBLE TAKES COMMAND	98
8	TO THE SHORES OF TRIPOLI	108
9	ACTION IN THE MEDITERRANEAN	136
10	CHANGE OF COMMAND	150
11	INTERIM	160
12	FREE TRADE AND SAILORS' RIGHTS	171

13 THIN ICE 191

14 CRY HAVOC 203

15 ARMS AND THE MAN 215

16 TWISTING THE LION'S TAIL 230

17 R.H.I.P. 246

GLOSSARY OF NAUTICAL TERMS
AND SHIPBOARD DEFINITIONS 260

BIBLIOGRAPHY 276

INDEX 281

ILLUSTRATIONS

Launching in Boston Harbor, 1787   85
Capturing pirates in Tripoli, 1805   86
Chart of the Mediterranean   86
Stephen Decatur capturing Tripolitan gunboat, 1804   87
Escaping from British squadron, 1812   88
Victory over the *Guerriere*, 1812   90
Captain Isaac Hull   90
Sailors celebrating victory over *Guerriere*   91
Constitution exchanging broadsides with *Java*, 1812   92
Course of battle with *Java*   92
Battle with *Cyane* and *Levant*, 1815   181
Constitution towing captured *Cyane*   181
Andrew Jackson figurehead   182
Drydock in Portsmouth, N.H., 1855   183
Training ship for Naval Academy, 1860   183
Anchored in Newport Harbor, 1861   184
As barracks ship in Portsmouth, N.H., 1898   185
In Boston Harbor before reconstruction, 1907   185
Entering New York Harbor, 1931   186
Aerial photograph of 1931 cruise   186
After restoration, in Boston Harbor   187
Spar deck with guns   187
Annual turnaround   188
Painting of *Constitution* now in White House study   188

Aye, tear her tattered ensign down!
Long has it waved on high,
And many an eye has danced to see
That banner in the sky.
—Oliver Wendell Holmes
Old Ironsides

Scarce one tall frigate walks the sea
Or skirts the safer shores,
Of all that bore to victory
Our stout old Commodores.
—Oliver Wendell Holmes
to Admiral David Glasgow Farragut

And so our Constitution's *might*
Upheld our Constitution's right!

1

THE SHIP

S E P T E M B E R 20, 1797, came up sharp and clear and
windy, with a hint of frost in the early morning air. All
through the city and across the Common and into the countryside beyond, the leaves of the trees were turning from the cool
green of summer to the flaming gold and red and yellow and
orange of autumn. The skies above were pale blue-white and almost cloudless, and the waters of the Charles River and of the
bay below sparkled with little whitecaps and were even bluer
than the sky. Up on Beacon Hill even the already well-aged red-
brick houses on Joy Street and Mount Vernon Place and in
Louisburg Square shone as if they had just been scrubbed
with soap and water, while above them the blue slate roofs
glistened in the sunlight.

The dazzling brilliance of the day came as no surprise to the
people of Boston and the surrounding area. To them it seemed
only right and proper and what was to be expected, for this
was the day they had long been waiting for. For weeks, months,
even for years they had been looking forward to the day when
the great ship was to be launched. From the very beginning,
from the moment that her keel was laid and her frames were
raised, they had watched her grow and take form—watched
with a strange fascination and an almost overwhelming sense of
pride. Now at last the great hull was finished and all that remained was her christening and her blessing, and then the long

slide down the greased ways to the water she was to rule so proudly.

It had been fifteen years since the end of the Revolution, and in that time a whole new generation had come to spread its wings. At the same time, as soon as the fighting stopped American merchantmen once again flocked to the seas to recoup their war-shattered fortunes. This was natural. The sea and the rivers that fed it and the great bays that opened at the rivers' mouths were their natural highways. Back of the narrow strip of coastal settlements, westward across the continent, there were few roads. The sea was the natural link between them and the one highway that led to the world outside.

The northern states, most notably Massachusetts, produced corn, lumber, fish—and rum now that molasses was again available from the West Indies. The more southerly states offered cotton, flax, tobacco, indigo, more corn and other varieties of fish, and lumber. Both found their wilderness frontiers to westward a profitable source of furs. It was not long before a lucrative coastal trade sprang up between the several states, and it was not long before this spread to the West Indies and from there to more distant seas. The merchants of Massachusetts and the rest of New England quickly found out that there was a demand abroad for all the ships that they could produce out of the forests that grew in their back yards. The lumber and masting and naval stores trades flourished and shipyards sprang up on every inlet. Shipwrights and ship carpenters were in demand, and it was not long before Yankee skippers were sailing out to distant ports to sell first cargoes and then their ships themselves, so that often as not they came back home in foreign bottoms with a double profit tucked firmly in their belts.

But alluring as the prospect might seem on the surface, it was not without its drawbacks. During the War for Independence there had been a navy of sorts and some protection also was provided by the various states' navies and the privateers that swarmed out from American ports. With the coming of peace, however, the Continental Navy had been disbanded and its ships sold or broken up. The privateers had ceased to exist —except where an occasional one, rendered rapacious by his years of profit, turned to piracy and spared no one—and the several state navies were reduced to a few armed sloops and schooners which guarded the coasts and kept an eye out upon the revenues of their own inshore waters. Out upon the broad oceans and far flung seas of the world at large, the only protection for an American merchant was the swiftness of his vessel and the few small deck guns that he might carry; and as is usually the case, there were those abroad who were not slow to take advantage of the weakness.

England, for example, was one of the worst offenders. Nor is it difficult to understand why. For one thing, she smarted under the humiliation of defeat. For another, she found it difficult to realize that the new American states were no longer hers to dominate as she willed. And for a third, she feared and resented American inroads upon her long-established overseas trade. As a result, England did everything possible to hamper the upstart rival. Nor was France, late ally of the United States, much better, especially after the outbreak of the French Revolution and the resumption of hostilities with England. France first assumed that America, despite its proclamations of neutrality, would naturally espouse her cause. At once she began to make such use of American ports as suited her purpose: fitting out and repairing privateers, recruiting, and even sending in prizes. When the United States protested the action and demanded that it stop, she grew arrogant and continued to make such use of American waters as suited her needs. Moreover, she began to harass American ships at sea and in her own ports, seizing many on the flimsiest of pretexts and imprisoning their crews in dungeons both in France and in the French West Indies.

Worst of all, however, were the Barbary pirates, the Moslem corsairs who swarmed into the Mediterranean and the Atlantic out of the ports of North Africa: from Morocco, Algeria,

Tunis, and Tripoli. Quick to discover the defenselessness of the young newcomers, they seized every American ship that came their way, selling their crews into slavery, from which they could be rescued only by payment of an exorbitant ransom. Future raids could be prevented only by further payments of huge annual tributes to the North African rulers.

Under such circumstances it soon became obvious that some steps had to be taken to protect American ships and men. But the idea of anything resembling a naval force aroused opposition in Congress, since it was feared that any strong, permanent military establishment, whether on land or sea, might tend to undermine the popular civilian government. Accordingly, for several years Congress attempted to meet the problem through negotiation. But the hopelessness of this was shown when, in 1793, the Algerine corsairs pushed out into the Atlantic and seized eleven ships and some 109 captives. A letter from Captain O'Brien, one of the captives, accompanying a petition signed by the masters of thirteen captured vessels, explained to the House of Representatives the great danger to American seaborne commerce if a fleet were not fitted out promptly for its protection. The petition read in part: "Your petitioners pray you will take their unfortunate situation into consideration, and will adopt such measures as will restore the American captives to their country, their friends, families and connections; and your petitioners will ever pray and be thankful."

One chronicler commented wryly that "some of them had already prayed through eight years of hard labor!"

This apparently was the straw that broke the camel's back. The opposition to a naval force remained strong and vociferous, but it was no longer possible to deny the facts. As a result, on March 27, 1794, Congress enacted, by the slim margin of two votes, a bill calling for the establishment of "a naval force adequate to the protection of the commerce of the United States." As adopted, the bill allowed the President—still George Washington at the time—to order the construction of four ships of 44 guns each, and two of 36 guns each, or to secure by purchase and equivalent force. Arms and equipment, stores and supplies and officers and enlisted men, were provided for at the same time. By way of compromise with the opposition, no doubt in order to ensure passage of the bill, it was stipulated that if a treaty should be concluded with Algiers before the completion of the vessels, all work on them would be discontinued. Since no separate Navy Department existed or was provided for, the entire operation was placed under the direction of Secretary of War Henry Knox.

The exactness of the specifications as to the armament of the several ships was significant. At that time the principal navies of the world were chiefly composed of three distinct classes of vessels. The largest of these were the ships of the line, or "three-deckers" as they were sometimes called. They carried from 60 to 120 guns on three or more decks and were, of course, the monsters of the sea; the "dreadnoughts" of the age. They formed the backbone of the major navies and did the heavy fighting at such great fleet actions as Trafalgar, the Saints, Cape St. Vincent, the Nile, and Copenhagen. But in point of fact such huge sea battles were comparatively rare, and when they were fought required far greater numbers of the huge sea monsters than the young nation was capable of building and sending to sea. Moreover, they were slow and unwieldy, and between major engagements could be used only for purposes of station-keeping and the maintenance of blockade. In short, they were usually more awe inspiring than effective, for when it came down to ship-to-ship action they were often as not unable to use their lower tiers of guns because the rough weather made it impossible to open their lower ports. In such circumstances they were reduced, in terms of armament, to equality with the frigates which they might be engaging, while at the same time they lacked the mobility, speed, and maneuverability of the smaller ships.

The frigates, which formed the second class, were smaller, lighter, and faster ships, carrying 28 to 60 guns on two decks. In modern terms they corresponded to today's cruisers, for there was hardly a task they could not perform. They could act as advance points for the main fleet. They could serve as guards for large convoys, or they could patrol extensive areas. They could maintain communications between larger blockading vessels, or they could perform the full duties of blockaders themselves. On the other hand, they were fast and handy enough to slip through a blockade and preserve and secure communications with allies or neutrals, or simply prowl the seas singly or in groups in search of legitimate prey. On occasion they could even attack and overcome ships of the line, especially in rough weather and when they acted in concert.

The third class of vessel was the sloop of war, or, as it was sometimes called, the corvette. In ordinary civil parlance the word "sloop" usually meant a small, single-masted, fore-and-aft-rigged vessel. The sloop of war, however, was, like her two more powerful companions, ship rigged; that is to say, she carried five to seven square sails on three masts—fore, main, and mizzen—stepped in that order. She was more lightly built than a frigate, but even sharper and faster, and carried up to 30 guns on a single deck. The corvettes were also sometimes known as "ship-sloops," which was probably the best technical description of them. In point of service, the duties they performed corresponded roughly to those of today's destroyers, destroyer escorts, and coast guard cutters.

There were other types of warships of course—brigs, brigantines, schooners, ketches, cutters, and even conventionally-rigged sloops—and on occasion whaleboats—but they fell into no single regular classification, and in the main were useful only in onshore waters and local defense. The three described formed the stout backbone of the world's principal fleets.

The stipulation that the ships to be built or purchased should be 44's or 36's suggests that Congress had made a careful study of the matter. It was out of the question for the United States to build enough ships of the line to hold her own in open combat with such ship-heavy navies as those of England, France, and Spain. Even Holland and little Portugal had more ships of the line in service than America could hope to float in a short time. The sloops of war, on the other hand, were scarcely powerful enough to command the respect demanded by the situation. The choice, then, fell to the frigates, and the immediate response showed that it was a popular one. After consulting with a number of prominent shipbuilders, Secretary Knox announced the acceptance of plans and models submitted by Joshua Humphreys of Philadelphia, calling for ships which, according to Knox's report, "separately would be superior to any European frigate of the usual dimension; that if assailed by numbers they would always be able to lead ahead; that they would never be obliged to go into action but on their own terms, except in a calm; and that in heavier weather they would be capable of engaging doubledecked ships." In short, from the very outset it was determined that American naval construction should be sighted to a standard superior to any yet achieved abroad. That the naval architects and builders who produced them were successful in their aim is attested by the somewhat disgruntled remarks of some British critics who stated categorically that the American 44's, though rated as frigates, were actually, in point of size, armament, and protection the equivalent of an English 60-gun ship of the line, while in point of speed they were equal if not superior to the largest British 50-gun frigates.

All that, of course, was for the future to prove. For the moment it is enough to say that the act of March 27, 1794, marked the real birth of the United States Navy. True, the Navy Department itself was not established until 1798 and it is from that time that the navy dates its existence. Nevertheless, it remains a fact that United States naval vessels were provided for and launched some time before the navy actually came into being.

There was to be more than one delay, however, in the proceedings. In accordance with the act bids were taken and the construction sites for the various vessels promptly allotted. The 44's were to be built at Boston, New York, Philadelphia, and

Norfolk, Virginia. The 36's were to be built at Baltimore, Maryland, and Portsmouth, New Hampshire. Later, for some reason, the vessel building at Norfolk was reduced to a 36. However, our interest here is in the ship allotted to Boston. Insofar as she was concerned, beyond sharing the general designs drawn by Joshua Humphreys and Josiah Fox, her keel was laid in the yard of Edmund Hartt, in Hartt's Naval Yard, in the North End, near what is now Constitution Wharf. In charge of material procurement was John T. Morgan, a master shipwright of Boston, who ranged the colonies from Maine to Georgia to secure the best timber—white and yellow pine; red, white, water, and live oak; red cedar; and ironwood for the hulls; and maple, cherry, and chestnut for fittings. General Henry Jackson was named naval agent, through whose hands all payments passed. George Claghorne was naval constructor, and dour Captain Samuel Nicholson was named as her first commander and general overseer and inspector for the government. The ship's gun carriages were built by Edmund Thayer at the South End. Her anchors were cast at Hanover, not far from Plymouth, and her sails were made in the old Granary Building at the corner of Park and Tremont streets. The Skillings brothers carved out the first figurehead of Hercules and several other ornaments for various parts of the ship, and none other than the redoubtable Paul Revere provided the copper for the hull. According to the record he received $3,820.33 for labor and material, which included copper bolts and spikes forged by a process which he alone knew.

Thus far everything seemed to go smoothly. By the end of 1795 the ship was well along. On November 28, 1795, however, a treaty with Algiers was signed at Lisbon. Accordingly, work on the vessels stopped, as had been stipulated in the resolution establishing the navy. It did not take long to prove, however, that in its eagerness for economy Congress had been penny-wise and pound-foolish. In hard cash the Algerian treaty cost the United States nearly a million dollars—enough to build and equip several frigates—and resulted in only a shaky truce rather than a lasting peace. At the same time it transpired that the corsairs of Barbary were not our only enemies upon the sea. In 1793 the uneasy peace between Great Britain and France was once again shattered, and once more the two mightiest powers of the world at the time resumed their traditional quarrel.

By all rights the neutral American merchants and traders should have profited from the struggle. So long as they did not deal in contraband of war they should have been free to deal with either side as they saw fit individually. Unfortunately, neither England nor France was inclined to take that view of the matter, and neither was in the least concerned for the rights of neutrals. Each declared the other's ports to be in a state of complete blockade, and any vessels caught trading with the enemy, even on the high seas outside the blockaded waters, were considered fair game and subject to search and seizure. The British, having emptied their jails and exhausted their supply of felons and convicts, and finding slim pickings for their press gangs ashore, added insult to injury by impressing American seamen from American ships they stopped at sea, under the pretext that the men were in reality Englishmen sailing under false papers. On the other hand, French cruisers and privateers made themselves equally obnoxious by ignoring the President's proclamations of neutrality—closing our ports to the use of belligerents and forbidding Americans to take service with either side—by openly refitting in our waters and recruiting crews on shore. Once they had filled and sailed away, they did not hesitate to lie in wait within American inlets for ships they had observed loading with cargo for ports in England or the British West Indies.

Thus within a year the United States found itself caught between the upper and nether millstones in a situation so intolerable that Congress was forced to do something about it. Fortunately a treaty with England at that juncture momentarily relieved some of the pressure from that direction, and the United States was able to turn its attention to the French, who seemed quite put out that the Americans would not take sides with them against the English. Early in 1797 work was resumed upon the three ships nearest to completion—those at Boston, Philadelphia, and Baltimore.

Quite naturally the rivalry among the cities selected for the honor of being first to set its ship afloat ran high, but in spite of everything the Boston builders could do, Philadelphia won the race. As early as July 10 her builders sent the big frigate *United States*, a 44, smoking down the slippery ways. Bostonians, their ship still a-building, took what comfort they could from the fact that in their haste the Philadelphians had made their ways too steep, as a result of which the *United States* was injured at the outset and had to be hove down immediately for repairs. They took a reef in their belts and went back to work, confident that theirs would be the second ship to leave the ways. Moreover, they assured one another, when their turn did come the launching would run off smoothly, all shipshape and Bristol fashion, as the saying goes; nothing so slipshod and sloppy as those cunny-thumbed Philadelphians had managed.

But here again they were doomed to disappointment, for on September 7 Baltimore sent the little *Constellation*, a 36, sliding smoothly into the sparkling waters of Chesapeake Bay. This time there was no accident from which Bostonians might take cold comfort. But it was a fact that the *Constellation* was a smaller ship than their own and consequently, they told themselves, scarcely counted.

So once again they went back to their work, putting on the last finishing touches now, and here at last the great day was come and it was Boston's turn. By nightfall of the nineteenth everything was in readiness. The stands were in place. The ways were greased. The caulker's mallet had tapped home the last bit of caulking, and Hercules flourished his mighty hammer ferociously over the launching platform. In her cradle the great ship lay waiting—204 feet in over-all length and 175 feet at the waterline; 43 feet 6 inches in the beam, with a draft of 21 feet forward and 13 feet aft; 1,576 tons finished, a mighty behemoth, the largest ship that Boston had yet built. When she was launched and rigged, her masts would tower 90 to 105 feet above her deck, and her lower yards would spread 60 to 95 feet of canvas across them. Nothing else remained to be done aboard for the moment. That night she rested. In the morning, all the world was confident, she would shake herself a little, with an anticipatory shudder, and then slip smoothly but with gathering speed down the ways to the waiting water and her destiny.

All through the early hours of the day the crowds gathered; thousands of them, trooping in from the countryside around, from as far away as Fitchburg and Worcester, while many came from as far away as Springfield. Even before the sun rose the workmen were at the yard making the final preparations for the great event. By sunup there were enough early onlookers to get in their way, and an hour later the stands were beginning to fill. When there was no more room there, the crowds began to overflow to the nearby wharves and jetties and the neighboring roofs; any place that offered a good view of the proceedings. Small boats, overladen and packed with spectators, began to choke the channel outside. Colonel George Claghorne, the naval constructor, and Captain Nicholson, the general overseer and sometime first commander, were the first celebrities to arrive; Claghorne suave, elegant, courteous, the perfect politician; Nicholson rock-faced and hard-bitten, rough-cut and rough-spoken, with a cold, piercing eye and the harsh manner of a martinet. The colonel glanced at the already-crowded wharves and choking cluster of small boats and sent orders to the constables to clear the way. A ship of this size, at launching, was likely to send up a small tidal wave that could sweep many watchers from the wharves' edges and swamp unwary small boats that crowded up too close. Nicholson merely growled his approval of the preparations and ordered that no one was to touch the signal halyards without his command. He planned to hoist the first flag over her with his own hands.

But the tide was still making, scarcely yet up to the quarter mark, and not until the water had reached its full September peak could such an immense ship be launched. There was time for breakfast and a toddy, and the captain hinted that his vitals could stand some warming. They took advantage of the opportunity, and when they returned they found that some prankster had seized the chance to hoist a huge American ensign at the fore. According to the record it was Sam Bentley, a caulker, who raised the flag. Nicholson had served as a lieutenant with John Paul Jones aboard the *Bonhomme Richard* in her engagement with the *Serapis* during the Revolution, and for this he was entitled to respect. But he was never popular, either in the yard or aboard ship later. At this time he swore, in fine seafarer's language loud enough to be heard throughout the yard, that he would have Bentley flayed alive and hung at the yardarm. But the caulker survived in Boston, full of years and respectability, until 1852—which is more than could be said for the captain by many a year.

For all his fuss and bluster, however, Nicholson did not haul down the flag once it had been raised. The hour finally arrived. The tide was high, and the speeches—such as could be heard in that day before loudspeakers—were over. A hush fell on the waiting throng. Captain Nicholson, as the ship's first commanding officer, stepped forward.

"I christen thee *Constitution!*" he shouted, and smashed a bottle across her overhanging cutwater.

An expectant silence fell over the gathered throng. One could almost feel them step back a pace. The mauls swung and the holding wedges squirted out. The ship shuddered, moved, and began to slide and gather momentum, and as she moved the sound of the great crowd's breath, indrawn for a lusty cheer, was like a gusty wind on forest leaves.

But it was a cheer that never came. Ten—fifteen—twenty feet the big ship slid with evidently increasing speed, covering that distance as quickly as it takes to tell. Then suddenly it lost momentum, and at twenty-seven feet it shuddered to a grinding halt. The pent-up breath of the crowd escaped in a sort of moaning sob.

Even before Colonel Claghorne could order them to it, the workmen of the launching crew were swarming down. With screws and wedges, bars and hammers and prayers they labored for more than two hours to free her and start her on her way, but she would not budge. By that time the tide had turned and had ebbed so much that the colonel deemed it unsafe to continue the effort, and he sent down orders to shore her up and set blocks to prevent any further movement until a complete examination could be made to determine the cause of the failure and what damage, if any, she might have suffered.

Only then did the flag come down and the captain, mortified and crestfallen, stump off home to an extra dram of Medford rum. Behind him the multitude sighed and shook its collective head and slowly melted away. Disappointment would have been the mildest word to describe the general mood. Chagrin, humiliation, hurt would have been more apt. There were some who said it had been an ill day for Boston and a worse one for the ship. An evil omen, they called it, for, they argued, what ship could ever be a lucky one with such a start?

2

COME, BULLY BOYS!

BOSTON'S MEN are notoriously stubborn and hard-headed. It would be surprising if the ships she produced, as well as the men that sailed them, did not partake of the same rock-ribbed character. The initial failure of the *Constitution*'s launch was a disappointment. More, it was a sore humiliation, for instead of making Philadelphia eat crow they found themselves facing much the same dish. There was only one thing to do: eat it and at least pretend to like it. After all, whatever the circumstances, there was no doubt in their minds that theirs was the better ship.

There was another attempt at a launch on the following day. But once again it ended in failure. Careful examination then showed that the ways on which the *Constitution* had been built, never intended for a ship of such size, had settled under her weight to such an extent that there was not enough incline left to allow free passage to the water. A further examination showed that her keel had suffered some slight damage, which must also be repaired before another attempt could be made. Such things take time, however, and it was not for another full month that she was finally ready.

There is an old story, still extant in the navy, regarding the launching of the *Constitution*. In substance it tells how, at the first attempt, a bottle of brackish Charles River water was used for the christening. The ship shivered indignantly and then moved grudgingly a short distance down the ways and came to an immovable halt. The next day a second effort was made, this time using good salt water from the lower harbor. This time she shivered again, and moved about thirty feet farther. There she stayed and would not budge again until some thirty days later, when the jovial old sea dog Captain James Sever came down from Portsmouth, New Hampshire, with a bottle of fine old Madeira which he smashed across her bows, showering the beard of Hercules with the good grape juice.

"Now then!" some say he snapped. "Take a lick o' that and git down there where ye belong about yer business. Let's have no more o' this nonsense!"

And to the amazement of all she shook herself once more and then slid off into the bay. Whether or not it was the Madeira that made the difference, the *Constitution* finally was launched on the 21st of October, 1797. All the difficulties and embarrassments of the past few weeks were forgotten, and Boston men could give a smile of pride and relief and go home to drink another cup, this time in toast to a gallant ship. Might she enjoy a long and glorious career and serve notice on the world that she and the nation for which she stood were not to be taken lightly!

But there was yet much to be done. Even today ships are not launched fully rigged and manned ready for sea. The *Constitution* was scarcely an exception. Her masts had yet to be fished—that is to say, spliced—for in the sailing vessels of that day none of the masts stood in a single solid piece. Only the lower sections of the fore, main, and mizzen masts were solid from their rests upon the keelson to a point that ranged anywhere from 70 to 105 feet above the keel, depending upon the size of the ship itself. (In the case of the *Constitution* the dimensions of these foundation masts were: foremast, 96 feet; mainmast, 105 feet 6 inches; mizzenmast, 90 feet.) The topmasts, which were the next section, overlapped these tall stumps by several feet and were fastened securely in place by a complicated system of *fids* and *bibbs, trestletrees* and *crosstrees,* each one of which had its own bracing function. Topgallant, royal and skysail masts were fitted together and secured in much the same manner, so that the main trunk was extended several times over. The ultimate height of the *Constitution*'s masts, for instance, from truck to keelson, was: fore, 198 feet 3 inches; main, 220 feet; mizzen, 178 feet 10 inches.

After all, however, when the ship's masts had been fished, fidded, and bibbed, there was good reason for the procedure however strange the nomenclature might sound. In the first place, it was next to impossible to find a flawless single stick of the necessary over-all length in all the forests of New England. In the second place, had such a spar been found and installed and the vessel sent to sea, it would have been nearly impossible to replace had it been carried away by a storm or an enemy's shot. By the piecemeal construction then in use, however, a broken section could be replaced with materials carried on board, even while the ship was still at sea.

But this was only a small part of the work that was yet to be done to ready the ship for sea. She had to be rigged from stem to stern, alow and aloft, her yards set and braced and canvas bent on. Her hull, of course, had been painted before she was launched, but there was still painting and carpentry to be done on deck and below. She must be armed, victualled, provisioned, equipped with everything necessary for sound navigation from tar to charts, cables to lead lines; log chips, binnacle, lines and brass. She must have two anchors forward and a bower stowed by the foremast with two extra spares in the boatswain's locker. The wardroom and officers' quarters must be precisely built, and it needed a cabinetmaker to finish the interior of the captain's quarters and the several staterooms for official passengers, for in those days it was customary for public, armed vessels to carry diplomats and government emissaries to and from their posts, or sometimes even to accommodate the senior officers' families.

Arming the big ship was scarcely less complicated than rigging her, and was probably much more frustrating. Certainly it has since confused a good many latter-day historians, for no two seem to agree upon her original armament. The small arms—muskets, cutlasses, pistols, pikes, and the like—of course, were stowed in the armorer's locker, while the magazine and shot locker were placed far in the bowels of the ship, next to the bread locker, the spirit locker, and the cockpit—the bloody, butcher station of the surgeon and his mates during action, since down there, just over the bilges, there was the least chance of being hit by the shot that whizzed overhead. This much was simply routine and similar in all men-of-war, so that it presented little problem.

Up above, on the quarterdeck and the forecastle and on the gun deck where the main batteries and the great guns were ranged, it was apparently not so simple. The original plans called for some thirty long 24-pounders on the gun deck plus twenty to twenty-two long 12's on the forecastle and the quarterdeck and two more long 24's on the forecastle as chase guns. This seems to be pretty generally accepted and presents no problem beyond the fact that had the plan been carried out she would have carried fifty-two to fifty-four guns instead of the forty-four she was rated. However, at that time it was common practice for a man-of-war to carry several more guns than she was rated.

What she actually did carry, however, is less clear. In accordance with the foregoing plan, twenty-eight of the long 24's were mounted on the gun deck, and perhaps two more on the forecastle as chase guns. The battery for the upper decks—the quarterdeck and the forecastle—however, is less generally agreed upon, and in this connection it should be remembered that not until nearly seven months after the *Constitution* was launched did the Navy Department, as a separate branch of the government, come into existence. Prior to that the work had been carried out under the aegis of the War Department, and consequently some confusion of records is understandable.

Somewhere along the line the plans for the upper batteries had been altered to call for twenty to twenty-two 42-pounder carronades to replace the original long 12's. For the benefit of those unfamiliar with the terminology, the "long guns" had a much greater range and were far more accurate than the carronades, but the latter could throw a much greater weight of metal for a shorter distance and were accordingly invaluable when it came to the close infighting that most ship-to-ship engagements eventually boiled down to.

But here is where the discrepancies begin to appear. One authority simply states that the *Constitution* appears to have carried 32-pounder carronades instead of 42's during her early career, and lets it go at that. A second authority states that the carronades on the upper decks were replaced by a battery of ten long 12's, and that these were the guns she carried throughout what has since come to be known as our "quasi-war with France." Still a third authority, Mr. Bruce Grant, in his biography of Isaac Hull, fourth lieutenant on the *Constitution* at the time of her commissioning and destined to become perhaps her most outstanding commander in time to come, gives us yet another account. According to this, when the guns for the upper decks did not arrive—long 12's by his account—Captain Nicholson went in search of guns to take their place. At Castle Island, in Boston Harbor, he found nineteen long 18's, evidently designed for ship's use but mounted for harbor defense and belonging to the State of Massachusetts. To give the story in its bare bones, the governor of Massachusetts agreed to release the 18's to the *Constitution* on the War Department's promise to replace them with 32-pounders.

Since Mr. Grant cites chapter and verse, even to the extent of quoting correspondence between Captain Nicholson and Mr. McHenry, the secretary of war, and between the latter and the governor of Massachusetts; and since 18's would be a much more logical arm for a vessel of the *Constitution*'s size than 12's, I for one am inclined to credit Mr. Grant's findings, and accept it for a fact that the big ship's first battery consisted of twenty-eight or thirty long 24's and nineteen 18's, giving her a maximum over-all armament of forty-nine, not counting the smaller guns mounted in the tops.

The point is that commanding officers at that time were given great latitude in such matters. Over the years the ship's batteries were changed many times in accord with the theories most favored by the man who happened to be in command of her at the moment. As much as one can hope to do here is to give some idea of the new ship's fire power. It would be fruitless, not to say tedious, to list every change that was made in the years that followed. Accordingly beyond this we will note only the batteries she carried during her major campaigns and principal actions. For the rest it may be assumed that she was adequately armed.

The job of arming the vessel was only half of what had to be done, for no ship could sail without a crew, and no crew could work efficiently as a team without proper officers to direct it. By the same token the day had not yet arrived when guns could be pointed by remote control and fired at the push of a distant button. In short, before she could go to sea the *Constitution* had to be manned; a crew shipped and at least partially trained. That is to say, they must be seamen, of course—bluewater sailors—but even they would have to be shown the ways and whys and wherefores of life in a man-of-war.

In all fairness it must be said that the problem had not been entirely unanticipated. As early as June 1794, after the six new ships had been authorized by Congress, steps had been taken to appoint fully qualified commanders for them. At that time six captains were named and listed in their order of precedence. All were veterans of the Revolutionary service, which was, after all, the only yardstick that could be applied at that date. They were John Barry, who had commanded the *Lexington*, the *Raleigh*, and the *Alliance;* Samuel Nicholson, who had commanded the cutter *Dolphin* and the frigate *Deane;* Silas Talbot, who had not commanded a Continental vessel but had rendered valuable aid by capturing, in a Rhode Island cruiser, the British schooners *Pigot, Lively, King George, Adventure, Elliot,* and *Dragon* in Long Island waters; not to mention helping to transport Washington's army from the siege of Bos-

ton to Brooklyn and the Battle of Long Island, spending time
as a prisoner of war in the old *Jersey*, the British prison hulk
of evil fame in Wallebogt Bay, and in the Old Mill Prison,
whence with Richard Dale he was one of the few who managed
to effect an escape. He had also served with the Revolutionary
army, and held the rank of major.

Joshua Barney ranked fourth by list. He had served with
the Continental Navy from its inception, and he distinguished
himself in many ways, especially in his action with the *General
Monk* and his contacts with the American commissioners
abroad: Franklin, Deane, and Lee. It was he who brought back
to America the news of the Treaty of Paris, that brought the
Revolution to a close, and he, too, was one of that select fra-
ternity—an escapee from Mill Prison.

Whether or not jealousies ran higher in those days in matters of rank it is difficult to say, but from the present point of
view a lot of fine men wasted a great deal of time—not to mention impairing their subsequent careers—in wrangling about
who had priority over whom! It was the feeling that he had
been passed over, for instance, that prompted Benedict Arnold
to turn his coat. John Stark packed up and went home in 1777,
after the Battle of Princeton, when he felt that younger, less
experienced men had been passed over him, while Gate's jealousy of Washington is well known. Fortunately only Arnold
took the course he did, but the pattern speaks eloquently of the
day. It was a time when men were bitterly jealous of their
"honor" and would brook no slightest reflection upon it.

So it was in Captain Barney's case. Though he was a friend
of Talbot's and both had been friends in captivity, still he
maintained that Talbot had never served under regular commission, and that therefore he should not be ranked before him.
Reasoning so he declined to serve, and his place was taken by
James Sever, who seems to have had less in the way of experience than either of them to offer!

Fifth on the list of captains was Richard Dale. As one time
master on the *Lexington* at the time of her capture, and later
first lieutenant of the *Bonhomme Richard* in her memorable

battle with the *Serapis,* he was surely as well qualified as Sever to step up into Barney's vacated spot, but apparently he offered no objection and accordingly stayed where he was for the time being.

Last on the list was crusty old Thomas Truxtun who, like Talbot, had never served under any regular commission, but who had given a brilliant account of himself as a privateer.

Each of these captains was allowed the privilege of selecting his own lieutenants and other officers, and these were to take precedence according to the standing of their commanding officer. Captain Barry's first lieutenant outranked all others down the line. Lieutenant Russell, who served as first lieutenant under Samuel Nicholson—second on the captains' list—was second on the list of lieutenants. The system was confusing enough, but one thing is clear: Isaac Hull, who was fourth lieutenant of the *Constitution* under Captain Nicholson, was well down the line. Nevertheless we will hear more of him—much more!

All of this, though it was calculated to solve the problem, scarcely went off without a hitch. Each of the new ship's captains encountered more or less personal jealousy and jockeying for position. Indeed, some even contributed to it in more ways than one. Truxtun, for instance, quarreled with the commander of the marine detachment aboard on the issue of divided command, and even went so far as to write a letter to the secretary of the navy—the Navy Department by then had come into existence—threatening to throw the marines assigned to the *Constellation* ashore unless they recognized his supreme command and did equal duty with the seamen. He would appoint his own marines from among his crew, he said, and they would be responsible solely to him. Whether or not he was right is beside the point. The case is cited simply as an example of the sort of dispute that some skippers were involved in.

The *Constitution* was no exception. As has already been more than hinted, Captain Nicholson was not a popular man. The best proof of the fact is that the first appointment for first lieutenant was offered to Edward Preble of Falmouth (now

Portland), Maine. Apparently, at first, Preble was satisfied, perhaps even pleased, at being selected. He even got as far as Boston. But on arrival there he learned that he was to serve under Nicholson and lost no time in declining the commission. Lieutenant Charles C. Russell ultimately filled the post, and did so most creditably. The second lieutenant appears to have been either John Blake Cordis or Benjamin Lee—records do not agree. Richard C. Beale was third, and as already noted, Isaac Hull was fourth.

These officers had their duties on board. They stood watch. They supervised the final touches of rigging and construction. (I speak now of the duties immediately following the launching. Later, at sea, their duties would be no less stringent, though they might be much less diversified.) In addition it was part of their task to build up a crew, and this called for ingenuity and wit, and sometimes conviviality. They took turns. Recruiting stations were set up in Boston and north, through Lynn, Swampscott, and Newburyport; south through Duxbury and Plymouth and out on Cape Cod; while the hinterlands where farm boys might long to escape the plough—Worcester, Marlboro, and even Springfield—were not ignored. The following poster, circulated throughout New England, is worth quoting:

FRIGATE CONSTITUTION

To all ABLE BODIED and PATRIOTIC SEAMEN, who are willing to serve their Country and support its Cause:

The President of the United States, having ordered the Captain and Commander of the good Frigate CONSTITUTION, of 44 guns, now riding in the harbor of *Boston*, to employ the most *vigorous exertions* to put said ship, as speedily as possible, in a situation to sail at the shortest possible command.

Notice is hereby given, that a HOUSE OF RENDEZVOUS is opened at the sign of the FEDERAL EAGLE, kept by Mrs BROADERS in Fore-street;—where ONE-HUNDRED and FIFTY able Seamen, and NINETY-FIVE ordinary Seamen, will have an opportunity of entering into the service of their country for One Year, unless sooner discharged by the President of the United States.—To all able bodied Seamen, the sum of SEVENTEEN DOLLARS; and to all ordinary Seamen the sum of TEN DOLLARS per month will be given; and two months advance will be paid by the Recruiting Officer, if necessary.

None will be allowed to enter this honorable service, but such as are well organized, healthy and robust; free from scorbutic and consumptive affections.

A glorious opportunity now presents to the brave and hardy Seamen of New England to enter the service of their country—to avenge its wrongs—and to protect its rights on the ocean. Those brave lads, are now invited to repair to the FLAGG of the CONSTITUTION, now flying at the above rendezvous; where they will be kindly treated, handsomely entertained, and may enter into immediate pay.

SAMUEL NICHOLSON

Commander, United States Frigate CONSTITUTION.

At the above rendezvous Lt. Clark of the Marine, will enlist three Sargeants, three Corporals, one Armourer, one Drummer, one Fifer, and fifty privates to compose a company for the ship CONSTITUTION. None can be inlisted who are not five feet six inches high.

BOSTON, MASSACHUSETTS, MAY 12

In connection with that postscript, it is of some interest to note that the marines received only $6 per month and were the lowest paid living souls on board with the possible exception of the boys. Actually the Marine Corps was not officially established until July 11, 1798, and at that time only the pay of officers was increased slightly.

In spite of the alluring prospects held out by the posters and handbills and the blandishments of the recruiting officers, the free grog and the good fellowship, the task of filling out the crew went forward slowly. Obviously, for all the pride Bostonians took in their spanking new frigate, and for all their impatience to see her float, few were so enthusiastic as to want to sail in her. Obviously Captain Nicholson's reputation as a "sundowner" (the term originally was applied to a strict skipper who insisted upon all hands being on board by sunset, but it was later expanded to apply to any martinet or strict disci-

plinarian, a stickler for form, one who goes by the book) had
gone before him and even the hardiest seamen were reluctant to
serve under him. When the *Constitution* had first been authorized in 1794, her crew had been officially designated by Congress at 359 officers and men. Upon the formation of the Navy
Department in April 1798, however, the ship's complement was
expanded to some 400 all told: 22 officers and 378 men, listed
as follows:

Commander	1
Lieutenants	4
Lieut. marines	2
Sailing master	1
Master's mates	2
Midshipmen	8
Purser	1
Surgeon	1
Surgeon's mates	2
Clerk	1
Carpenter	1
Carpenter's mates	2
Boatswain	1
Boatswain's mates	2
Yeoman of gun room	1
Gunner	1
Quarter gunners	11
Coxswain	1
Sailmaker	1
Cooper	1
Steward	1
Armorer	1
Master-at-Arms	1
Cook	1
Chaplain	1
Able seamen	120
Ordinary seamen	150
Boys	30
Marines	50
Total	400

This number was increased to nearly 500 about the time the carronades were added to the battery.

But it is one thing to authorize a ship's crew on paper. It is quite another to cajole them aboard. The fact remains that by the time Captain Nicholson at last deemed his ship ready for sea, in July 1798, seven months after launching, her total complement numbered 388 men, officers, and boys.

3

SHAKEDOWN

I T had been many a long and weary month from the moment when the detailed plans for the *Constitution* were first laid down on the drawing boards to the day when, at last, she rode confidently to her cables, fully rigged and armed, victualled, manned and officered, and ready for sea. Indeed it had been close to four years since the pencil had first been put to the drawings, and during those years a good many tides had ebbed and flowed, both nautically and politically. The complexion of American policy had shifted with them. So had the foreign political climate changed, in ways over which we had no control but which still had a profound effect upon our overseas relations. That effect was felt throughout our political structure, but perhaps it was most emphatically felt in the destiny of our navy as a whole, and upon that of the frigate *Constitution* in particular.

Perhaps the most striking illustration of that fact is that, although she had been first conceived with the principal thought of asserting American power in the Mediterranean against the Barbary corsairs, by the time she was completed and sent to sea the pirates of North Africa had become a forgotten issue for the time being. When the *Constitution* finally sailed, she sailed against the nation's erstwhile allies—the French. The paradox calls for explanation. So does the three-year delay in the vessel's completion.

Long before the passage of the Naval Establishment Act, in

1794, authorizing the construction of the six frigates, ominous clouds had been gathering over Europe. In 1792 the French Revolution, actually begun in July 1789 with the destruction of the Bastille, came to a violent head in the storming of the Tuilleries and the September massacres; the arrest and trial of the king, Louis XVI, and the establishment of the National Convention and the Republic of France. In those times communications were often exasperatingly slow, and it was not until December that news of the coup d'état reached America. For three months and more after that a series of savage westerly storms lashed the Atlantic, cutting communications with Europe, at least westbound, so completely that no further news was heard of events in France until early in April, when it was suddenly learned that Louis XVI had been beheaded on January 21, 1793, and that France had declared war on England, Holland, and Spain on the first of February!

The first item, though grim and shocking, was of no immediate concern to Americans. The second, however, was of very great consequence, for it placed the United States squarely between two millstones and actually brought a war in which it had no stake to this nation's very shores. It is perhaps significant of the shape of things to come that even as the news of the Anglo-French clash was spreading through the nation—on April 8, to be exact—the new minister from the Republic of France to the United States, Citizen Edmond Charles Genêt, landed at Charleston, South Carolina, a considerable distance from Philadelphia, which was by then the temporary seat of government pending the construction of a new capital city on the banks of the Potomac.

It was also the most convenient *pied-à-terre*, for apparently Citizen Genêt was in no hurry to present his credentials. He had, it appeared, other fish to fry. He evidently believed that American gratitude for French aid during the Revolution, along with the Franco-American treaty of 1778, would incline the U.S. to the French side and blind American eyes to any treaties this nation may have signed with the English, for he brought with him a trunkful of blank letters of marque, which he was empowered to issue at his own discretion to "French" privateers, bought, fitted, and recruited in our ports. Furthermore, these privateers were to be based in American waters. Their prizes might be sent into American ports for adjudication by French consuls, who were empowered to sit as properly constituted courts of admiralty! Several such "commissions" were issued in Charleston even before Genêt's credentials were recognized, or even known, to the American government. Others were issued as Citizen Genêt made his leisurely way northward. The cloak with which they were covered was the contention that the treaty of 1778 permitted such action; but that Genêt and his government were well aware that that cloak was slightly threadbare is witnessed by the landing at Charleston and the long, slow journey north.

Such acts—and they grew steadily more flagrant as the Citizen journeyed up the coast—were in undeniable violation of United States national sovereignty. In the words of Alexander Hamilton:

The equipping, manning, and commissioning of vessels of war— the enlisting, levying, or raising of men for military service, whether by land or sea, all which are essentially of the same nature, are among the highest and most important exercises of sovereignty. . . .

It is manifestly contrary to the duty of a neutral nation to suffer itself to be made the instrument of hostility by one Power at war against another. In doing so such nation becomes an associate, a party.

The United States would become effectually an instrument of hostility to France against the other Powers at war, if France could, *ad libitum*, build, equip, and commission, in their ports, vessels of war—man those vessels with their seamen—send them out of their ports to cruise against the enemies of France—bring or send the vessels and property taken from those enemies into their ports—dispose of them there; with a right to repeat these expeditions as often as she should find it expedient.

(Hamilton Papers, May 15, 1793)

In other words, should the United States permit Citizen Genêt to continue his game, he must certainly jeopardize its neutrality, let alone insult its integrity, and quite possibly drag it into an unwanted war with England.

When the United States government protested, Genêt flew into a rage and threatened to appeal to the American people over the heads of the President and his advisers. Naturally there was nothing left to do but to demand Genêt's recall. This appeared to be quite agreeable to the French, who were aghast at the way in which the man who had been sent out with orders to make friends with the Americans had so ineptly managed to alienate us. Certainly the Citizen was not of the suave and slippery school of Talleyrand!

As a sequel, though it has little to do with the story of the *Constitution*, Citizen Joseph Fauchet was sent out to replace Genêt, with orders for the latter's arrest and return to France. However, Genêt apparently had a healthy regard for his neck and preferred to remain in America. Washington refused to extradite him on grounds of humanity. Genêt married a daughter of Governor Clinton of New York and settled down to the respectable and bucolic life of a country squire on the banks of the Hudson—where his name is still perpetuated. Fauchet proved little improvement over his predecessor, though he did eventually go back home.

Despite the Genêt episode, however, most Americans failed to recognize the full significance of what was happening. For the moment the whole force of American resentment was centered on the Barbary powers in general and Algiers in particular. But even at that, such was the American mistrust of military power, either on land or at sea, that the act authorizing the construction of the six frigates passed by only the narrowest of margins, and then only after the addition of a rider stipulating that if an agreement should be reached with Algiers all work on the ships would cease. (Incidentally, among those who voted against the bill was James Madison of Virginia, who was only too happy to have those same ships some eighteen years later, during the War of 1812.)

As matters fell out, scarcely more than a year later, in 1795, just such a treaty was concluded with Algiers. It was a treaty that brought little luster to American honor, for it cost close to a million dollars in tribute and ransom, arms, munitions, and naval stores, and even a fine frigate. Since the total outlay for the six ships, completed, manned and ready for sea, would have come to only a little more than a million, this was a sorry bargain. Had the U.S. rejected the Algerine terms and gone ahead with its plans, it would have had ships in service long before it did—probably in plenty of time to administer the drubbing to the Barbary states that it eventually had to give them anyway. However, the U.S. kept its end of the bargain. In the shipyards the creaking of block and tackle, the rasp of the hand-held wood saw, the clatter and thump of hammer and maul, and the hum of voices ceased and silence settled over the half-finished skeletons standing stark and lonely and seemingly abandoned on the deserted ways. That piece of short-sighted penny-pinching alone cost almost a year's time in the completion of the *Constitution, United States,* and *Constellation.* More in the case of the other vessels.

But, as an old saying straight from the sea expresses it: " 'Tis an ill wind that blows no man good." And it might be counted so in this case. While all this was going on, matters were not at a standstill in Europe, and having bought our way out of the Algerine impasse, we were allowed a brief moment in which to take off our blinders and look around. The English, at sea, grew ever more truculent as they themselves became more deeply involved in their fight with France. By orders in council they expanded their lists of forbidden articles destined for continental ports, and more and more frequently they halted American ships at sea, seizing them upon one pretext or another half the time, or impressing such men as they needed when they allowed the ships to continue on their voyage. At the same time the French were equally obnoxious. While they did not try to impress American seamen, they made it known by decree that neutrals—meaning specifically the United States— who dealt with their enemies might expect the same treatment from them that they were willing to accept from the English, and to emphasize their point they did not hesitate to make prize of American ships by fair means or foul, and in place of impressment flung their crews into foul French jails.

That was enough to make the situation unbearable, but the French went even further. When the United States sent a trio of negotiators to France to try to adjust matters the Directory, which had succeeded the National Convention, refused to receive them. Unofficially they were greeted by the French foreign minister, Talleyrand, and later approached by a trio of French agents, known best to history as X, Y, and Z, who suggested that a loan of some ten million dollars and a bribe of $240,000 would bring consideration of American claims. It was C. C. Pinckney who replied: "No! No! Not a sixpence!" (later distorted by the American press to "Millions for defense, but not one cent for tribute!") and broke off negotiations.

Meanwhile, tension with England had eased somewhat, though there were many who had advocated war, and for a time it had been touch and go. John Jay, in London, had managed to reach a somewhat ambiguous agreement in that quarter which, though it fell far short of what had been hoped for, did at least gain some concessions. Though the orders in council still remained on the British books, they were less rigorously enforced; certain areas of trade were reopened to American vessels, and both sides agreed to submit their claims to joint commissions for restitution.

Naturally the French were something less than pleased. They accused the United States of duplicity and threatened to send ships of war into American ports and waters to seize any vessel caught trading with the British or their colonial possessions no matter what their cargo. Obviously the situation was fast growing too hot to handle by peaceable means. Something had to give, and shipowners, pausing to take a second look, reminded themselves that the English at least made some recompense for the ships they seized. The French offered nothing at all.

In that situation Washington recommended and Congress

stirred to action. The original six frigates authorized by the Naval Act still stood in the stocks in stages of partial completion. They, at least, would be better than nothing as a means of defense. Accordingly the necessary appropriations were made, the orders were issued to complete the three frigates most nearly ready: the *Constitution, United States,* and *Constellation,* and life returned to the shipyards of Boston, Philadelphia, and Baltimore.

It was a beginning, and we have already witnessed its most immediate results. But there were others. On May 3, 1798, after a stiff fight in Congress, the Navy Department was established as a separate and distinct entity apart from the War Department and on the 21st of the same month Benjamin Stoddert was named as our first secretary of the navy. On July 7 all treaties with France were declared officially and legally at an end, thus terminating every vestige of alliance with that nation. Some congressional hotheads clamored for an immediate declaration of war, but John Adams, who had succeeded Washington as President, opposed any such action. To declare war, he argued, might be construed by the rest of the world as an act of aggression; an interpretation that would not only be erroneous, but might lead to even greater and more involved international complications than we were prepared to cope with at that moment. All that the United States wanted, he pointed out, was to protect its own rights upon the sea, and this it could and should do without a declaration of war. If efforts in this direction so infuriated other nations that they deemed recourse to war necessary, then let them be the first to declare it. In the meantime let Americans take every measure that they could to defend their ships, and their country's shores and its waters.

This was the thinking behind the undeclared naval war with France—or what has since come to be known as the "quasi-war." Undeclared it may have been, but it was certainly war nonetheless. Furthermore, this was our first challenge to an outside power since our birth as a nation. It was our first "shooting" war after the Revolution.

Such also was the situation when, on July 2, 1798, the frigate *Constitution* cast off from her moorings at the Long Wharf and stood down the harbor for her first test under sail. It was a moment of excitement and anticipation—excitement for what might lie ahead, anticipation to know how the ship herself would handle. There had been conflicting predictions, doubtless colored by the political leanings of the prophets. Some opined that she was too heavily sparred, and consequently would tend to be top-heavy and might even capsize. Others predicted that she was too heavily ballasted, too broad in the beam, too ponderous for her rate, and that she would be sluggish. Defenders replied that her rig was indeed extensive, but that it was proportioned to her construction, which, in turn, was heavier than was generally true of vessels of her rated class. By American standards she was a 44-gun frigate, though she was capable of carrying at least ten or twelve more guns and usually did—this not counting the small-caliber guns in her tops and similar strategic places whence a blast of grape or langrage would be most effective. In general bulk she was much stouter than British frigates of a similar class. But at the same time she was extraordinarily fast—faster even, as it proved, than many of the sharp French frigates, at that time considered the fastest ships afloat. British naval historians have often called her a heavy, frigate-rigged ship, and compared her arms and power with those of one of their own smaller ships of the line, which is probably fair enough. On more than one occasion she showed herself capable of standing up to ships rating as 50's and even more, but the basic difference was not altogether in her comparative armament or structure. The officers who commanded her and the crews that manned her were equally to be credited. War is not like a game of cricket or football, to be played by a set of rules laid down beforehand, though it has often been considered in that light by armchair strategists. Actually it is a grim business of the survival of the fittest—and the most ingenious. Americans have always been noted as innovators, adapting whatever came handiest at the moment to the immediate needs. In this case they set the pattern, and certainly there could be no complaint about the *Constitution*'s first performance.

This is not to suggest that this was a "glory voyage." Far from it! Actually it was just plain, ordinary, everyday sheer routine, humdrum as ham and eggs, but there was not a man aboard who thought of it that way. There were 390 ship's people on board. This counted only the ship's properly signed company, not the "supernumeraries" or possible women, for in that day it was fairly common for a sea-going man, whether officer or foremast hand, to take his "wife" with him. Many a brawling babe was born between the batteries on the gun deck while the ship was at sea—whence the well known term "son-of-a-gun." The roster, of course, showed only those officers and men who had signed the articles and were legally attached to the ship. "Supernumeraries" were those "young gentlemen of family and ability" who for one reason or another were not quite ready to sign as either officers or crew but who wanted to go along for the adventure, and whose social or political futures might be more or less involved with the success of the cruise. That is to say, they paid their own way, maintained their own mess, ate their own food, drank their own wine—all of which they brought on board with them and paid for out of their own pockets. They were treated generally as passengers, but might be called upon—and usually were—to act as members of the crew, to work or fight as the need arose. Many a fine officer, it should be added, grew out of such a start. But at the same time more fell by the wayside.

The day was fair, with the wind coming moderately from the west by a little north, which meant that she would have it almost squarely abeam at the start, then over her starboard quarter as she swung into the channel, and finally almost dead astern as she turned into the King (now President) Roads, about as fair a breeze as any skipper could ask. To offset this advantage the tide was setting in strong, so that it would be against her all the way. In ordinary circumstances Captain

Nicholson would probably not have chosen that moment, but would have waited for a time when both wind and tide were in his favor. But this time it was something in the nature of a test of ship and crew, and it could hardly be considered a fair one if all the elements were in their favor.

At that it was not a long or exhausting voyage. Indeed, it lasted exactly twenty minutes. But that was all the time Captain Sam Nicholson needed to find out what minor adjustments were needed to make her fit for sea. It was exactly 1250 hours when she cast off from the Long Wharf and stood downstream under topsails and her fore-topmast staysail until she had swung round into the main channel and come abreast of Castle Island, where she was duly saluted by the guns of Fort Independence, and though there seems to be no record of the fact it is reasonable to suppose that a correct response was returned. At the same time she shook out her topgallant sails, and the gesture brought thunderous cheers from the crowds ashore, who had come to watch, and from hundreds of small harbor craft and pleasure boats that had thronged to escort her seaward. Beyond that point her speed increased under the added press of canvas and, leaving her swarming convoy behind, she sped on into the Roads, where at 1:10 P.M., she came to anchor beyond Spectacle Island, twenty minutes and three short miles from her point of departure. Not a long voyage, or a spectacular one, but it proved a number of points in addition to bringing out those small defects that must be adjusted before the ship would be entirely ready for sea. For one, it gave a good foretaste of her sailing qualities, showing that she handled well even in constricted waters and against the tide. It also hinted at her speed, for under such light canvas in the face of an adverse current of considerable strength her nine miles per hour, while nothing hair-raising today, was a respectable rate for a sailing ship in those days. It could be taken for granted that she would do much better than that at sea under a full spread of canvas and with the wide ocean's wind in her favor.

But if the good burghers of Boston thought that crusty Sam

Nicholson was about to be hurried off, they had plenty of time to revise the notion. The *Constitution* lay for nearly three weeks at anchor in the Roads while such adjustments as the captain deemed necessary were made. Some of those were more than likely products of the skipper's whim, temper, and temperament. They may or may not have been needed, depending altogether on how he planned to sail and fight her. But others were certainly well worth the wait. New rigging, for instance, tends to slack off after its first use, and that slack must be adjusted carefully, not taken up so tautly that it will yank the sticks out of her when the first warm, dry day at sea shrinks the ropes. At the same time, in a wooden ship there is last-minute caulking and ballasting; masts and spars to be dressed, aligned, and stayed so that they will not shift. A certain amount of movement in the top hamper of a wind ship is inevitable, even desirable, but every care must be taken to see that it does not go beyond the bounds of tolerance.

In those days all this could not be done by slide rule and exact mathematical calculation. It was largely dependent on the captain's instinct, experience, and common sense—and no doubt it accounted much for the old-time skipper's reputation for crust and irascibility! In any case these were the matters that principally preoccupied Captain Nicholson during that interval. His junior officers no doubt groused and complained and chafed at the delay, but still they had their duties to perform. Apart from the routine of shipkeeping there were still supplies of food and ship's stores and ammunition to be lightered aboard, not to mention additional guns, for it was not until the sixth that Nicholson reported that he had received the battery of 18-pounders from Castle Island, and that he had sent the gunner and some of his men up to fill cartridges and obtain enough 18-pound shot to prove the guns.

Not until July 22 did the *Constitution* finally weigh anchor. By that time almost three weeks of constant drill and duty without shore leave, even though lying immobile within sight of land, had undoubtedly honed nerves and tempers of both officers and men to a fine edge—which may well have been a part of Captain Nicholson's plan. More than one commanding officer has found that a touch of irritation often drives men to their best if only as a matter of minor vengeance.

In any case it was a fine, fair day, and the fogs that sometimes roll down in the morning on Boston's harbor had long since melted away. There is a legend that someone, presumably young female visitors, aboard while the fine new ship was on public display, had slyly slipped a handful or two of nails into the binnacle. There is no doubt that someone did, for the ship's log reports their discovery on August 1. It could have been a grim and costly prank, for even a few bits of iron so placed could have caused the compass to swing from its true, and even end for end so as to show south for north and north for south, possibly causing the vessel to pile up on one of the jagged reefs that abounded in those still imperfectly charted waters.

They sailed late in the afternoon, taking full advantage this time of both wind and tide, and threading their way past the islands of the Lower Harbor and through the Narrows, dropped their pilot off Nantasket and headed for the open sea. It was dusk when they took their last bearing on Boston Light. By dawn they were well away, with the great, green, rolling ocean all around them, and the land not even a smudge on the horizon.

The sun was hardly an hour up when Captain Nicholson summoned all hands on deck and mustered aft where he read to them his instructions from Bejamin Stoddert, secretary of the newly created Navy Department. How much of this was already well known to the officers of the quarterdeck is not clear, but it is probable that it was the first inkling that the men before the mast had that they were now part of a separate and distinct arm of the government. Captain Nicholson's announcement that "We are now at war with the public and private armed ships of the Republic of France only!" was greeted with an outburst of cheers.

But this strange undeclared war was with France only.

"Should you even see," Nicholson continued, quoting from Secretary Stoddert's letter, "an American vessel captured by the armed ship of any nation at war, with whom we are at peace, you cannot lawfully interfere to prevent such a capture."

The captain went on from there, probably the more grimly because of his own sense of disappointment, to give them a brief summary of events thus far. The *Constitution*, he told them, was not the first ship of the young navy to get to sea, much as he had hoped that that would be their honor. As early as May the converted merchantman *Ganges*, 24, Captain Richard Dale, had been the first to get away to sea. A month later the new frigate *Constellation*, 36, Captain Thomas Truxtun, had cleared from Baltimore, almost immediately followed from Philadelphia by the converted former merchantman *Delaware*, 20, Captain Stephen Decatur (senior, the father of a son by the same name who was destined to become much more famous); and the frigate *United States*, 44, Commodore John Barry, the navy's senior officer. First honors had already fallen to the *Delaware* when, on July 7, off Egg Harbor, New Jersey, she had surprised and captured the French privateer *Croyable*.

Thereafter the *Constitution* seemed to drop from sight, and it was almost a month to the day before she reappeared. In these days of swift communication and almost constant radio contact with the shore, it seems inconceivable that a large ship with nearly four hundred men on board could vanish utterly and completely from sight, and yet remain safe and self-contained. But in the days of sail, before the invention of wireless, it was an accepted fact, one of the hazards and uncertainties of seafaring that both the men who sailed the ships and the men ashore who owned them and their cargoes took for granted. Once a vessel had dropped below the rim of the horizon she was gone as completely as if the ocean had opened up and swallowed down every stick, stitch, and man on board—as it not infrequently did—without leaving so much as a bit of wreckage to mark her grave. From that moment until she spoke some other ship at sea or reached some distant port, no one on shore could say where she might be or what might have happened to her. That was why the ships' logs of the day, ordinarily so laconic and tersely to the point, seem to have gone out of their way to report every sail sighted and every vessel spoken in complete detail—her identity, her home port, the name of her captain, her port of last departure, her cargo, her destination, and even pin-pointed the location of meeting. For example, such an entry in the log as "Lat. 31′ 05″ N. Long. 45′ 30″ W. At midday spoke the ship *Zephyr*, Captain Eccles, of Salem, ten days out of Funchal with wine for Boston," etc., etc., was commonplace. Not only might it serve as a report of the last known whereabouts of the *Zephyr*, it might also be their own last contact with the outside world and would be duly reported when, as, and if the *Zephyr* came safely to her destination.

Even such small diversions, however, appear to have been missing from the *Constitution*'s bill of fare during that first month at sea, doubtless as a matter of deliberate policy on the part of Captain Nicholson. After all, it was his first duty to whip ship and crew into an efficient fighting machine, and until that had been accomplished all outside contacts were to be assiduously avoided. Apart from the terse comment in the ship's journal on the second day out remarking that "Ship sails remarkably, and Well and Works Easy," the record is primarily a list of each day's position at sea and of the state of the wind and weather and the distance run at stated intervals.

But all of this should by no means be taken to suggest that she was but "a painted ship upon a painted ocean." Far from it! The entry "Beat to Quarters and Exercised the Guns" appears almost as frequently and loses pace with the others only by weekly interruptions of the notation "Observed the Sabbath." The practice of "beating to quarters"—that is, of summoning all hands to battle stations—at any hour of the day or night, tumbling out the crew, slinging hammocks and nettings, and sending each man to his battle post—surgeons and loblolly boys to the cockpit, marines to the tops, gunners and their crews to the guns, powder monkeys to the hoists, etc.—was much the same in all navies, for the outcome of any battle would depend upon the speed, precision, and coordination with which all hands fell to their appointed tasks. Only in American ships, however, was such emphasis laid upon gunnery, and as dreary and tedious as it must have seemed after the first twenty or thirty summonses, it was to prove a policy that earned good dividends in days to come.

When, on the twenty-first of August, the *Constitution* suddenly reappeared at Newport, Rhode Island, she was well shaken down, honed fine, and ready for action.

4

AND MAIDEN VOYAGE

THE DAYS of test and trial were over. The first training and what today's navy calls "indoctrination" were done, though the daily drills and exercises at the guns would go on endlessly as long as the ship remained in active commission.

There were orders awaiting them at Newport, orders to stand southward and patrol the coast from the Virginia Capes to Florida in company with the four revenue cutters already on duty in those waters, and a tremor of excitement ran through the ship as the word seeped down from the quarterdeck, for it was in that area that the French privateers had been most active. Perhaps there was action in store for them. At last it seemed to the crew that they were about to justify their existence. This was what they had signed on for.

Nicholson stayed at Newport only long enough to take on fresh supplies of food, ammunition, and water to replace what had been expended in the last month's training cruise, and then sailed for the Capes.

The run southward was uneventful. Despite doubled watches and constant vigilance, they sighted nothing more exciting than a scant handful of plodding merchantmen, inbound and outbound. Those that were heading seaward they allowed to pass unquestioned. The inbound vessels they detained long enough to question closely. But even they could give them no clue as to the enemy's whereabouts. Their voyages, too, had been unremarkable. They had seen nothing suspicious during the entire passage, let alone having been chased. It was all very frustrating!

Off Cape Henry, Captain Nicholson sighed and remembered his orders to join company with the four revenue cutters already at sea and presumably patrolling somewhere between his present position and the entrance to Cumberland Sound, at the then southernmost limit of the United States. That left him some seaway for search and some leeway for hope that he might yet fall in with a prize that would be theirs alone. But his orders were specific enough, and they left him no choice but to look first for his consorts and leave to chance the possibility that an unwary fish might swim into his net as he did so.

They continued on their southward course, keeping well off shore in order to avoid the notoriously treacherous shoals of North Carolina's Outer Banks and still maintaining their constant vigilance. Now, however, as their eyes swept the rim of sea around them, they watched for friend as well as foe. But it was not until early in the morning watch on September 8, 1798 that the long-awaited cry came ringing down from the foremasthead lookout station:

"Sail Ho-o-o-o!"

As if by magic the ship suddenly burst from a state of torpor into pulsating life. Men leapt for the shrouds, where they shaded their eyes against the rays of the rising sun and stared forward; the watch below tumbled from its hammocks and came swarming on deck to see if it were true. The officer of the deck made a quick, cursory study of the distant stranger through his spyglass and sent a boy racing to the captain's cabin. Nicholson came on deck a few moments later with his glass under his arm and his breakfast napkin still tucked under his chin. Doubtless he glared around him in frank disapproval.

The captain removed his napkin and raised his glass to his eye. Tense silence reigned throughout the ship as he made a close and careful and prolonged study of the stranger, a large topsail schooner. Suspecting the vessel might be a French privateer, Nicholson gave the order to call all hands to quarters and clear the ship for action. The drums rolled in the waist and the responding thud of running feet bore witness to the thoroughness of the weeks of drill. Clouds of canvas tumbled from the yards and billowed and filled in the wind as the *Constitution* crowded on all sail. Her bows lifted and the seas creamed beneath her forefoot as she started in pursuit. No topsail schooner, however heavily she might be armed, could be a match for a frigate in weight of metal. But such vessels were noted for their speed, and it was here that the first test must come.

But here, too, the *Constitution* proved herself superior. The chase that followed was long but by no means as exhausting as such dogged pursuits frequently were in those days. When it became apparent that she could not outrun the frigate, the stranger sought refuge in evasive tactics, but the *Constitution* matched her turn for turn, and long before midday drew abreast of her, within easy gunshot, hoisted the American ensign, and threw a warning shot over her. Thereupon the stranger broke out British colors and fired a gun to leeward as a signal of submission. At the same time, however, he continued on under full sail, obviously plotting some trickery.

Only after Captain Nicholson had snatched up his speaking trumpet and shouted across to the stranger that he was ready to fire a broadside did the other vessel docilely spill the wind from her fore and mainsails and bring her topsails around against the wind, so that they served as a brake to check her way, and lie quietly waiting. Nicholson told Lieutenant Beale, the third officer, to cross over with a boat's crew, board, and drive the stranger's men from their guns. At the same time he shouted orders to the captain of the other vessel to hoist out a boat and come on board the *Constitution* with his ship's papers.

For a long, pregnant moment then the two vessels lay cheek by jowl, lifting and falling in the long swells, close enough for the gunners, standing at the ready with lighted matches, to stare out through the open gunports at one another.

Noting that the schooner's gun crews remained ready at their posts despite their commander's protestations of submission, Captain Nicholson hailed once more, warning that he would "sink them and give no quarter" unless his orders were immediately carried out.

In response to this, at last, a small boat with four men and an officer put out from the stranger and pulled toward the frigate. When they came alongside it proved to be only the second officer. Nicholson was livid. He refused to allow the officer to board and sent him back with peremptory orders for the captain himself to come with all his papers, at once. As they waited for the boat to make its return trip to the schooner, Lieutenant Beale hailed to say that the enemy's crew had been prepared to blow up their ship, for he had found a powder train laid to the magazine which he had, of course, removed. At that a second boat was despatched from the *Constitution* with reinforcements for Beale.

In due time another, larger boat put out from the "enemy," and presently Captain George du Petit-Thouars, wearing the uniform of a French naval officer, stepped on board the *Constitution*.

According to the papers he brought with him, the vessel he commanded was the British privateer schooner *Niger*, 24, from Jamaica for Philadelphia, and Captain Petit-Thouars offered what appeared to be a properly executed letter of marque and reprisal, issued by the British government, in substantiation of the fact.

Captain Nicholson examined these credentials with some skepticism. In the first place, there was that uniform. Captain Petit-Thouars sought to explain that by saying that, yes, he was a Frenchman, a former officer of the French navy. But he was a royalist—an emigré—cruising against the ships of the French Republic. Captain Nicholson dismissed the story with a snort, pointing out that Petit-Thouars was wearing a French, not an English, uniform. The French captain replied that it was the uniform of the royal navy that he was wearing, and added that he had been in the English service for the previous five years and in command of the *Niger* for the last three.

Nevertheless, Nicholson persisted, doubtless in great part driven by his desire to bring home a prize. Asserting that papers carried by Petit-Thouars were forgeries, Nicholson required the Frenchman to hand over his dirk, the nearest thing to a sword that he carried.

The *Niger*'s people were brought on board the *Constitution*, and a prize crew sent aboard the schooner with orders to accompany the frigate into Norfolk. It came as something of a shock to the captain to find that the paymaster of the *Niger* was an English army officer, en route to Philadelphia with his family, and that there was also a passenger on board—an American named Garts, of Baltimore. Both of these supported Petit-Thouars' claims. But on the other hand there remained the uniform, the obvious evasive actions, the failure to abandon the guns until driven from them, and the powder train. Added to this were the evidence of considerable loot and the villainous appearance of the crew, which led Nicholson to wonder if he had not stumbled on something more than a mere privateer— though it must be admitted that his view of them may have been somewhat colored by his own glasses. The problem was finally clinched when one of the *Constitution*'s crew, a seaman, Martin Rose, identified the *Niger*'s boatswain as one of the crew of a French privateer which had captured the *Masy* of Portsmouth, in which Rose was then serving. According to the affidavit which Rose made at Nicholson's request, Rose had been robbed at the Frenchman's orders, stripped naked, and carried prisoner to Guadeloupe.

After that there was no room for doubt left in Captain Nicholson's mind. The two ships proceeded in company to Norfolk, whence the captain reported to the secretary of the navy the capture of "a very fast sailing ship mounting completely 24 guns ready for immediate use, and 400 tons burthen."

Alas for Nicholson's luck. The Navy Department, the State Department, and even the President, well removed from the scene of action and so able to view matters somewhat more objectively, took a somewhat different view of the event. To cut through a mass of correspondence and report, the powers that be ultimately found the *Niger's* papers in order and her capture "wholly unwarrantable," and consequently damages were decreed to the captured men. Furthermore, they declared that Captain Nicholson's "eagerness to procure a condemnation savored of rapacity."

In short, like so many others before and since, in his efforts to justify his position, Nicholson had stepped on unsuspected toes. And to add fuel to the fire, having deposited his prize in the hands of the shoreside authorities, he had not the wit to return immediately to his station. On the contrary, he persisted in remaining in port for weeks in idleness while the dispatches flew back and forth between Norfolk and Philadelphia. Such inactivity scarcely endeared him either aboard ship or with the Navy Department.

All of this, of course, was his own doing and may be regarded with a certain sympathy—with reservations. But worse fortune—and this time not of his own making—lay in wait for him.

In those days yellow fever was by no means a stranger to the East Coast. Epidemics of the disease went as far north as New York, though the worst outbreaks were at Philadelphia in 1793–94, and 1797–98. Whether it was this which struck the *Constitution* as she lay at anchor in Hampton Roads is not known definitely, though it seems probable. The fact remains that on September 25, while the ship was at anchor, an entry in the log read: "died Midshipman Samuel Nicholson, Jr, 16, son of Captain Samuel Nicholson, of the fever."

It is understandable that not long after that, the *Constitution* weighed anchor and returned to her duty station. There, off Charleston, South Carolina, she fell in with the U.S.S. *Baltimore*, 20, Captain Phillips (formerly the merchant ship *Adriana* of Baltimore) gathering a convoy for Havana. Captain Nicholson, as senior officer present, took command, and together the two men-of-war began herding their totally undisci-

plined and more than a little recalcitrant charges southward
through waters that could only be considered hostile.

Hostile they were in more ways than one. Not only were they
a favored hunting ground of French privateers, they were also
hurricane seas, and though it was late in the stormy season, and
the worst of it might be considered past, there was always a
chance of a dying gasp that could scatter the convoy and
wreak heavy damage upon them all.

And apparently the weather was far from settled, though
whether or not they encountered anything as savage as a hurricane the record does not show, but evidently it was bad enough
to give them some trouble, for on October 7 the *Constitution*'s
journal notes "twenty-seven sail of the convoy in sight. Many
of the masters shamefully neglectful of their duty." And on the
twenty-eighth, three weeks later, by which time, given any sort
of decent weather, they should long since have reached their
destination, the *Constitution* sprung her bowsprit and foremast
in a gale and was forced to withdraw from the operation. Captain Nicholson turned the convoy over to Captain Phillips, in
the *Baltimore*, and the *Constitution* limped home to Boston,
where she arrived on November 10. There she remained, undergoing repairs until early in January 1799, when she sailed
under new orders to join the squadron of Commodore John
Barry in the West Indies.

While she was lying thus unavoidably idle in Boston, a curious and rather unhappy sequel was being enacted by her
former consort, the *Baltimore*, far to the southward; a sequel
that shows only too forcefully the frequently contemptuous attitude of the great sea powers toward the United States Navy
during the first years of its existence and demonstrated the
need for maintaining a sufficient force afloat to maintain the
nation's rights.

Following the departure of the *Constitution*, Captain Phillips, in the *Baltimore*, continued southward with the convoy.
On the sixteenth of November he fell in with a powerful British

squadron under the command of Captain Loring, consisting of three ships of the line: the *Carnatic* (flagship), 74; the *Queen*, 98; and the *Thunderer*, 74; and the two 32-gun frigates *Maidstone* and *Grayhound*. That added up to a total of 310 guns as opposed to the *Baltimore*'s scant 20, and that without taking into consideration the fact that the *Baltimore*'s batteries were composed of 9- and 4-pounders while the English ships mounted nothing smaller than 18's, and doubtless carried heavier batteries ranging up to 42's.

In the face of such odds it is hardly to be expected that the *Baltimore* should stand and fight. Neither was she swift enough to outrun the frigates. As a matter of fact, she was noted as a sluggish sailer. However, in view of the fact that Great Britain herself was at war with France and at peace with the United States, Captain Phillips might be excused for regarding all that as academic. When a signal summoned him aboard the flagship he responded without the least anticipation of trouble.

On his arrival on board the *Carnatic*, however, he was bluntly told by Captain Loring that every man aboard the *Baltimore* who was not provided with an American "protection" would be impressed. Captain Phillips naturally protested indignantly that the *Baltimore* was a public armed vessel, belonging to and representing the government of the United States; that England and America were not at war—in fact they might even be considered allies against the French—and that any such action as Captain Loring proposed could only be regarded as the grossest of insults to the American flag and nation, if not, indeed, an actual act of war.

He might have saved his breath. His objections met only with derision from Loring, who is even reported to have had the bland effrontery to boast that there were already a number of impressed Americans serving on board the *Carnatic*. When Captain Phillips swore that he would surrender his ship rather than submit to such an outrage, he was brusquely reminded that since a state of war did not exist between them such a surrender could not be accepted, his sword was refused, and he was returned to the *Baltimore*.

There he found a British lieutenant already in the act of mustering his crew. He took the muster roll from the Englishman, ordering him to the lee side, and sent the *Baltimore*'s men to quarters. But it was a futile gesture. In the face of such odds and such an attitude resistance was obviously impossible. The *Baltimore* could not outrun the frigates; she could not even hope to stand and fight one of them, let alone all five ships of the squadron. To stand and fight would mean suicide, not alone for Captain Phillips but for many of his men as well. It could only mean the unnecessary sacrifice of lives and probably the ship, and though there might be a measure of glory in sheer bravado, experience has shown that glory pays small pensions. In the end Captain Phillips was forced to surrender the roll and call up his men once more for inspection.

Out of that crew—duly enlisted men in the service of the United States—fifty-five were selected and taken on board the *Carnatic*. Fifty of these were later returned to the *Baltimore*, but five of the men removed were retained. After some delay in obtaining the release of three American vessels of the convoy, which Loring had detained under his own interpretation of the rules of blockade, Captain Phillips proceeded with his charges to Havana. Upon his return to the United States in January 1799, he was censured for "his course of non-resistance" and declared most culpable. He was court martialled and dismissed in disgrace from the service.

The British, of course, felt their actions were entirely justified. The crews of American vessels, both merchantmen and ships of war, included many British sailors who had deserted from their navy in search of better pay and treatment. It was a simple matter for deserters to assume false names and swear that they had been born in the United States and, as a rule, American captains would not question a new hand's word. But neither the British nor, for that matter, the United States, then recognized the principle of expatriation, so the deserters

were unable to protect themselves when challenged by claiming
that they had become naturalized citizens. The British thus did
have a legal basis for retrieving deserters from their navy.
Americans, however, violently objected to having their ships
stopped at sea by another power and claimed, in addition, that
British officers were not overly particular when it suited their
purposes about the true nationality of the sailors they impressed.

Meanwhile, the *Constitution* underwent repairs in Boston,
departing for the West Indies at about the same time poor
Captain Phillips returned.

The island of Dominica, 29 miles long by 16 broad, is the
largest of the Leeward Islands. It lies about midway between
the two largest islands of the French West Indies, Guadeloupe
and Martinique—each about 30 miles away—and is even closer
to Marie Galante and Les Saintes. Its capital, Roseau, lies on
the leeward side, on an open roadstead near the southwest end.
But northward it boasts two fine fresh streams; Morne Dia-
blotin, the highest peak in the Antilles; and, at the northwest
corner of the island, Prince Rupert's Bay, one of the finest harbors in the West Indies. The northern arm of the bay, domi-
nated by the jungle-clad slopes of the Cabrits, protects the anchorage from the prevailing weather, while beaches overhung
with coconuts and manchineel, ideal for careening even large
sailing ships, ring the inner and southern sides. The entrance
was guarded by strong fortifications. The barracks of the garrison straggled up the hillsides on the north, while the little
town of Portsmouth nestled at the head of the bay, inland. It
was English and an obvious thorn in the French side, and as
such it was a logical point of rendezvous and headquarters for
the American naval forces in the West Indies. It was there that
Captain Nicholson, in the *Constitution*, reported his arrival on
station to Commodore Barry, in the flagship, the frigate
United States, 44.

Even in so short a time the American navy had grown to respectable proportions. By the first of January, 1799, including

the vessels of the revenue marine which had been ordered to duty with the navy, the United States had some twenty-two ships in active service, ranging from the little 10-gun cutter *General Greene* to the 44-gun frigates *United States* and *Constitution*. With the onset of winter and the coming of the seasonal, savage North Atlantic storms it was reasoned, and probably quite correctly, that the French were not likely to prowl our coast in such weather. Accordingly it was decided to seek them out on their own grounds, the West Indies, where they were known to swarm in winter. For this purpose all of our ships but one were ordered south, the 20-gun converted merchantman *Montezuma* alone being left behind to patrol the coast. The ships ordered south were divided into four squadrons, all with a common rendezvous at Prince Rupert's Bay, on Dominica, but each separately having a base of its own from which to operate while on station. Captain Stephen Decatur, senior, in the ship *Delaware*, 20, patrolled the waters to the northward of Cuba in company with the revenue cutters *Governor Jay*, 14, and *General Greene*, 10—small vessels, indeed, but, as it proved, far more effective craft than the bigger and far more powerful frigates in these shallow, narrow seas. Farther east Commodore Tingey, in the *Ganges*, 24, covered the Windward and Mona passages and the waters between Cuba and Puerto Rico. In his squadron were the *Pinckney*, 18, and the revenue cutter *South Carolina*, 12. A third squadron under Commodore Truxtun, in the new 36-gun frigate *Constellation*, was based on Saint Kitts and covered the inner and outer waters of the northern sector of the Leeward Islands, from Antigua up past Anguilla; the Sir Francis Drake Channel, one of the main lanes of traffic between Europe and the Indies; the Virgin Islands and the Culebra Passage to Puerto Rico. This was an especially important point, not only on account of the Drake Passage, already mentioned, but also because it included the islands of Saint Martin, which was half French and half Dutch; Saint Bartholomew, which had been ceded by France to Sweden on paper some time since, but which still retained a strong French coloring; and Saint Eustatia—better known in the Islands even now as "Statia"—which today belongs to the Dutch but at that time was momentarily held by France. Truxtun's squadron included the *Baltimore*, 20; *Richmond*, 18; *Norfolk*, 18; and the revenue cutter *Virginia*, 14. Commodore Barry's own squadron was based on headquarters at Prince Rupert's Bay and covered the Atlantic of both the Leeward and Windward Islands, from Anguilla to Barbadoes and Trinidad and even to Georgetown and Demerara on the South American mainland. His squadron was the largest of all and included, besides the 44-gun frigates *New York* (his flag) and *Constitution*, the *George Washington*, *Merrimack*, and *Portsmouth*, all rated as 24's; the *Herald*, 18; and the revenue cutters *Pickering*, *Eagle*, and *Scammell*, each 14; and the *Diligence*, 12.

The gathering of United States forces in the West Indies almost amounted to a convention of officers who were later to become commanders of the *Constitution*. Isaac Hull, as fourth lieutenant, was already familiarizing himself with the ship which under his command was to win her immortal nickname— "Old Ironsides." Edward Preble, by many considered second only to John Paul Jones in American naval annals, commanded the *Pickering*. Hugh Campbell commanded the *Eagle*, while the able but eccentric Daniel McNiell was in command of the *Portsmouth*. John Rodgers was lieutenant aboard the *Constellation* with Thomas Macdonough, one day to be the hero of Lake Champlain, serving under him as a very junior midshipman. Charles Stewart was a lieutenant on the *United States*, while Stephen Decatur, Jacob Jones, and Richard Somers were midshipmen on the same ship. At the same time, though not on board one of the vessels enumerated, William Bainbridge, undoubtedly one of the unluckiest officers ever to climb to the top of the naval heap, was already a captive on the island of Guadeloupe.

Unfortunately, the *Constitution* met with little glory during that season's campaign. She was too large to follow the fleet little French privateers and picaroons in the shallow waters and tortuous channels that threaded close among the islands, and offshore, where there was ample sea room for a fight, she had not the luck to encounter a willing enemy. Once, indeed, she did go in chase of the French frigate *Insurgente,* a ship that was destined to fall prize to the *Constellation* not long afterward.

On this occasion, however, the Frenchman showed no inclination to stand and fight. Instead he cracked on all sail and fled with the *Constitution* hot on his heels. The *Constitution* might have overtaken her and forced a fight, but as luck would have it, at the very moment when action seemed imminent, once again she sprung her foremast and was forced to withdraw from the chase.

Unfortunately the incident did not end there. In her flight the *Insurgente* had been forced to abandon one of her prizes, the *Spencer,* an unarmed English merchantman, and she, of course, fell prey to the *Constitution.* Having been once burned, however, Captain Nicholson was twice shy, and to the disgust of his officers and crew he returned the *Spencer* to her French prize crew on the ground that she was not armed.

Apparently the officers and crew of the *Constitution* were not the only ones who were displeased. The administration lost no time in expressing its displeasure, and Congress promptly passed an act "further to suspend the commercial intercourse between the United States and France and the dependencies thereof." A few weeks later the Navy Department issued a circular order to all captains calling for the strictest enforcement of the act. Further, it called for increased vigilance in the surveillance of French ports and the search of all suspicious vessels even though they might be under a foreign flag. It also ordered the recapture from the French of the vessels of other nations, and specifically mentioned the case of the *Spencer* as a "misconstruction of authority" on the part of Captain Nicholson.

Not long afterward the *Constitution* was ordered to return to Boston in company with the small frigate *Merrimack.* When she arrived there in May, Samuel Nicholson was disposed of by the time honored departmental method of "kicking him upstairs." It seemed that Congress had authorized the construction of six ships of the line, and the Navy Department, after noting that he had been a good deal absent from his family, asked that he take charge and supervise the building of the one assigned to Boston.

Thus Captain Nicholson at last—and doubtless to the relief of those he left behind—bade farewell to the *Constitution*. His place was taken by Captain Silas Talbot, an old Revolutionary hero and a man of much different temperament.

5

*F*LAGSHIP OF THE
*W*EST *I*NDIES *S*TATION

I M M E D I A T E L Y upon the appointment of Captain Talbot to the command of the *Constitution*, the familiar "battle of the numbers" broke out among the junior officers with all its attendant jockeying for position. When the time came to count noses and examine qualifications, both on paper and in fact, it was found that Isaac Hull, who had served under Nicholson as fourth lieutenant, was actually the senior lieutenant on board. As a result he was—none too enthusiastically, it appears— assigned as first lieutenant and executive. Whether or not the other lieutenants who had served over him during the first cruise resigned or were transferred to other posts does not appear in the record. In any case, all that matters is that, after the smoke cleared and the clamor died away, the *Constitution* found herself provided with a complete new set of officers. Hull alone had served on her before. Robert W. Hamilton was second lieutenant; Isaac Collins, third; and Edward Boss, fourth. Another newcomer to the ship at this time was Nathaniel ("Jumping Billy") Haraden, who was destined to serve for many years aboard as sailing master. It was he who, as master of the yard, at Washington in 1812, recoppered her bottom and restowed her ballast in such a way that her sailing trim was much improved and doubtless accounted for much of her success in the war that was then at hand.

When Captain Talbot was first appointed to command, Secretary Stoddert had in mind—rather nebulously as yet—a project to send the *Constitution* and some of the other, faster ships to cruise in the Bay of Biscay, off the coasts of France and Spain, where they were to strike such swift blows at both shipping and shore installations as they could, and then as quickly withdraw before they could be overwhelmed by superior force, and return homeward through West Indian waters.

But the *Constitution* was not ready for sea again until late in July, and the plan had to be scrapped. Perhaps that was just as well, for in August the frigate *Insurgente*, Captain Murray, crossed to Lisbon, cruised the coast of Portugal from Finisterre to Gibraltar, and thence returned to the Caribbean, but the cruise was a complete disappointment, netting nothing. A little later the *United States*, under Captain Barry, crossed to France. But her mission was not warlike. Instead she carried out two envoys who were to treat with the French for a peaceful solution of the quarrel.

In the meantime, however, there was action of a sort in store for the *Constitution*. She sailed from Boston early in August and put in at Norfolk, where Captain Talbot found specific orders awaiting him from Secretary Stoddert. These orders directed him to proceed southward to Cape Orange, on the north coast of South America, the easternmost point in French Guiana. From there he was to cruise in the vicinity of Cayenne until September 20, when it was estimated that the hurricane season in the islands would have passed, after which he was to proceed by way of Surinam and Guadeloupe to Cap François, in what is now Haiti, on the island of San Domingo, and there take command of the San Domingo station.

The outward voyage was uneventful save for the recapture of the swift Hamburgh packet *Amelia*, which had been captured by the French a few days before. A prize crew was placed aboard her and she was sent back to New York while Talbot and his officers went to bed that night to dream sweet dreams of prize money at last.

The *Constitution*'s luck, however, still seemed to be running bad. When it came to adjudication, it seemed the case involved certain fine points of international law, and it was carried all the way up to the Supreme Court. The decision finally handed down was that the *Amelia* had sailed under a neutral flag in the first place and that hence the capture by the French was not legal. Therefore, said the court, the *Constitution*, in recapturing the vessel, *rendered no service to the owners!* However, the Supreme Court ruled that "the *Amelia* and her cargo ought to be restored to the claimant on paying for salvage one sixth part of the net value after deducting therefrom the charges, which have incurred." This meant that instead of full prize money of some $180,000 to be divided among the ship's company, the award amounted to only some $30,000, which by regulation was split 3/20ths to the captain, 2/20ths to each of the five officers, and the balance evenly divided among the rest of the crew; in round figures, $4,500 to Talbot, $3,000 to each officer, and $26.50 for each member of the crew. In the light of their hopes it was not much; still, when one considers how far a dollar went in those days it was not to be sneezed at. Indeed, even that paltry share of $26.50 per man was a worthwhile bonus to an ordinary or able seaman, for it represented from two to three months' pay, according to his rate.

But none of this, of course, was forthcoming immediately. They would be lucky if the matter were settled by the time they returned home. In the meantime there was a cruise ahead of them. Late in August or early in September the *Constitution* arrived off the coast of French Guiana, where she stood off-and-on in the vicinity of Cayenne until the twentieth of September, as she had been ordered, without encountering anything worthy of notice. Then, in further compliance with orders, she hauled her wind and stood up for San Domingo. There, if she took no prizes, at least she should be able to find some other excitement of a different sort to break the monotony of shipboard routine, and it is scarcely to be wondered at that all hands looked forward to the change with a sense of relief.

In order to understand this air of suppressed anticipation, it is necessary to examine briefly the political situation in San Domingo, for it was largely the unsettled state of affairs there that prompted the navy to send Talbot in the *Constitution*, supported by almost half of our force in the West Indies, into that area.

As far back as the year 1697 the western part of the island of Hispaniola had been ceded to France by Spain by the Treaty of Ryswick. For a time it had been primarily the haunt of *boucaniers* and piratical freebooters from nearby Tortugas, but by 1722 a flourishing plantation society had grown up; a society in which a handful of white planters controlled the lives and destinies and even the mating of thousands of Negro slaves. Even in an age when brutality was a commonplace the planters of Saint Domingue, as the colony had come to be called, were noted for their cruelty, which often took the form of sheer sadism in the guise of sport. And nowhere in the world, outside of France itself, did the news of the Revolution of 1789 strike with more chilling effect. At first the planters refused to recognize the handwriting on the wall, but whether they admitted it or not made little difference. Their days were numbered.

The first note of grim warning came when the "freemen of color," i.e., the mulattoes and others of varying degrees of mixed blood, who were despised by the pure blacks and looked upon with contempt by the whites, demanded that the principles of the Revolution be extended to them. To the consternation of the planters, they were granted French citizenship in 1791. But such a wail of protest went up from the French colonists that the decree was reversed in the same year, and when the slaves broke out in open insurrection the mulattoes sided with them against the whites. Most of the white planters and their families were massacred out of hand and their homes and plantations burned. Out of this chaos emerged the one outstanding figure of Haitian history, Toussaint L'Ouverture, black, a former slave and leader of the blacks; wise, intelligent, politically acute and an instinctive military tactician and strategist. He vigorously opposed the more violent rebels and managed to bring a semblance of order out of the prevailing anarchy of the time. When the English, at the desperate urging of the dispossessed planters, invaded the island in 1795, L'Ouverture sided with the French Republicans, was named commander in chief of the French armies, and in 1798 finally succeeded in driving the English out. By the treaty of Basle all of the eastern part of the island was ceded to France, only the little town of Porto Plata on the north coast stubbornly clinging to its allegiance to Spain on the ground that no formal surrender of that place had ever occurred. Thereby hangs a tale —as we shall presently see.

But peace in Santo Domingo was still a distant dream. A quarrel now broke out between Toussaint L'Ouverture and Sonthonax, the French governor appointed by the Directory. The latter accused Toussaint of plotting to make himself head of the state—an accusation which in the light of revelations long afterward was undoubtedly true—and L'Ouverture promptly responded by descending upon Cap François and forcing Sonthonax to flee to France. But still the way was a thorny one. Several native leaders rose to dispute Toussaint's power, especially André Rigaud, the leader of the mulattoes, who held most of the southwestern part of the island.

Toussaint was well aware of the importance of trade with the United States. The Americans brought all manner of sorely needed supplies as well as money in return for island products —mainly sugar, molasses, and "muscovado," as the crushed cane by-product of the sugar mills was called; the coarsest, low-grade brown sugar, which was the basis of New England's "blackstrap" and trade rum. This had fallen off considerably both as a result of the constant bloody free-for-all ashore and the dangers from freebooters, picaroons, and privateers who swarmed in the waters surrounding the island. Because the loss had been severely felt, Toussaint at this point appealed to the government at Philadelphia to help re-establish their former trade relations. The United States, in response, had offered to send ships of war to help patrol the island's waters and to encourage traders provided Toussaint would co-operate to suppress privateering and piracy from his ports and inlets.

This was the reason for Talbot's orders to that station, and it was at this time that he appeared there to take command of the American squadron which was based at Cap François, or "Le Cap" as it was more generally known. Commodore Barry, in the *United States,* was already gone from Prince Rupert's Bay and the Guadeloupe station, but his place had been taken by Commodore Truxtun, in the *Constellation,* 36, who was in turn some time later to be succeeded by Commodore Decatur. Fortunately their commands were separated by a considerable distance and their courses did not cross, for there was some difference of opinion between them as to who outranked whom and there was little love lost, each one considering himself the other's senior.

Commodore Talbot and the *Constitution* arrived on the Santo Domingo station in October, but for several months their duties were little more than a round of routine activities. As the flagship on the station, of course, there were other excitements than fell to the lot of lesser vessels—official visits and receptions of foreign dignitaries, assistance to refugees and their transportation to points of safety, and the like. But if these are mentioned in the record at all it is only in a laconic note, and while such minor events may have provided some entertainment for the officers, they meant little to the crew beyond extra duty.

One event, however, appears to have provided excitement and satisfaction for all hands. The word "appears" is used advisedly, for nowhere in the official record is there any mention of the event. No one involved seems to have spoken of it in his letters—at least those that have survived—nor does it seem to have been noticed in the press. All subsequent accounts apparently have been based upon James Fenimore Cooper's article "Old Ironsides," published in *Putnam's Monthly* in 1853, and even he does not give the date of the event or name the other ship involved or her commander. As everyone knows, Mr. Cooper is more famous as a novelist than an historian, though his *Naval History* was the definitive and indeed the only work on the subject for many years. For the sake of all on board the *Constitution*, one hopes that the story is true, for the event must have provided a welcome break in the monotony. Cooper's account appears now to be generally accepted as accurate.

The *Constitution*, according to Cooper, on her first appearance in West Indian waters had been the subject of a good deal of speculation and adverse criticism and the butt of many jokes among the officers and men of the royal navy on station in the same area. Naturally these aspersions and sneers were hotly resented by the Americans, and it was as well perhaps that contact between them ashore was infrequent, else there might well have been blood spilled. It was a time when the Code of Honor was taken seriously, and insults, whether in earnest or in jest, were not taken lightly. Encounters at sea, however, appear to have been fairly commonplace and, with one or two exceptions such as the affair of the *Baltimore* and that of the *Leopard* and the *Chesapeake*, much later, were usually quite amicable.

Such a meeting occurred one fine day when the *Constitution* was on routine patrol in the waters just northward of Santo Domingo. There she fell in with an English frigate whose name is not given but which was reputed to be one of the royal navy's fastest and finest. Upon exchanging the private signals agreed upon between the Americans and the British to avoid the chance of costly errors, it was discovered that Commodore Talbot and the English commander were acquaintances of long standing, having served on opposing sides during the Revolution and broken bread at the same table more than once while one or the other was being held as a prisoner. Upon learning the Englishman's identity—though the record makes a secret of it—Talbot invited the other to come on board and inspect the *Constitution*.

The British captain was nothing loth to renew his old

friendship, for it seemed that even Talbot's enemies came to like him. But even if that had not been the case it is probable that he would have been quick to accept, if only to get a closer look at this new ship of which he had heard so many and such conflicting reports. He came. He saw. He even admired—her size, which he conceded to be considerable for her rate, her stout timbers, her roomy decks, her formidable armament, her masts and spars and the immense spread of sail that she could carry. But it was not for any Englishman—especially an officer of His Majesty's Navy—to be entirely uncritical of anything American. He granted most of the *Constitution*'s good points, but he dared say that being so heavily built she must be a dull sailer. He added, prodding, that she must be especially unhandy in beating to windward, i.e., in sailing upwind.

But Talbot was not to be badgered into a show of temper, as his predecessor might well have been. Out of long experience Talbot had learned that the best way to deal with an Englishman is to arouse his sporting instinct. He glanced aloft and then looked down at the deck, and finally admitted that his ship might be pretty heavily built. But at the same time, he said, she was a pretty good sailer. In fact, he concluded, she should have little difficulty showing her heels to the Englishman if he would care to make a little wager on it.

One can almost hear the Englishman's response as he took the bait.

"Oh, come now, Captain! You can't really be serious?"

And the commodore undoubtedly assured him that he was never more in earnest. The upshot of it all was that the challenge was made and accepted. The Englishman was fresh from Madeira where he had taken on a large store of fine wine for his own use, and he offered to bet a pipe of the finest against an equivalent in money on the outcome of such a contest. Since the Englishman was due to report without delay, probably to Kingston, in Jamaica, which would have been the nearest royal naval dockyard, to refit and heave down for scraping, the matter could not be settled forthwith, but a date was set for a rendezvous some two weeks thence off Le Cap when the race would officially be run. With everything thus arranged the Englishman continued on his way, while the *Constitution* proceeded to maintain her duties on patrol.

When the appointed day came around, sure enough, there came the Englishman to the rendezvous looking bright and shiny as a new silver dollar. Her rigging had been thoroughly overhauled and she wore a suit of new white sails; she had been painted alow and aloft, and the barnacles and other marine growth had been scraped away so that her copper bottom was clean as a whistle. It had been ten months since the *Constitution* had undergone such an overhaul, though undoubtedly she had been hove down at convenient intervals during her tour of duty and given a lick and a promise by her crew. But Silas Talbot was not a man to quibble about such things. When the Englishman came up he was as ready for the race as his rival.

But for all their readiness there were yet some details to be agreed upon. Once again the Englishman came on board and over the wine they settled the terms and conditions. When he was gone Talbot summoned Lieutenant Hull, who had already established an enviable record for ship handling, and turned over complete charge of the ship during the race. Hull had already discussed the matter with the commodore and for several days had had picked crews aloft, running through drills calculated to have them working in perfect harmony when the time came. At the same time the men themselves, from the lowest powder monkey up, were perfectly well aware of what was afoot and were as eager as the officers to win. Nevertheless Lieutenant Hull would not be satisfied until he had made one final and very thorough inspection. All that night the two ships sailed close together on parallel courses under reduced canvas. When the sun rose dripping from the sea ahead, burnishing the sea with gold and copper, the hoped-for breeze came with it and they squared away to their positions. The crews aloft lay out along the yards while on deck the waisters stood by their lifts and braces, sheets and downhauls. For a moment the two tall ships lay neck and neck, a cable's length apart, their forefeet gently slicing the rippling seas. Then the Englishman, as agreed, fired the ready gun. Aboard the *Constitution* an answering thump signified her corresponding readiness, and at that signal they were off. Simultaneously the white canvas cascaded from the yards of both vessels, filled and bellied in the wind and swung as the waisters hauled the yards around to catch the full drive of the breeze. The ships heeled and leapt forward, each with a creaming bone in her teeth as she sliced the seas aside. On board the *Constitution* the full ship's crew not working on the sails, under Hull's direction, moved to the weather rail, trimming the ship by their combined weight so as to take fullest advantage of the wind—a little trick that Hull had long ago learned as a merchant skipper.

The race lasted all day, beating up by short tacks that for a long time were so precise and nearly identical in length and timing that it would have seemed to an onlooker that they were sailing in exact formation. By midday, however, the *Constitution* had opened a perceptible gap between herself and the Englishman, and by sundown, which was the signal for the end of the race, the latter was hull down, far behind, only her topsails and lower courses showing over the rim of the horizon. Commodore Talbot fired a gun as a signal that the race was ended, and a long moment later—the time it takes for sound to carry over and back across the water—an answering dull thud came from the direction of the Englishman and a wispy cloud of smoke was seen to rise above the distant sails.

At that signal Talbot brought the *Constitution* about and squared away before the wind and ran down to meet his recent rival. As they rounded to under the Englishman's lee and brought their topsails aback to check their way, the latter put over a boat and presently the English captain came aboard with his agreed upon payment in acknowledgment of his defeat. He stayed to dine, of course, and according to the yarn toasts were drunk by all hands, both forward and in the ward-room, to Commodore Talbot and the *Constitution*, Lieutenant

Hull, and the English captain and his crew, and probably even the President of the United States and the king of England—which is probably all quite accurate and true, since at that time a pint of grog was an official part of every seaman's ration. As for the lack of official mention in the record, one can easily understand that a full day spent upon such a sporting event might not be considered a suitable entry for the ship's log.

Not all of the *Constitution*'s adventures during that tour of duty, however, were confined to routine patrols and sporting events. She rescued more than one hapless merchant ship from her French captors, escorted others to safety, and though she herself was too large to venture into the shallow shoreward waters and tortuous channels amid the reefs and mangroves in pursuit of the swarming picaroons and privateers, her boats frequently took part in such operations in conjunction with those of other ships. What proved to be her greatest adventure, however, was the cutting out of the privateer *Sandwich*, in the harbor of Porto Plata, on the northeast coast of Santo Domingo in the late spring of 1800.

The *Sandwich*, which is said to have been a corvette, had once been an English mail packet and was constructed accordingly. She was well timbered and coppered, fast, and armed with four 6's and two 9's—no match, of course, for the *Constitution* in weight of metal, though she might have been able to show her heels in a chase. Some years before she had been taken by the French and for several years had given a good account of herself in the English Channel and the Bay of Biscay. Now she was employed as a letter-of-marque, carrying much-needed sugar and coffee between the West Indies and France.

As a private armed ship of war sailing under French license and wearing French colors, the *Sandwich* was certainly fair game for the *Constitution*. But Commodore Talbot was well aware of her reputation for speed and he preferred not to risk having her give him the slip once she got to sea if it could be avoided. That left him only one alternative—to slip into the harbor and cut her out at her moorings, under the protection of the heavy guns of the fort on shore, and bring her out. At this point, however, an ugly technicality reared its head. Bearing in mind the steadfast claims of Porto Plata to its allegiance to Spain, since there had been no formal surrender of that place to France under the treaty between the two countries, was Commodore Talbot justified in such a move? The United States was not at war with Spain. Indeed, technically, insofar as other powers were involved, we were not actually at war with France since there had been no actual declaration to that effect. In such circumstances might not such action as Talbot proposed be regarded in some quarters as an unjustified invasion of neutral rights—the very thing against which we were fighting?

Moreover, it was quite possible that to invade the little port and bring out the privateer might be resented by Toussaint, even though he had agreed to cooperate in the suppression of privateering from his island's ports, and Talbot had been instructed above all else to maintain cordial relations with the Negro leader.

It was a tangled situation that called for some study, and while the *Constitution* warily patrolled the area, keeping a weather eye open for the *Sandwich* should she attempt to run for it, the commodore gave it careful consideration. In the end he came to the conclusion that whether or not the Porto Platans liked it, the fact remained that under the treaty of 1795 Spain had ceded the entire island to France. That there had been no formal surrender of the port in question was, to his way of thinking, a mere splitting of hairs. Porto Plata was on the island of Santo Domingo. The island had been turned over to the French. Therefore it followed that the port was also French, and since the United States was to all intents and purposes at war with France upon the sea, ships of war under French colors and in French waters were fair game. As for Toussaint, he decided, if he could not maintain his end of the bargain—as he clearly could not or would not in this case—he could scarcely object if we offered assistance to that end. Accordingly Commodore Talbot took matters into his own hands, and under cover of darkness the *Constitution* slipped in toward the little port.

It was the commodore's original plan to slip into the port in the *Constitution* and bring his ship into position where his heavy guns could cover his small boats as they made their attack. As they came on soundings, however, it quickly became apparent that even here the frigate's draft and size made such a course impossible without exposing the ship to dangers far beyond the value of the prize. In consequence Talbot sent in Lieutenant Hull in the barge with a picked crew of volunteers to reconnoiter. On his return Hull reported that the privateer lay close inshore, well under the protecting fire of the heavy guns in the fort, that she was anchored fore and aft, and had moved her entire battery to the seaward side so that she might be able to bring all her guns to bear upon an approaching enemy. She had handed down her topmasts and upper rigging, so that she now lay under bare poles, and would have to be re-rigged before she could be brought out. He confirmed the commodore's suspicions regarding the hazards of trying to go in with the frigate herself. Even at the flood there was not enough water to float her alongside. Nor, he felt, would it be advisable to try to cut her out with the ship's boats, as they would be bound to be recognized and brought under fire before they could approach near enough to effect a boarding.

On the face of it the prospects for success at that moment seemed a little dim. But then Talbot recalled a small American sloop that had been observed on several occasions entering and leaving the harbor of Porto Plata. Indeed, she had slipped out only the day before, and to judge from her previous actions she would probably be returning again within a short time. On board the *Constitution* they had every reason to suspect that she was engaged in contraband trade with the French, which was strictly forbidden, but since they were out for larger game, and because she had so far sailed only between island ports, they had not moved to intercept her. But now the situation was somewhat different. She was well known in the port and apparently came and went as she willed. Such a craft might approach the *Sandwich* without arousing suspicion, and that was exactly what was needed.

They went in search of the sloop and found her lying at anchor in a little bay some fifteen miles or so to the westward. Once again Lieutenant Hull manned his barge with volunteers, and at two in the morning slipped in and boarded the sloop where she lay. The master and his small crew offered a stout resistance, but they were no match for the armed sailors who soon had them all clapped under hatches, slipped the cable, and made sail to rendezvous with the *Constitution*. The prize proved to be the *Sally*, Captain Thomas Sanford, out of Providence, Rhode Island, and there was enough evidence in her hold to prove that Commodore Talbot's suspicions in regard to her had been entirely correct.

However, she had another role to play now. Upon reaching the *Constitution*, the sloop's crew were taken on board, and Captain Sanford was informed that he would have to make one more visit to Porto Plata before he returned home to face the music. Once more volunteers were called for, and since every man aboard offered to go it became a matter of selection. Some ninety sailors and marines were told off for the duty—doubtless just about all that could be packed into the sloop's tiny hold. Arms and provisions were set on board and Lieutenant Hull named to over-all command. Captain Daniel Carmick and Lieutenant William Amory were to command the marines under him.

They cast off shortly before midnight and made their way at an easy pace alongshore, for they had timed their attack for midday. At that time the Frenchmen would be at their Sunday dinner, and there would be light enough for the marines to storm the battery on shore swiftly and for the seamen to rerig the prize for sea.

For all their care, however, there was one moment when it seemed as if all their work had gone for nothing. They were not far on their way when out of the darkness to seaward loomed the black silhouette of a large ship. A gun roared and orange flame stabbed through the night. A ball whined over the *Sally*'s bows. Hull promptly hove to and fired a pistol to leeward in signal of compliance, though his heart must have sunk at thought of the possibilities. Was the stranger a Frenchman, of whose presence they had been unaware? Certainly there was no doubt that she was a man-of-war.

Presently a longboat came sliding toward them over the long, sleek rollers that were hardly ruffled by the catspaw breeze. A moment later an English lieutenant came over the side and all but rubbed his eyes at the sight of so many men and officers in obvious naval uniform crowded in so small a vessel. When Hull, drawing the Englishman into the cabin, explained his identity and mission, the young officer was only partly mollified by the inevitable glass of wine, and explained that the British, too, had only been waiting for the *Sandwich* to complete her cargo before cutting her out themselves. He had the grace, however, to wish the Americans luck and send them on their way.

The Americans were still some distance from the mouth of the harbor when the dawn came, and by deliberately clumsy sailing they were able to delay their arrival off the port until well after mid-morning. They were still beyond reach of any possible watchful eyes when Hull sent all hands save himself and Captain Sanford and four or five hands, necessary to work the vessel, below. Naturally those who remained on deck discarded their uniforms and donned disguises. At the same time it was impressed upon Captain Sanford that he was there merely as a decoy since he was known in Porto Plata and his presence would allay suspicion. However, any overt move on his part to warn the enemy would result in the most drastic penalties.

It was almost noon when they reached the entrance to the tiny harbor and turned their bows directly toward the anchored privateer. With a spanking breeze from dead astern they went in at a good clip. In the stern of the *Sally*, with a light anchor pre-rigged to drop the moment the two vessels came together, Hull had for the first time a good, full, daylight view of the situation. The *Sandwich* lay close inshore, with the guns of the shore battery looming on the hillside beyond, so placed as to be able to shoot over the privateer at any hostile force approaching her. At the same time all eight guns of the *Sandwich* herself also bore directly upon the *Sally*. However, there was no sign of life on board. Apparently all hands were below—either at dinner, unsuspecting, or forewarned and lying in wait to spring a trap. Lieutenant Hull could only hope for the best.

Aboard the sloop the same appearance of innocence predominated. Hull lounged against the after rail. A naval quartermaster disguised as a somewhat ragged New England seaman held the tiller, while a few others similarly disguised tended the sheets and jib halyard. Captain Sanford braced himself on a bobstay, where he would be sure to be seen. But below decks the armed officers, sailors, and marines crouched in readiness to pour forth at a signal, while under the bulwarks, close hidden under what only appeared to be a slovenly tangle of gear, lay spare spars and canvas for use aboard the *Sandwich* in case they were needed. Hull was comforted to have them, for now in full light he could see that the privateer had indeed been stripped to her lower masts.

Even when the *Sally* drew within hail there was no challenge. Incredible as it may seem on a man-of-war—even a privately owned one—not a single man had been left to act as lookout while the others went below for the midday meal. Not until the little sloop crashed into the *Sandwich*, entangling her stubby bowsprit in the Frenchman's jib boom rigging, were the privateersmen aware that they were being attacked, and then it was too late. As the grappling irons flew and his men swarmed on deck and began to pour over the Frenchman's rail, Lieutenant Hull let go the stern anchor and raced forward to join the boarders. As they poured across to the *Sandwich*'s deck, a dozen or more of the privateer's crew tumbled up from below to take one startled glance at this unexpected company, then turn and dive again for cover. There was a quick spatter of musketry and a popping of pistols to speed them on their way, and almost in a twinkling the decks were cleared, the hatches battened on the hapless Frenchmen below, and guards stationed at the companionways.

While this was taking place, Captain Carmick and Lieutenant Amory with their detachment of marines tumbled into two of the *Sandwich*'s boats which lay conveniently alongside and pulled for the shore. So eager was the landing party to carry out their end of the exercise—for it was really little more—that they leaped from the boats before they were beached and waded ashore, up to their chins in water, with their arms held over their heads to keep them dry. Once on dry land they scrambled up the short but steep and brush-choked hillside and fell upon the fort before the small guard stationed there could gather itself together for resistance.

Once over the parapet it was only the work of a moment to disarm the garrison, spike the rusty, unloaded cannon and smash their carriages, and withdraw once more to the boats. In the meantime Lieutenant Hull, aboard the *Sandwich*, had turned to and cleared the privateer's decks of its accumulation of trash, restored the starboard battery to its proper place so that it bore upon the town, and sent up the topmasts and top hamper, bending on new canvas and making all ready for sea. In moving the starboard battery back in place, it was discovered that the guns were not loaded. Indeed they had not been fired in a long time and were full of rust and scale, and this was cleaned out by firing a blank charge, after which they were swabbed properly and reloaded.

All of this—the activity of the marines on shore and the sudden burst of life on board; the clatter of musketry and the banging of the guns, even though only charged with blanks— could scarcely escape notice in the town. Ashore the church bells began to toll and presently, singly and in small groups at first and then all in a crowd, the villagers began to stream out along the meandering footpath that led along the shore to the battery until they reached the point closest to the still anchored *Sandwich*, where they stopped and gathered, nearly five hundred strong, men, women and children, and stood staring out at the little drama taking place aboard the captive privateer. They did not shout or even seem to talk much among themselves. They simply stood and stared. But their attitude seemed ominous, and Hull ordered some of his men to stand by the guns.

Presently a pair of boats put out under a flag of truce and made for the *Sandwich*. The stern sheets of the foremost were occupied by the local priest and the alcalde, recognizable by their official dress. The other seemed to carry a number of lesser local officials, though no one aboard the *Sandwich* had any way of identifying them. Lieutenant Hull allowed them to come within hailing distance and there ordered them to heave to and state their business. There followed a moment of hasty consultation among the men in the boats. Then the alcalde stood up and delivered a long, impassioned harangue in Spanish—of which the Americans understood scarcely a word.

It seemed clear to Hull, however, that they were protesting the Americans' action in what they considered Spanish waters. Cagily, not to become embroiled in any delicate matters of international diplomacy, Hull merely replied in blunt English that he was simply carrying out his commanding officer's orders to cut out the French privateer *Sandwich* and bring her out to the *Constitution*. Whether or not the Spaniards understood the words any better than the Americans had understood theirs makes little difference. Lieutenant Hull seemed to have made his point clear. There followed a few moments of bilingual argument, complete with gestures which several times threatened to overturn the officials' boats. But when it became apparent that no amount of argument would move the Americans from their purpose the boats withdrew amid sour looks and muttered but incomprehensible imprecations.

In the meantime the task of rigging and bending on new sail had been completed, and at Hull's command both the *Sandwich* and the *Sally* weighed anchor and stood out to sea, to rendezvous with the *Constitution* off Cap François.

Considered in its full perspective the raid, though boldly conceived and executed, was little more than a minor diversion. But it was a powerful boost to American morale—especially on board the *Constitution*. For months they had cruised in those waters with nothing more exciting to buoy their enthusiasm than routine patrol and escort work, and in such circumstances even so minor a bit of action went far toward rekindling their spirit of eagerness. Commodore Talbot's report of the affair was glowing in its praise of Hull, Amory, and Carmick and their men, and even the secretary of the navy unbent sufficiently to commend them on their enterprise. The *Sandwich* and the *Sally* were both sent north to New York, in charge of prize crews, for adjudication.

Alas for all that! Apparently the diplomats took a different view of the matter and the *Constitution*'s luck ran true to form. According to the findings of the court Porto Plata was still technically a Spanish port, and the capture of the *Sandwich* was a violation of the laws of neutrality. The privateer was released from custody and returned to the Spanish minister with apologies and damages—which were deducted from the prize moneys due the *Constitution*. As for the *Sally*, she was condemned as having been engaged in illegal contraband traffic with the enemy and sold as a proper prize. But the officers and men of the *Constitution* saw none of the money realized from her sale. Every penny of it went to pay for the *Sandwich!*

Possibly Secretary of the Navy Stoddert felt a little conscience stricken about it all, having already praised the adventure in glowing terms. At any rate, in reporting the finding of the court to Commodore Talbot, he did close with a small sop:

I cannot withold my intire approbation of the spirit which dictated and the gallantry which achieved an enterprise which reflects honor on the American Navy; and knowing as you did that Puerto Plata was substantially French, tho' legally Spanish territory, a formal surrender not having been made under their treaty, no part of the merit of making the capture can be taken from you by the relinquishment of the Vessel.

6

HIGH BARBAREE

THERE is an old English sailor's song that tells of

> . . . *sailing down along the coast*
> *Of the High Barbaree!*

Although they did not know it yet, Americans were soon to have their chance at that, and one of the ships that played a part in the game was the 44-gun frigate *Constitution*.

For more than a year American commissioners had been at work in Paris seeking a solution to the dispute that would be acceptable to both parties. Late in 1800 they came to such an agreement, and on February 3, 1801, Congress ratified the treaty and the quasi-war with France came to an end. In March the *Constitution* was recalled from the West Indies and made her way home to Boston.

Had Congress and the new administration of Jefferson, which replaced that of Adams, taken a more realistic view of what was happening elsewhere in the world, they must have seen that America was not yet out of the woods by a long shot. But now that the immediate danger appeared to have been removed, those responsible for the national safety reverted to penny-pinching ways. While the *Constitution* drove northward Congress started paring, and on March 3, 1801, passed the Peace Establishment Act, by which the strength of the army was slashed drastically and the navy all but eliminated. Even those small parts that were retained were relegated for the time being to mothballs.

At the close of the war with France the navy, starting from scratch, had been built up to a force numbering some seven hundred officers and five to six thousand men, while the marine corps was composed of some eleven hundred officers and men. Thirty-four ships, exclusive of auxiliaries, were in commission. The Peace Establishment Act reduced this to 195 officers, including some 150 midshipmen, while the enlisted personnel was completely disbanded and only as many as were needed for maintenance re-enlisted. Of the ships twenty were disposed of, leaving only fourteen in service. These were immediately sent into various shipyards along the coast and laid up in ordinary. Clearly Congress fondly hoped—if it did not actually expect —that their services would never again be needed.

That such a millennium would be desirable is hardly to be denied. Unhappily, it was no more to be then than it is now. In the beginning the very genesis of the navy had been the need to protect America's burgeoning commerce in the Mediterranan from the savage corsairs of the North African coast. The treaty with Algiers had bought the United States a costly and precarious sort of truce that only lulled it into complacency, and the quarrel with the French had served to divert American attention from that area. As a result the ink was hardly dry on the treaty of peace with France when the United States was somewhat rudely jolted out of its smug little dream world by the sudden news that the pasha of Tripoli, Yussuf Karamanli —a gentleman who had hitherto given little trouble—had expressed his jealousy at the favored treatment of Algiers, ousted the American consul, James Cathcart, chopped down the American flagstaff in front of the consulate, and declared war. It was not possible, of course, for Tripoli—even aided by Tunis, Algiers, and Morocco—to carry the war to American shores. But United States trade with the Mediterranean, which had increased to an annual value of nearly $12,000,000, was unprotected and extremely vulnerable. Thus, to all intents and purposes, the United States was back once more at almost exactly the point from which it had started.

The treaty of November 1795 with Algiers had cost close to a million dollars, an astronomical sum for a new nation already burdened with staggering obligations. The other Barbary states had been apparently satisfied with lesser sums, but it was not long before their greed was tickled by jealousy and they began to cast about for excuses to increase their demands. This nation's mistake, of course, was to have knuckled under to Algiers to the extent of granting her more than the others. Nor was the American position improved when, as a result of other problems and obligations that beset the new nation, payments under the treaty were so delayed that the United States "peace" commissioners were forced to toss in as an additional sop a spanking new 32-gun frigate, a brig, and two schooners. The brig, the *Hassan Bashaw*, mounted eighteen 6-pounders and was built at Philadelphia. The schooners, also built in that city, were the *Lelah Eisha*, mounting eighteen 4-pounders, and the *Skoldebrand*—named for a Swedish diplomat who had been of assistance to the United States during the negotiations— carrying twenty 4's. The three smaller vessels were completed in 1798, though the exact date of delivery is not clear. The frigate *Crescent*, however, was the most important. She was built at Portsmouth, New Hampshire, in 1797 at a cost of $100,000 and was delivered the following year, apparently with the first payments under the treaty. The following excerpt from the *Portsmouth Gazette* gives some of the story:

CRESCENT FRIGATE

Portsmouth, Jan. 20th (1798)

On Thursday morning about sunrise, a gun was discharged from the *Crescent* frigate as a signal for getting under way; and at 10, A.M., she cleared the harbor, with a fine leading breeze. May they arrive in safety at the place of their destination, and present to the Dey of Algiers, one of the finest specimens of elegant naval architecture which was ever borne on the Piscataqua's waters.

Blow all ye winds that fill the prosperous sail,
And hush'd in peace be every adverse gale.

The *Crescent* is a present from the United States to the Dey, as compensation for delay in not fulfilling our treaty stipulations in proper time.

Richard O'Brien, Esq., who was ten years a prisoner at Algiers, took passage in the above frigate, and is to reside at Algiers as Consul General of the United States to all the Barbary States.

The *Crescent* has many valuable presents on board for the Dey, and when she sailed was supposed to be worth at least three hundred thousand dollars.

Twenty-six barrels of dollars constituted a part of her cargo.

It is worthy of remark, that the captain, chief of the officers, and many of the privates of the *Crescent* frigate, have been prisoners at Algiers.

Officering and manning the frigate to the greatest possible extent with former prisoners of the Algerine pirates apparently was a gesture on the part of the American government; an attempt to flatter and mollify the dey that did no credit to the United States government.

Whatever the effect upon the dey of Algiers, however, the arrival of the *Crescent* at that port heavily laden with presents and tribute scarcely had a soothing effect upon the other piratical potentates of North Africa. In Tripoli the pasha promptly summoned Cathcart—himself a former prisoner of the Algerines and the survivor of eleven years of enslavement in the dey's palace—and demanded similar presents, an enlargement of the annual tribute, and the gift of a frigate or a brig such as had been sent to Algiers. He would wait six months he told Mr. Cathcart, and if the United States did not agree to his demands by that time he would declare war. The pasha further implemented the interview with a letter to the President in which he scolded the United States for its "empty words" and lack of "deeds," and threatening that "if only flattering words are meant without performance, everyone will act as he finds convenient."

The bey of Tunis became similarly recalcitrant, complaining that some of the naval stores sent him as part of the American tribute fell short of specifications. He, too, wrote to President Jefferson demanding a present of forty cannon of different calibers, and still later he summoned William Eaton, the American consul at Tunis, and demanded an additional ten thousand stand of arms.

"Tell your government," he said arrogantly, "to send them without delay; peace depends on compliance."

Even as this sort of tension was mounting elsewhere in Barbary, the state of American relations with Algiers was scarcely improving. In June 1800, the United States sloop of war *George Washington*, 24, Captain William Bainbridge, sailed for Algiers with the regular annual tribute for the dey. She arrived in September, coming to anchor, in compliance with the orders of the port authorities, close under the guns of the batteries on shore, where her official cargo was duly landed and placed in the care of the American consul, Richard O'Brien.

Having thus discharged his unsavory duty, Captain Bainbridge was only too ready and anxious to depart. Before he was allowed to do so, however, he was to learn by bitter experience the truth of the old rhyme:

> *Great fleas have little fleas upon their backs to bite 'em,*
> *And little fleas have lesser fleas, and so ad infinitum.*
> *And the great fleas themselves, in turn, have greater fleas*
>   *to go on;*
> *While these again have greater still, and greater still,*
>   *and so on.*

In the hierarchy of the fleas the pashas, the beys, and the deys stood somewhere in the middle, for though they were fond of looking upon themselves as sovereign and independent, nevertheless, even as they demanded tribute so were they in turn obliged to pay tribute to the sultan of Turkey as the price of *his* peace. At that particular juncture it so happened that the dey of Algiers was seriously out of favor with the Sublime

Porte, for he had rather stupidly concluded a treaty with France, with whom Turkey and Great Britain were at war. Napoleon and his armies were presumably trapped in Egypt, and the sultan had been rather counting on Algiers to help block the Corsican's only escape route, westward through the Mediterranean between Italy and Africa. Consequently the dey was anxious to forward to Constantinople a sufficiently munificent gift—say some five or six hundred thousand dollars, horses and lions, houris, slaves, and eunuchs and two hundred or more envoys—to placate the Grand Turk's wrath.

In the presence of the *George Washington* in his harbor the dey believed that he had found an ideal solution to his dilemma. She was fast enough and large enough for the purpose. She was well armed and stoutly manned. Moreover, it would add considerably to his own stature in the eyes of the sultan if he should demonstrate in such a practical way his power to commandeer the public vessels of less favored nations. Accordingly he somewhat arbitrarily requested that the American man-of-war be placed at his disposal and take on board the presents and envoys that he wished to send to Constantinople.

As he might have suspected, Captain Bainbridge was incensed. He refused flatly to entertain the proposal, whereupon the dey discarded his pretense of diplomacy and changed his request to a flat demand, at the same time threatening to blow the *George Washington* out of the water with all hands if Captain Bainbridge persisted in his attitude.

"You pay me tribute," he argued, "whereby you become my slaves and gives me the right to order you to act as I wish!"

It was a delicate moment, especially as the shoreward batteries were entirely composed of heavy caliber guns and bore at almost point-blank range. They were quite capable of pulverizing the ship and all on board at a single blast if the dey only gave the word. At this point the consul, Mr. O'Brien, intervened. He had long been acquainted with the devious ways of Moslem politicians, and his advice was not lightly to be ignored. While he agreed that the demand was outrageous, he pointed out that it was by no means unusual. British, French, and similar nations had complied with like requests; and he added that the dey would have no compunction about carrying out his threat. Indeed, continued refusal would not only lead to their own probable annihilation, it would also result in a declaration of war against the United States.

Bainbridge had no choice but to clamp his teeth on his anger and comply. The following extract from the log of the *George Washington* for Thursday, October 9, 1800, gives some indication of the feelings on board:

Commences with Light winds & Fair weather. This day we were big with Expectation of returning to the Land of Liberty—had every thing prepared for the voyage. at this instant of Anticipated [departure] we receive a postive command from a Dispoctic Dey of Algiers that we must be the porters of savage Tygers & more Savage Algerines Ambassadors in Compliment to the Grand Seignior at Constantinople. At 2 P.M. the Capt. Consul & the Dey's executive Juncto [Junta] came on board. The pendant of the United States was struck and the Algerine Flag hoisted at the Main Top Gallant Royal mast head. 7 guns were fired in Compliment. Some tears fell at this Instance of national Humility [*sic*] The Compliment was answered from the Castle.

Some ten days later the United States consul general to Algiers, Richard O'Brien, in a letter to William Eaton, the United States consul at Tunis, expressed his own reaction in considerably more explicit terms and at greater length. Some of his side comments are worthy of remark:

Sir, I wrote you & forwarded you letters announcing the arrival of the *Geo. Washington* at Algiers the 17th Sept. On the 9th Inst said ship was ready for Sea & would sail on the 10th for the U.S. but the dey in a great fury declared to me that if said ship did not proceed with his ambasador & Regalia for Constantinople That he no longer held to his friendship with the U.S. we had no alternative but to acquise [*sic*] or War would be the result and I am convinced Detention to the Ship and Crew, besides every other loss from a sudden surprise. It is a forced business—the ship is under sail and is to return here god knows when I supose in 5 months—I would make no responsibility, but Sir, if any accident happens depend on the *first* news said Potent dey will send out his Corsairs—and take all Americans in order to repay himself—the ship is the Peace of the U.S. with Alg'rs—I have had a Severe Squall.

On the 14th Inst arrived the ship *Brutus* capt Brown from Livorn in 10 dayes—the dey will insist the Said Ship will proceed to Rhodes to bring him a cargo of Turks—Observe said Ship has 1056 cases of Oyle and Soap on board—the dey told me if Said Ship did not go he would oblidge her per force—no pay No Consideration but the dey's own dispotic will—I will expect a Successor in the next vessel and the U.S. will give the outfit to me if I will ask it the 2d time I am too Heart Sick and tired of Barbary to be tempted to stay any longer even the Out Fit should be—20 Thous'nd Dollars—At least after the *General Washington* returns I shall Certainly leave this Country whether the U S sends a Consul or *not*.

Crew of *Washington*	. . . .	131	
Ambassador & suit .	. . . .	100	331
Negro men women & children .	.	100	

4 horses 150 sheep 25 horned cattle. 4 lions,
4 tygars. 4 antilopes 12 parrets. funds &
Regalia amt nearly one million of dol'rs. I have Sir,

6 weeks past been very sickly. The Child has been twice very unwell, and in fact never more irritated than I have been. We want 6 frigates in this Sea. to wait the event of the *Washington* making the voyage Safe or Not.

/s/ O'Brien.

In view of what he reports one can certainly forgive Consul O'Brien for his mood of the moment, and for his impulse to throw up his hands and go home. But obviously his reaction was only a mood, justified or not, for it was to be four long years before Richard O'Brien resigned his post, packed up his traps, and returned to the United States. In the meantime he clung to the courage of his convictions, served his country and

his countrymen faithfully and well, and in the end helped dic-
tate the terms of the peace.

As for Captain Bainbridge and the *Washington*, humilia-
ting as the enforced duty was there were some compensations. He
had already taken pains to observe the western Mediterranean
during his voyage from Gibraltar to Algiers. Now, on the further voyage eastward, he had opportunity to observe conditions
of sea, weather, and navigation throughout the eastern part of
that sea—waters hitherto unknown to any American keel. The
George Washington was the first American ship—let alone the
first public man-of-war, to penetrate the Dardanelles and the
Bosporus and drop anchor off the legendary city of Constantinople. Contrary to his expectations, the Grand Turk and his
officers had only contempt for the envoys from Algiers, whom
they received like flea-bitten scavengers, while at the same time
they were eaten with curiosity and even respect for this first representative of the new nation beyond the seas to visit their shores.
The crew was feted. Bainbridge dined with the Turk himself,
and with as many of his captains, paschas, beglerbegs and high-
muck-a-mucks as he was able. At their insistence he held open
house on the *Washington*, and was himself the first American to
sail upon the Black Sea. In short, he was met with respect and
consideration such as was due his rank and official position, and
on leaving he was provided with dispatches for the dey of Algiers and with a Grand Turkish firman entitling him to the special protection of the sultan in any part of the Turkish Empire.
The dispatches to the dey were much less pleasant. He, having
just entered upon a treaty with the Turk's enemies, the French,
was arbitrarily allowed sixty days in which to cut down the
French flagstaff and declare war on Napoleon.

Of course, the fact that the United States at this time was
also presumably at war—even though undeclared—with
France, may have had something to do with the Turk's almost
heavy-handed friendliness. In any case Bainbridge returned to
Algiers with paper weapons, and a new appreciation of the
weakness of the dey.

On November 17, 1800, Bainbridge wrote to the secretary of the navy, from Constantinople:

. . . should a demand be made . . . of the frigate's remaining 5 or 6 months in this place, I shall consider myself justifiable [*sic*] in not complying . . . a refusal may be attended with the threat of war which I candidly believe will never be put into execution, would 6 of our frigates appear before Algiers. . . . A list of their whole marine force, I had the honor of enclosing you from that place, you can see the pitiful force of the *All Powerful Algiears*, to which is to be added they have only 2 ports on their whole coast. . . . Believe me Sir, my information of that Country is so correct, that I do not hesitate in saying that 6 or 8 frigates in the Mediterranean Sea, would give us more permanent security than any treaty that can be made with the States of Barbary. . . .

Having once succeeded in his little wiles, the dey of Algiers was sure that he had carefully and craftily set the stage for more to come. The Americans were naive. The Grand Turk was far away, and an old man. But he reckoned without two things; the determination of the Americans, and the long arm of the Turk. It was the dey's plan to have his port officials bring the *Washington* to anchor on her return as before, close under the guns of the shore batteries. There, under any pretext he might be able to devise, he would seize her, enslave all her officers and men, and then declare war upon the United States. Having thus secured the upper hand he would force the Americans to their knees by threatening to torture and then butcher all of the several hundred prisoners in his hands. By this means they would be forced to agree to an exorbitant increase in the annual tribute and at the same time to pay a tremendous ransom for the captives—a sum sufficient not only to reimburse him for the fine the sultan had just imposed but also to cover his own tribute to the Porte and leave a handsome profit for himself. To cap it all, he would stipulate that the American ship, the *George Washington*, must make a second trip to Constantinople with the fine and the tribute for the sultan.

On his return from Constantinople on the twenty-first of January, however, Captain Bainbridge tossed the first wrench into the dey's scheme by refusing to anchor within range of the shore batteries. The dey was furious, but Bainbridge was adamant. He would not move, and it was only after much pleading on the part of Consul O'Brien that he would even consent to go on shore and wait upon the dey. Then he went only after he had been given solemn assurance of his personal safety. Not that he placed any faith in the dey's pledges, however solemn, but he meant to have the record clear!

On his arrival at the palace he found the dey in a ferocious mood. At the outset he was frosty and hostile but no worse. But control was short-lived in the face of Bainbridge's firm attitude of defiance. Before the audience was more than a few minutes old he burst into a tantrum of ungovernable rage and threatened the American with captivity and torture. Bainbridge heard him out for a few brief moments and then, when it seemed apparent that the dey was about to order his seizure, calmly produced the firman of the sultan which had been given to him in Constantinople by Capudan Pasha. Instantly all the wind drained from the dey's sails. Bainbridge was released at once with every show of fawning friendship and given full leave to come or go as he pleased. The next day, in compliance with the sultan's orders, the flagpole at the French consulate was cut down and war was declared once more against the French. At the same time some 400 Venetian, Maltese, and Sicilian prisoners who had been taken while presumably under British protection were set free and were taken aboard the *George Washington.*

Although he believed the United States to be still at war with France, Captain Bainbridge, in the name of humanity, also took on board the French consul and his family and staff and as many French nationals then in the city as could be found, and transported them in safety to Alicante, where he landed them on the eighth of May. Having thus earned the gratitude of Napoleon and the French, Bainbridge at last felt free to

The *Constitution* was launched in Boston Harbor on a clear day in 1787. The builder spoke of his "conducting into the ocean a powerful agent of national justice which hope dictates may become the just pride and ornament of the American name."

". . . to the shores of Tripoli." In 1803 the *Constitution* sailed to the Mediterranean to lead an expedition against the Barbary states. There, in 1805, assisted by the fleet, she first blockaded and then bombarded the corsairs' stronghold at Tripoli, thus forcing its surrender and ending the dreaded power of the Barbary pirates forever.

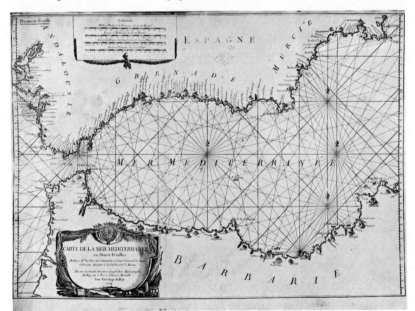

Charts of the Mediterranean, although decorative, often omitted important land and shoal areas. In the harbor of Tripoli the frigate *Philadelphia* went aground and was captured by the Tripolitans.

To avenge the death of his brother, Stephen Decatur chased, boarded, and captured a Barbary ship. In this romanticized painting, one of Decatur's men, Reuben James, steps in to save him from an attacking pirate.

Early in the war of 1812, the *Constitution* was nearly trapped by a
squadron of five British ships. The wind died, and the *Constitution*

lowered her boats and oarsmen applied "white ash breeze" to tow her away. Finally, after a three-day chase, the American frigate escaped.

In its most celebrated victory the *Constitution* demolished the British frigate *Guerriere* off the coast of Boston in the War of 1812. The *Guerriere* was blown up and sunk since there was no hope of getting her into port as a prize.

Captain Isaac Hull—stalwart commander of the *Constitution* in the battle with the *Guerriere*.

Rejoicing that the British were no longer invincible, the *Constitution's* men hail their victory over the *Guerriere*. An old legend says one of them yelled as a British cannon ball hit the American vessel's hull and bounced off, "Her sides are made of iron," and thus christened her "Old Ironsides," the name which Oliver Wendell Holmes immortalized in his famous poem.

On December 29, 1812, the *Constitution* destroyed the British frigate *Java* off the Brazilian coast, Commodore William Bainbridge fired the opening broadside with long 24-pound guns before coming in range of the *Java's* carronades. Within an hour all of the *Java's* spars were shot away. The chart below shows the winding course of the battle.

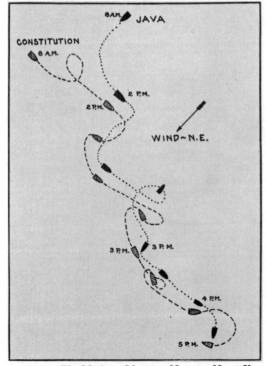

The Mariners Museum, Newport News, Va.

turn his ship toward home, where he arrived early in the summer of 1801.

In the meantime matters in America had not been at a standstill. Neither the news of Tripoli's declaration of war nor of Commodore Bainbridge's difficulties with the Algerines reached the United States until almost summer. However, there had been numerous other and earlier reports of a disturbing nature to warn the government that all was not well in the Mediterranean and to suggest that as it appeared to be developing the situation was likely to grow worse before it was better. Obviously steps had to be taken to give some protection to our growing commerce, and for this purpose the secretary of the navy had already ordered a squadron "of observation," under the command of Commodore Richard Dale. This squadron was composed of the frigates *President*, 44 (flagship), Captain James Barron; *Philadelphia*, 36, Captain Samuel Barron; and *Essex*, 32, Captain William Bainbridge, and the schooner *Enterprise*, 19, Lieutenant Andrew Sterrett. They sailed on the twentieth of May—all but the *Essex*, which perforce remained behind to await the arrival of her commander. Poor Bainbridge had hardly had time to set foot once more in his beloved home before he was turned about and ordered to his new command, and by late summer he was back again in the Mediterranean waters he so heartily detested.

Had the *Constitution* been in readiness for such duty she would undoubtedly have been included in Dale's command at that time. In fact she had actually been listed as one of the ships of the squadron. However, she did not get back from the West Indies until too late, and consequently had to be scratched from the list. When at last she did return she was found to be badly in need of repairs and was ordered to Boston where she was laid up for that purpose. Captain Talbot returned to his home, leaving his first lieutenant, Isaac Hull, in full charge. When he retired in September, Hull was left in command as acting captain.

For some unexplained reason the *Constitution* now lay a full two inactive years in Boston. At the outset, to be sure, the delay may be laid to the fact that following her long tour of duty in West Indian waters she was in need of considerable repairs. The winds, the weathers, and the warm waters of those seas are notoriously unkind to wooden ships, to say nothing of sails, spars, and rigging. Still it seems incredible that the damage to her should have been so extensive as to require so much time. More likely the delay in returning her to active service was the result of several shifts of command and their attendant red tape.

Hull remained in charge though he was not then upgraded to the rank of captain. Shortly before Christmas, Hull received orders to speed the work on the *Constitution* as she would prob-ably be called upon for service about the first of February, 1802. That date arrived and passed, and either the ship was not ready for sea or for some other reason was passed over for the moment. Lieutenant Hull was ordered to join the *Adams*, 28, at New York, and his place aboard the *Constitution* was taken by the aging Sam Nicholson—the same man who had been her original commanding officer. There seems little doubt that the appointment was something in the nature of a political consolation prize, for by the death of Barry, Nicholson had in-herited the number one position on the captains' list, and since at the time he was in command at the Boston Navy Yard—or, that is to say, its forerunner since the Navy Yard per se had not yet come into existence—it seemed as good a time as any to give the old veteran a final fling at command on his own deck. Nicholson himself had requested command of the frigate and active sea duty some time since, but it is doubtful if it was ever intended that he should take her out.

In any case, during the slightly more than a year in which he was in command of her the *Constitution* did not leave her berth, nor was a full crew shipped. The work of repairing and refit-ting continued, but hardly at a pace that suggested any sea service immediately pending.

In the meantime matters in the Mediterranean boiled down

to virtual stalemate. Commodore Dale, having sailed before the news had been received in the United States, was unaware until he reached Gibraltar of Tripoli's declaration of war. At the same time, however, he was not unprepared for the possibility, for Mr. Cathcart's letters had warned the President bluntly of the bashaw's belligerent attitude, his treachery and bad faith. Upon arriving at Gibraltar, Dale found two Tripolitan men-of-war, a ship of 26 guns and a brig of 16, under the command of a Tripolitan "admiral"—a Scottish renegade who called himself Murad Rais—at anchor, obviously only awaiting an opportunity to slip out into the Atlantic. The "admiral" pro tested vigorously that there was no war, but reports from a number of sources ashore and from merchant vessels lately arrived from the central Mediterranean were sufficiently convincing to put the commodore on his guard. His orders, under which he had sailed, were not specific enough to permit him to take the offensive. Neither was the force at his command enough to make any such action effective. Yet he did the best he could, leaving the *Philadelphia* at the Straits to keep a close watch on the two Tripolitans while he continued eastward with the rest of his squadron. He appeared off Algiers and Tripoli with apparently chastening effect, for the dey—according to O'Brien, who was still there—tempered his truculence considerably at the sight of them, while at Tripoli the corsairs stayed prudently in port, close under the protection of the forts, so long as he remained in those waters.

For the most part, however, the squadron's activity was confined to convoy duty, in which respect it is worth noting that not a single American vessel was taken during the rest of that year. Only one action worth noticing took place. This occurred when the schooner *Enterprise*, 12, Lieutenant Sterrett commanding, fell in with the Tripolitan polacre *Tripoli*, 14. A bloody three-hour battle ensued in the course of which the corsair lost 20 killed and 30 wounded out of a crew of 90 officers and men, while on board the American vessel there were no casualties of either description. The fight ended when the Tripolitan

captain hauled down his flag and threw it into the sea and surrendered.

However, Lieutenant Sterrett was not authorized to bring in
his prize. Accordingly, after tending the wounded, he threw
overboard the Tripolitan's guns and ammunition, stripped her
of everything but a single sail and a spar and such food and
water as she might need for the voyage, and set her adrift, to
make the best of her way home to Tripoli.

Commodore Dale remained on station until December, when,
the term of enlistment of most of his men having expired and
the weather having turned seasonably bad, he returned to the
United States in his flagship, the *President*, 44, and the *Enterprise*. The following spring he was relieved by Commodore
Richard V. Morris, who went out in his flagship the *Chesapeake*, 36, Acting Captain Isaac Chauncey; accompanied by
the *Constellation*, 36, Captain Alexander Murray; the *New
York*, 36, Captain James Barron; the *Adams*, 28, Captain
Hugh Campbell; the *John Adams*, 28, Captain John Rodgers;
and the *Enterprise*, Sterrett. On arrival in the Mediterranean,
Commodore Morris was to be joined also by the *Boston*, 28,
Captain Daniel McNiell, which had been sent out some time
previously to carry our new minister, Robert R. Livingston, to
France. Captain McNiell, however, was notoriously a "lone
wolf" to the point of eccentricity, and on this occasion he seems
to have had his own plans, for he almost studiously avoided
meeting with his superiors, cruised for a time in the Mediterranean, appeared fleetingly before Tripoli, offered independent convoy to a number of merchant ships, and ultimately
returned alone to the United States, where he was promptly
dismissed from the service, though he does not appear to have
been severely censured for his conduct.

The commodore's case was somewhat different. Even without
the *Boston*, he commanded the most formidable American force
yet to enter the Mediterranean. Furthermore, the term of the
seamen's enlistment had been extended to two full years, so that
now at last a ship could be kept long enough on station to be

really effective. In addition, he was empowered to make prizes and send them in, and he was instructed to treat specifically with the pasha of Tripoli for peace on terms honorable to the United States.

In the hands of a more aggressive commander undoubtedly such a force could have been used with telling effect. Commodore Morris, however, evidently lacked the drive and initiative needed to make the best possible use of it. Though he gave the appearance of bustle and activity, keeping his ships moving constantly from port to port—as often on the European side of the sea as on the African, it must be said—the campaign was a dismal disappointment and accomplished practically nothing. Indeed, so ineffectual was it that in the spring of 1803 orders were issued for his recall and the command of the squadron was turned over temporarily to Captain Rodgers.

At almost the same time in Washington, which had by now supplanted Philadelphia as the seat of government, orders were issued to Captain Edward Preble to take command of the *Constitution* at Boston, make her ready for active service at sea, and proceed at the earliest possible date to assume command of the Mediterranean squadron.

7

PREBLE TAKES COMMAND

EDWARD PREBLE, who succeeded Samuel Nicholson in command of the *Constitution*, might be considered something of an anomaly. In point of age he was almost young enough to have been the old commodore's son—had the commodore been such a gay dog. In point of sea service and command he was virtually contemporaneous. But he died in 1807 at the age of forty-six, while the older man survived him to the age of seventy. In point of rank, as counted by the naval system of numbers, he was far below Nicholson. Yet in his brief span he carved for himself a niche next to that of John Paul Jones in the navy's Hall of Fame. Few outside the service even remember the name of Nicholson. Paul Jones has been called—and rightly so—the "Father of the American Navy." It was he who established American naval traditions, fostered a fighting service, and pointed the way. Preble has been given the same title in respect to the United States Navy, as distinguished from that of the Revolution. It might be more appropriate, however, to speak of him as the "headmaster of the United States Navy," for it was in his "school," under his close, almost personal guidance, that the first generation of naval heroes was trained and ultimately brought to the fullness of their abilities.

Indeed, he looked and acted the part—which is in no way meant to detract from his ability or his genius. He was spare. He was balding. He was dour and dyspeptic, severe of countenance and demeanor—the very picture of the strict pedagogue.

Disliked at first, though never despised, for his insistence on perfection, he was later loved and honored for that very reason. Once, like a schoolmaster, he referred to the officers who served under him as "mere boys," which was in the main quite true for they were all considerably junior to him in years. At the time more than one of them resented the remark, but when long after he added the comment "but they were all good boys" they began to understand and loved him for it.

In other words, it was his destiny to be placed in charge of a heterogeneous and inexperienced group of youngsters which he was to weld into a competent and efficient group of officers, capable of commanding respect for the United States abroad and maintaining the rights of Americans in every sea. At the same time he furnished this country a naval foundation that has ever since served as a basis of pride and inspiration.

He was born in Falmouth (now Portland), Maine, in 1761. Apparently his people were not essentially seafaring folk, but the pull of the sea was strong for him. It is said that he ran away in 1778, entered the Massachusetts navy as a midshipman in 1779, and continued in that service through the Revolution, when he was mustered out with the rank of lieutenant. From then until the establishment of the United States Navy he commanded ships in the merchant service, grew thoroughly familiar with the principal commercial routes, and established himself firmly as an outstanding seaman of the day. In 1798 he was recalled to naval service and given command of the *Pickering*, in which he served in the West Indies. When the *Essex*, 32, was launched at Salem, Massachusetts, in 1799, he was placed in command, and in convoy of a large number of merchant ships took her around the Cape of Good Hope and across the Indian Ocean to the East Indies—the first time an American man-of-war had been seen in those waters.

In those days, in stiff weather, even the stoutest of ships was notoriously wet and uncomfortable. Fire was the most dreaded of all hazards in those wooden sailing vessels, and when the gales blew and the storms raged it was more often than not the

rule to draw the galley fires and subsist for days on end on rum
and raw rations, cold salt pork or beef and water-soaked hard-
tack. Duff, a soggy mixture of flour and water, was a staple
article of diet, and on Sundays and holidays some dried raisins
were added to it and it was called "plum duff." Weevilly bis-
cuits were also standard fare, and there is an old navy legend
that the midshipmen made pets of the worms and raced them
upon the tables in the cockpit after supper—those same tables
that were used by them for eating, and by the surgeon and his
mates for operating on the wounded in times of action. Add to
this the constant change of climate, from arctic to tropic to
subarctic, and it will be understood why they who manned those
ships had to be made of iron.

Edward Preble was lean and wiry, but he was not iron. Under the circumstances one can understand why, after such a
voyage, he should be furloughed for reasons of health. After
the return of the *Essex* he spent several months recuperating
at home and was then ordered to the command of the *Adams*,
28, at New York. But his health was still poor, and in due
course he was relieved by Captain Campbell and his furlough
was extended.

By the spring of 1803, however, Captain Preble felt himself
sufficiently recovered to report for active duty and was promptly assigned to replace Nicholson on the *Constitution*. He took
command on May 31 and immediately set to work to fill out his
crew, put the final necessary touches on the ship in preparation
for active duty, and take on board his stores, ammunition, and
supplies. By midsummer he was ready, and on August 14 he
sailed, carrying with him as passengers Tobias Lear, the new
consul general to the Barbary states, and his wife.

The voyage out was pleasant enough and uneventful save for
one incident which told much of the mettle of the man. It was
an inky night and they were under Cape St. Vincent, bearing
east-southeast for Cadiz and the lips of Gibraltar. As usual in
those waters at that time of year, there was little wind, only a
light breath of air from shoreward that carried with it the

strong smell of the land hard by. It was a welcome scent in a sailor's nose after weeks of smelling nothing but salt and spray. Overhead the tackle and rigging creaked and groaned almost comfortably with the lift and fall of the ship in the swells, and the sails filled and occasionally flapped slightly as they dropped into the trough between seas. The usual lookouts were posted, but a man could scarcely see his nose if he looked at it cross-eyed let alone a vessel a gunshot's distance away. But these were wartime waters—or at least, in those days of delayed communication no one was quite sure that they were not. England and France had signed a peace at Amiens only the year before, but already there were rumors that the war had been resumed, and who could tell which way the Spaniards would turn? In any case it behooved a sailor to watch and beware.

But how was a man to watch in this? Eyes were no good in such pitch blackness, and a lookout came quickly to know that he must depend on his senses of smell and hearing if he were to be effective.

It was true that a man's own ship could be uncommonly noisy on such a still night. But there is a difference in sounds. The creak of the rigging, the grumble of the masts, the protests of a man's own ship, become familiar to him. He knows instinctively when they are a part of the deck he treads. On the other hand, any sound from outside of the ship, from over the water, is instantly recognizable. Even though its source cannot be seen, a lookout knows they came from somewhere "out there." That's what his task is. If he cannot keep a lookout with his eyes, he must do so with his ears.

That was the situation on that night when the *Constitution* ran down her easting. There were lookouts posted as ordered, fore and aft and aloft, and when one—the record does not say which—heard the faint splash of water on a nearby hull the word was passed silently—also as ordered—to the "Old Man," who came on deck in his carpet slippers, and with speaking trumpet in hand.

Bare feet whispered on sanded decks. There was a faint rumble as the guns moved on their carriages; a creaking as the gun ports opened. When the silence was once again complete Preble raised his trumpet.

"What ship is that?" he barked into the blackness.

There was a moment in which those aboard the *Constitution* could almost feel the surprise of those aboard the stranger. Then came back the usual counter-hail.

"What ship is that?"

Preble replied that his vessel was the United States ship *Constitution* and asked again "What ship is that?"

After a long pause, the stranger echoed the same question. "What ship is that?"

Commodore Preble raised his trumpet once more, identified himself again and repeated his original question.

A reply came faintly through the night:

"What—ship—?"

Preble was quickly losing patience. At the top of his voice he told the stranger that he had already given the name of his ship several times. He now would hail the stranger once more. Unless a proper answer was returned, Preble added, he would fire a shot.

Before he could name his ship, the other interrupted to warn that a shot would be returned by a broadside.

The stranger then identified himself as His Britannic Majesty's ship *Donnegal*, 84, Sir Richard Strachan, commodore, and ordered Preble to send one of his boats on board.

This was too much for Preble, who bellowed back that he was Edward Preble, an American commodore, commanding the United States *Constitution*, 44 guns, and that he was not about to send his boat on board any other vessel. Turning toward the waist, he commanded the gun crews in a tone that could not but be heard by the other ship to blow on their matches.

There was a long moment of silence. Then through the dark came the sound of falls and the noise of a boat striking the water. Oars rattled, and presently came the rythmic creak and splash as rowers pulled toward them. A few moments later an obviously embarrassed English lieutenant clambered apologetically aboard.

With a face that shone an almost fluorescent pink in the dim light of the battle lanterns the young officer admitted that the ship from which he came was not the *Donnegal* at all but the frigate *Maidstone*, whose course had crossed that of the *Constitution* more than once in the West Indies and was destined to do so again before their fighting days were done. Although she was rated as a frigate she was a much smaller and more lightly armed vessel than the American, and would have been hardly a match for her had it come to a fight. The reason for the deception, the lieutenant explained, had been because the *Constitution* had caught them entirely off guard in the darkness with their crew snoring in their hammocks, their guns in slings, and their gun ports dogged down, and consequently it had been necessary to spar for time in which to get their men to quarters, especially as it was obvious that the challenger was not English and they had had no inkling of any American man-of-war in those waters.

It was a minor incident, of course, though if Commodore Preble had not kept his head it might have had rather serious international repercussions. As it was they parted on a friendly basis, and because of his firm stand and prompt decision Preble's popular status in the *Constitution* was much improved.

One other event occurred during that voyage which, while it seemed scarcely worth mentioning at the moment, proved to be of much greater significance later on. They were still some distance from Cadiz when they fell in with a strange sail which from the cut of her jib was not a peaceful merchantman. Neither did she resemble any man-of-war that the commodore had ever seen before. Accordingly he called his crew to quarters, prepared for action, spoke the stranger, and sent a boat aboard her. She proved to be the *Maimounia*, a Moorish cruiser of 30 guns and a cutthroat crew of some 150 men. They were clearly up to no good, but her passports and credentials were examined by Consul Lear and found to be all in order, having been endorsed by the United States consul at Tangier, James Simpson. Since she was directly the property of the emperor of Morocco, with whom so far as Preble knew the United States was not at war, he had no choice, despite his inclinations, but to let her go about her business while the *Constitution* continued to Gibraltar.

Upon his arrival there on September 12, 1803, Preble found Captain William Bainbridge in the *Philadelphia* already at anchor with a prize, the Barbary corsair *Mirboka*, 22, Ibrahim Lubarez commanding, and an American brig, the *Celia* of Boston, which had been retaken from the *Mirboka*. At the same time he was informed that Lieutenant Hull was cruising to the eastward, off Cape Ghat on the Spanish side of the Mediterranean, in search of two Tripolitan cruisers which had been reported seen in that vicinity. Also lying at Gibraltar was the Tripolitan cruiser *Meshouda*, which had been blockaded in that port by Dale on his first arrival and had been unable to move since, her crew having dismanteled her and returned home to Tripoli overland.

On the face of it the presence of the *Mirboka* and the *Meshouda* at Gibraltar in the custody of the Americans might have seemed like something of a feather in their caps. Actually, however, the situation was somewhat awkward, for it posed certain rather knotty international complications. So far as the *Meshouda* was concerned there was no doubt in the Americans' minds but that she belonged to Tripoli, though ever since her internment at Gibraltar she had been claimed by the emperor of Morocco. Politely but firmly successive American commanders had offered to surrender her to the Moors on presentation of adequate proof of ownership. Since this was not forthcoming they continued to hold her and, indeed, considered her case virtually closed.

The case of the *Mirboka*, however, was more complicated. When she had first been laid aboard by the *Philadelphia*, her papers had seemed in order and she appeared to be the property of Morocco. The identity of her prize was unknown and so far as Bainbridge could tell might well have been legitimate. But the commander of the corsair himself gave his game away when, under the impression that the *Philadelphia* was an English frigate, he stated that the prize was an American which had been sailing under his protection for several days. The circumstances aroused Bainbridges's suspicions, since the sailing of the brig seemed to suggest a prize rather than a vessel under escort. Accordingly, after some altercation with the prize crew he managed to put a boarding party into her when she was found to have—prisoners battened under hatches—the American captain Richard Bowen and seven American crewmen of Boston.

Captain Bowen and his men were, of course, released and transshipped to the *Philadelphia,* where the cruiser's captain was confronted with them. Upon what grounds, he was asked, had he seized the *Celia* and imprisoned her captain and crew? Was the United States at war with Morocco?

Ibrahim replied that he had no authority, but that when he had left Tangier there had been serious trouble between the emperor and the American consul, and it was in anticipation of a declaration of war that he had undertaken to sieze the brig.

In that case, Bainbridge informed him coldly, since no state of war existed he was guilty of an act of piracy, and unless the Moor could produce some evidence of authority he would have no alternative but to hang him from his own yardarm. No further threat was necessary. Ibrahim Lubarez begged that such action be postponed, and drew from an inside pocket a secret document signed by the Moorish governor of Tangier— presumably in the name of the emperor, though there was actually no other indication that he had authorized it— authorizing the capture of American ships.

Naturally Captain Bainbridge carried both brig and cruiser to Gibraltar where, no doubt, he was quite content to deposit the whole tangle in Commodore Preble's lap.

To many a man of action the situation might well have ap-

peared no more than another nuisance with its roots in proto-
col. Commodore Preble, however, was more perceptive. In the
first place, he was aware that the United States treaty with
Morocco, insuring peace between the two nations, was about to
expire. In the second, he was well aware that there had been
certain hostile rumblings from the emperor. In the third, he
was only too conscious of the fact that all supplies, both of food
and ammunition—not to mention reinforcements—must pass
through the narrow Strait of Gibraltar, only thirteen miles
wide and guarded at the south, from end to end, by the Moorish
Empire. If that were cut, as it could be by a hostile Morocco, it
would be like severing the umbilical cord of an unborn child,
and the American fleet—the fetus would be left to shrivel and
die in the barren Mediterranean womb. Only by keeping the
line open could he even hope for success, and it was possible
that the capture of the *Mirboka* had placed in his hands the
necessary instrument for that accomplishment.

Wisely he sent off the *Philadelphia* and the *Vixen*—the latter one of the new shallow-draft vessels specifically designed for
operations in those waters and recently arrived—to continue
the blockade of Tripoli. With the rest of his fleet, Captain
Rodgers having since joined, he stood across to Tangier where
with the *Mirboka* as evidence he opened negotiations for a renewal of the peace.

In view of the evidence the emperor could hardly pretend innocence, and the American show of force at Tangier was
enough to make him think twice. The upshot of it all was the
renewal of the treaty of peace, insuring free passage for American ships through the Straits. At the same time the usual payment of tribute was waived, the *Mirboka* was returned, presents
were exchanged, and there was feasting, dancing, and celebration.

The Americans, however, were not to be caught off guard, as
the following entry from the *Constitution*'s log for October 5
makes amply clear!

"At anchor in Tangier Bay. Men sleeping at the guns all

night before. In the forenoon saw fully ten thousand Moorish inhabitants marching in from different directions." Whatever the purpose of the ten thousand Moors may have been, it was evidently not hostile for they made no move against either the American officers on shore or the warships at anchor before the town. At the same time the governor of Tangier, for his part in the *Mirboka* affair and his presumption in issuing licenses in the name of the emperor without authority, was sentenced to the bastinado and his estates confiscated.

By mid-October Preble and the *Constitution* were back again in Gibraltar, where he found former Commodore Morris only waiting to turn over his official portfolio of charts, orders, and other documents pertaining to the station before he departed for home in the *Adams* to face a general board of inquiry, investigating his inactivity and lack of initiative. Rodgers, too, who had served as commodore during the interval following the receipt of the orders relieving Morris of his command, also surrendered his official papers, hauled down his broad pendant, and sailed in the *New York*, accompanied by the *John Adams*, for the Chesapeake. Behind them the sole command of the Mediterranean station fell upon Preble, and the full responsibility for the future rested in him.

8

To the Shores
of Tripoli

I T is not too difficult to put oneself in Commodore Preble's place at that time and suspect that his strongest feeling was one of relief, probably tinged with more than a little satisfaction. Not that he had any quarrel with his fellow officers or objected to their presence. He had an especially high regard for Rodgers, and there is nothing in the record to suggest any scorn for Morris. But he was a man who preferred to shoulder his responsibilities alone. Consultation irked him, for in his eyes it weakened his position of command. He liked to make his own decisions and he stood by them. Now, at last, he was on his own, free to act according to his own best judgment. To a man of his temperament and disposition such independence could only be pleasing.

But at the same time he was not imprudent. Having appeared upon the coast of Morocco, as far south as Mogador, with gratifying results, and secured the southern side of the Straits, he was well aware that it was equally important to make sure that there were no interference from the north. Gibraltar itself, of course, was English; officially friendly, but personally—as often as not—arrogant and contemptuous toward the "Yankee upstarts."

In view of the touchy relationship between the English and American forces, it was evident that Gibraltar could be a spot for trouble, especially between hot-tempered junior officers who had been weaned, so to speak, on the "Code." Preble himself was a state of Maine man who held with no such nonsense. But he was too sensible an officer not to recognize that most of his juniors were Southerners who regarded the duel as the only proper way of settling differences between gentlemen, whether differences of a personal or a national nature. Accordingly he felt it best for all concerned to stand as far clear of potential complications as possible, and on his return from Tangier he anchored at Algeciras, on the Spanish side of the bay, rather than at Gibraltar. As a matter of fact, the little Spanish city, even today, is far more interesting to anyone who cares to look beneath the surface, but it is hardly likely that the crew of the *Constitution* appreciated the advantage.

Using Algeciras as a base and the *Constitution* as a vehicle, Commodore Preble prowled the seas and the coast south and west of Spain and made the name of the new, young republic across the Atlantic known, a power on the horizon to be reckoned with and a challenge to be met. A specific instance was his call at Cadiz.

Cadiz has been described as a silver plate set on a cloth of blue velvet. Her whitewashed walls and towers sprawled along a jutting point of golden sand surrounded by deep blue waters. Her houses, then as now, were all white or pastel shades of cream and pink and blue and yellow, and even her roofs and tiles seemed scrubbed in the southern sunlight. The brass cannon in the embrasures of the ancient stone fort on the point now are used only for saluting visiting dignitaries. Originally they had a more deadly purpose, for piracy was rife in those seas and freebooters did not confine their activities to ships afloat; seaport cities were equally fair game if they could be taken. From the earliest times she has been known as a seaport of prime importance.

The first city on the site was called "Gadir" by the Phoenicians, who had appropriated the name from the Iberian natives who had made use of it long before. That was about

1100 B.C. Next came the Carthaginians, about 500 B.C., who renamed the city Gades. It was there Hamilcar and Hannibal fitted out their fleets and armies against the Romans, and Scipio followed their example in the second Punic War. Meantime, even in Alexander's time there was a sizable colony of Greek merchants there. The Romans fought for and conquered it, and after they had won it they savored its justly renowned sea foods and its even more famous dancing girls—the "*Improbae Gaditanae*" they were called, doubtless the forerunners of today's "Gitanas," the gypsy dancers that haunt the caverns of Andalusia. Long before the golden age of exploration Greeks, Romans, and Carthaginians were familiar with its spectacular tides and wondered what lay beyond the deep, seemingly endless waters that washed its shore. It was from Cadiz that Columbus sailed on his second voyage of discovery to the New World, and as late as 1770 it was one of the most important ports of Europe. Indeed, by all accounts, at that time it was an even wealthier place than London in point of commercial interests. Clearly, in something less than thirty-five years it could hardly have declined to a state of complete insignificance.

The point is important in our account for it was on the twenty-third of October that Commodore Preble in the *Constitution*, accompanied by Lieutenant Hull in the *Enterprise*, paid the first official American visit to that port. As they rounded the point and stood into the harbor both vessels saluted the Castillo with the correct number of guns called for under the rules of international courtesy. The Spaniards responded promptly enough apparently, but scarcely to Preble's satisfaction, for no sooner had they come to anchor than the commodore launched a formal and emphatic protest with the American consul, Josef Yznardi, and the Spanish captain of the port, complaining that the forts had failed to return his compliment properly, gun for gun. The port captain was effusively apologetic but explained that he could do nothing since he had received no royal order containing "Instructions Respecting the American Republick." At the same time the consul promised to get a ruling in the matter from the court on his next visit to Madrid.

The answer was hardly one to mollify a man of action, but Preble could only snort and fume. The gift, from the captain of the port, of an old and rusty anchor which had been left there by an American man-of-war—unnamed—at some time during the Revolution more than a quarter of a century before scarcely salved his feelings. For all his stiff acceptance of the gesture, however, Preble was probably more pleased than he admitted, for a salute could only be answered by wasted gunpowder but an extra anchor was something that could be used. As a matter of fact, in this case it was actually doubly welcome for only a few days before, in an open roadstead off the Moorish coast, the *Constitution*—notoriously hard on her cables in a seaway—had lost her bower anchor, and this token of Spanish esteem would take its place nicely.

On his return to the Straits, Preble found that the new brig *Argus*, 16, Lieutenant Stephen Decatur commanding, had arrived. Like the *Vixen* she had been built with a particular eye to service in the Mediterranean and her appearance there created a considerable stir, not only among the Americans but also among the British on that station, for even they had to admit that for the purpose she could scarcely be improved upon even by their own designers and builders. Commodore Preble himself, in a letter to the secretary of the navy reporting the new addition, wrote: "The *Argus* has arrived and is without exception the handsomest vessel of her rate I have ever seen. She is very much and very justly admired by every officer . . . a Vessel . . . so well calculated and armed for the service I shall want her before Tripoli." The comments of Lieutenant Henry Wadsworth, namesake and uncle of the poet Longfellow, an officer on board who was destined to die in the coming campaign, are perhaps even more interesting. To his cousin Nancy Doane he wrote:

The *Argus* is universally allowed to be the finest vessel floating upon the Mediterranean. The envy & jealousy of the British is excited by our fine ships and handsome manoeuvring; we meet on shore but to fight—& insult each other. The Politeness of the American Officers will always induce them to give the preference to such as *do not* claim it but we wage eternal war with those who arrogate superiority.

A rather revealing commentary, not merely upon the ships of the American squadron but also on the state of Anglo-American relations at the time. It had been nearly a quarter of a century since the fighting had stopped but the Revolution was still not ended, and it would take another war before Britain and the rest of the world would be convinced that the United States of America was at last come of age, a free and independent nation.

But such considerations did not consciously occur to Preble or any of his "boys" at the moment. Their concern of the moment was with Tripoli, and the season in which any concrete action was possible was already far advanced. It was already getting on toward the middle of November, and in a few weeks' time the blustery, cantankerous winter weather of the central Mediterranean would make it difficult if not impossible for sailing ships to maintain the blockade effectively. It had been nearly two months since he had sent the *Philadelphia* and the *Vixen* to the eastward, and since their departure he had heard not a word from them. Not that he felt any cause for alarm on that score. He had full faith in both Captain Bainbridge and Lieutenant Smith and the officers and men who were with them. True, they might be a little young on the whole, for there was scarcely a man of them who was over thirty-five. Preble himself was only forty-two and he was considered an old man, while most of the junior officers were in their early or mid-twenties. But that was nothing extraordinary in an age when boys went to sea as midshipmen—officers, expected to command mature men—before they were ten years old and frequently commanded their own ships by the time they turned twenty. Moreover, communications were notoriously slow in those days and seas. All ships depended on the wind, and a fast vessel sailing

eastward from Gibraltar with the wind at her heels could make
Italy in a fortnight or less. But her return was a very different
matter. Indeed, in that very season the *Argus* made the run
from Gibraltar to Leghorn in nine days—and that with two
slower merchant ships in convoy. Her return, however, beating
against the wind, took sixty days. Small wonder that the long
silence from the eastward seemed as yet hardly a cause for
alarm. Fundamentally there were more practical reasons for
Preble's impatience, and an entry in the *Constitution's* log,
made later as they approached the Tripolitan coast, explains
much:

The weather to the N'ward has every appearance of a strong
breeze from that quarter. A heavy gale from the N.E. or N.N.E.
would make our situation very disagreeable. It would expose us to
an enemy's coast, the angular position of which to the Northward
and Westward makes it necessary to avoid that part by standing
to the Eastward. We could only lay the coast along and of course
afford no drift or leeway. The horrors of shipwreck added to irre-
trievable slavery makes the coast very dangerous in winter. If any
[one] cruises on this coast in a heavy gale on shore, they have no
other safety but their sails, and if they once lose them they lose all
hopes of a retreat.

Clearly, if the blockade were to be effectively maintained
through the winter months it would be imperative to have as
many American men-of-war, of whatever rate, as possible on
station and available for duty. With this in mind Commodore
Preble began gathering up all the loose ends, planning to get
on down to Malta where he first intended to establish a new
rendezvous closer to the scenes of possible action than Gibraltar. His first move was to send the brig *Siren*, 16, under command of Lieutenant Charles Stewart, to the eastward, up the
Mediterranean, as escort to several American merchantmen
bound for Barcelona, Marseilles, and Leghorn.

This Lieutenant Stewart was no Johnnie-come-lately in
naval circles. At twenty-five he was looked upon by both sub-
ordinates and seniors as a respectable and efficient officer. He

had gone to sea as a cabin boy at thirteen, and by the time he
was twenty he had commanded an Indiaman with no discredit
to his record. At the age of twenty, in 1798, he had entered the
navy as a junior lieutenant and had served in the West Indies
aboard the *United States,* under Barry. Having set out as
"fourth luff," he was senior lieutenant, or more popularly "first
luff," by the time they returned. During the French War,
Stewart had commanded the U.S. schooner *Experiment,* 12, in
which he had made two outstanding captures—the *Deux Amis,*
8, and the *Diane,* 14—both well-known and dreaded French
privateers. He had also fought a long-drawn action at night,
when a man could not tell whether he was firing into friend or
foe, with the British privateer *Louisa Bridger,* 8, in which the
Englishman had been badly mauled. That had been an error,
of course, but not one of cowardice or indecision, and Stewart's
reputation was not damaged by what his superiors considered a
regrettable but justifiable mistake. After leaving the *Experiment* he did a tour of duty in the *Constellation* and was then
given command of the new brig *Siren,* 16, and was ordered with
the equally new *Argus,* 16, Lieutenant Stephen Decatur commanding, to join Preble in the Mediterranean.

Having thus disposed of the *Siren* for the moment, Commodore Preble indulged in some slight shuffling of his command.
Since Isaac Hull was the senior lieutenant present, he was
ordered to the command of the *Argus,* while Decatur was
shifted to the "lucky little" *Enterprise,* 12. Richard Somers remained where he was, in command of the *Nautilus,* 12. It is
worthy of remark that of these four young officers, only one of
whom had reached the age of 30, only one was not destined to
command the *Constitution* at a later date. That one was Richard Somers, and he too would one day have shared the honor
had he not had the misfortune to be blown to eternity with the
ketch *Intrepid* in a vain attempt to invade the harbor of
Tripoli the following year.

Preble's final official act before sailing from Gibraltar was to
issue a formal circular proclamation of the blockade, copies of

which he sent to all the courts of Europe and which stated bluntly that

all neutral vessels that attempt to enter the Port of Tripoli, or are met with on the coast near that Port after this Notice is received by such Neutral Powers, will be stopped by the Squadron under my command and sent into port for adjudication.

The blockade had already been established by his predecessors in command, and Preble had every intention of continuing it and enforcing it to the hilt. His circular was meant not only to put the powers on notice of that intention but also, in a somewhat less direct way, to let everyone know that he was a man of action and that he would listen to no protests that might be raised on the grounds of ignorance. Now that everyone had been formally informed there could no longer be any basis for such excuses.

That was on November 12. The following day the *Constitution* weighed anchor and stood in through the narrow Strait of Gibraltar, between the towering Pillars of Hercules, for the broader reaches of the blue Mediterranean. Long before sundown Ceuta and the mighty "Rock" were far out of sight astern while away to southward, on the starboard beam, the ragged mountains of North Africa's Riff Coast loomed, hull down, as sailors put it, with their feet in the seas well below the distant horizon and their great, tumbled peaks hanging like motionless banked clouds, etched in gold against the blue-pink of the sky.

Their passage eastward was pleasant, but generally uneventful. For the most part his passengers—Colonel Lear, the newly appointed consul general, and his lady—were able to keep the decks in comfort. The commodore had ample opportunity to keep himself busy in his cabin with tentative plans for the coming campaign, while the sailing and routine of shipboard life, including the endless round of drill and gunnery practice, could be safely left to the officers and men.

In a week's time they reached Algiers, where the dey was as

truculently arrogant as ever. But he did receive Colonel Lear
and his entourage with a certain reluctant courtesy—and he
did not order his seaward battery of heavy guns to fire upon
them, as he had threatened to do. Preble stayed only long
enough to pay his respects and take on a few needed provisions.
Then, on the twenty-second of November, he weighed once
more and stood on eastward for Syracuse.

Undoubtedly it was some time in the next day or two—about
the first forty hours or so after their sailing from Algiers—
that the *Constitution*, hurrying eastward to the rendezvous at
Syracuse with the commodore on board, passed without sighting her the little schooner *Vixen*, 12, Lieutenant J. Smith commanding, which was battling lashing winds and contrary
weather westward for Gibraltar with grim dispatches and
ominous news for Preble, who was still believed to be at that
port. Whether they passed close aboard in the fog and the
darkness of night, or whether Preble took the *Constitution* far
to the northward, almost to Sardinia, to take full advantage of
the winds which were giving poor Smith such a hard time and
forcing him to hug the Algerian shore well to the southward, is
scarcely relevant. It matters only that it happened and is eloquent proof of the difficulties of navigation and communication
in those times.

As it happened, however, the incident was of small import
beyond the fact that it deprived Commodore Preble of one of
the vessels of his small squadron for several weeks, and that it
proved a rather mortifying experience for Lieutenant Smith
and his officers and crew, for not only did they fail to intercept
the commodore in passing. They did not even get to Gibraltar.
After battling headwinds and contrary weather for about a
third of the way, Smith found the little *Vixen* running low on
water and provisions, and he was forced to put about and run
back to Malta.

Meanwhile the *Constitution* continued on course, unaware of
what was happening to the southward. On the twenty-fourth,
not far from Cape Spartivento at the southernmost tip of

Sardinia, they sighted a tall ship bearing on a course that would intercept their own. The newcomer proved to be the English frigate *Amazon*, 36, on her way to Gibraltar, and after each was satisfied of the other's bona fides there was the customary exchange of courtesies, visits, and, most important of all, news. There was little enough that the Americans could pass on to the Englishman, since at the time of their sailing everything had been calm and quiet around Gibraltar and the west. On the other hand, the Englishman could and did pass on the news that the little *Vixen* had tried so hard to deliver.

Some days since, it seemed, the *Amazon* had lain at Syracuse. While she was there a packet had come from Malta bearing the news that the fine American frigate *Philadelphia*, 36, under Captain Bainbridge, had gone hard aground on the reefs off the harbor of Tripoli and had been taken with all hands by the Tripolitans!

There were no details. Nothing to explain or embellish the report. But this much was enough. American forces in the Mediterranean had suffered an almost crippling blow, and Preble's already pitifully small squadron had been reduced by nearly one third.

Before leaving Gibraltar in September, Captain Bainbridge and Lieutenant Smith of the *Vixen* had consulted with Commodore Preble, on board the *Constitution,* as to what action they should follow upon their arrival on station. A plan had been worked out which considered both the strength of the blockading force and the dispositions of the enemy. Tripoli held a strong position on a blunt, low-lying peninsula, nestling in a rough crescent shape around the bay and facing generally eastward. A ridge of rocks and shoals, which protected the harbor from the north, ran eastward from the northern tip of the peninsula. Several other reefs and shoals pocked the outer, eastward end of the harbor, so that only a seaman familiar with the channels could find his way in safely. None of the shoals were charted, but their presence and their approximate location was at least suspected. It was also known that there were some passages—apart from the regular channel which led in from the east—that led out to open sea, though exactly where these were only the Tripolitans knew for sure.

Obviously, lacking charts or even reliable soundings, these were not waters to be blithely entered by a vessel of the *Philadelphia*'s size and draft. The little schooner *Vixen*, however, had been specifically designed and built for just such an operation. She was well armed for her size, her draft was shallow, and she already had a reputation for a good turn of speed under the proper conditions. Accordingly, the plan finally adopted was for the *Philadelphia* to patrol well offshore, maintaining her distance outside the treacherous reefs, with an eye to intercepting larger vessels attempting to enter or leave the port. The *Vixen*, on the other hand, was to lie in closer to shore and cut off the steam of general traffic ordinarily maintained by smaller craft carrying fish, plunder, or provisions to the city.

The scheme was apparently effective, for there was little activity during the first weeks. But it is axiomatic that no blockade is ever 100 per cent airtight. Late in October, a Neapolitan homeward bound from the eastern Mediterranean reported having sighted a Tripolitan corsair which had evidently just gotten to sea.

According to their original arrangement, Bainbridge, in the frigate, should have been the one to go in pursuit of the pirate since it would be, primarily at least, a deep-water operation. But perhaps Bainbridge felt that the schooner's superior speed and maneuverability would count for more than the larger vessel's heavier armament. Perhaps he anticipated that the corsair would try to take cover in the shoal waters closer inshore, where he would be unable to follow. Or perhaps he simply felt that after so long a tour of duty without so much as a shot fired the officers and men of the *Vixen* deserved the first chance. After all, it will be remembered, the *Philadelphia* had already made one prize in the western Mediterranean, near Gibraltar.

Whatever his reasoning, the fact remains that Captain

Bainbridge sent the *Vixen* in pursuit while he himself stayed on station in the *Philadelphia* to maintain the blockade. He was so engaged on October 29 when a strong westerly gale forced him from his station and drove him far to the eastward. As soon as he was able he fought his way back, and early on the morning of the 31st, as he once again approached his former post, the lookout caught sight of a Tripolitan vessel, probably the very same corsair that the *Vixen* was seeking, trying to slip into the harbor close alongshore.

Captain Bainbridge immediately ordered the *Philadelphia* to the chase, which lasted for some hours. By 11 A.M. the frigate had drawn close enough to open fire with her bow guns, but though some of the shots came close none were really effective as the range was still extreme and the steadily increasing number of rocks and shoals as revealed by constant sounding forced the ship to shift and twist on such an erratic course that accuracy was almost impossible. By the same token their rate of gain was less than it had been.

Actually, what was happening was that Captain Bainbridge was being drawn into a trap. What neither Captain Bainbridge or any of his officers knew—though it was well known to the Tripolitans who were born to these waters—was that a long reef, known as the "Kalinsa," extended from a point almost opposite the city far to the eastward and almost parallel to the shore. Between this reef and the shore there was ample water for a vessel of the *Philadelphia*'s size and draft, and so long as they approximated the enemy's wake they met with but little trouble. But they were unwittingly being drawn into a cul-de-sac. There were a few passages through the reef, well known to the corsairs, but they were narrow and tortuous and irregularly spaced, and in between lay the jagged shoals.

The chase continued until shortly after noon when it became apparent that despite their best efforts the Tripolitan, with his superior knowledge of the water and his shallower draft, would have no difficulty in reaching the safety of the harbor before they could possibly overtake him. Nevertheless they chased

him to within three miles of the forts before Captain Bainbridge ordered the helm hard up and stood out toward the open
sea.

But it was much too late. The *Philadelphia* was scarcely on
her new course before the water began to shoal swiftly and
alarmingly. Desperately Bainbridge tried to check the ship's
way and fetch her head around once more on a safer tack, but
she was already doomed. The orders had scarcely been given
when she struck with a force that threw many of the crew into
the scuppers and wrenched her bows five or six feet out of the
water. Immediate soundings showed that she had but twelve
feet of water forward and seventeen aft, while further examination of her position from a hastily lowered boat showed her
to be hard aground. Desperately they tried to float her free,
pumping out their water and even flinging her guns overboard
to lighten her, but to no avail. All the time she lay there, obviously helpless, the corsairs, emboldened by her plight, crept
closer and closer until at last Bainbridge gave orders to bore
holes in her bottom and the pumps choked to prevent her being
refloated. When that was done he surrendered in the slim hope
of saving at least the lives of his officers and crew.

In that, at least, he succeeded. They were robbed and beaten,
kicked, cursed, and spat upon, and finally dragged ashore and
flung into foul dungeons in the bashaw's castle. But their captors were careful not to offer them lasting harm. They were far
too valuable for that. Twenty-two officers and 293 men gave
the bashaw a powerful card with which to bargain.

Several days later the weather seemed to give him another. It
began to storm violently from the north, piling the Mediterranean seas high along the Tripolitan coast. The resulting
high tides enabled the Tripolines to refloat the wreck of the
Philadelphia and she was towed in and anchored under the
guns of the castle. Later her guns and anchors were raised and
she was rearmed, rerigged, and fitted. With the holes in her
bottom plugged and her pumps repaired and returned to work-

ing order, she was to all intents and purposes fit to take the seas
again under her new masters.

The news which the *Amazon* passed to Commodore Preble in
the *Constitution*, of course, included none of these details.
They reported simply that the *Philadelphia* had been taken
after running aground, and possibly added that she had been
refloated and towed into the harbor by her captors. The rest of
the story no doubt came to light piecemeal as details trickled in
from port to port, to be finally confirmed by Captain Bainbridge in secret correspondence via the Danish consul, a Mr.
Nissen, who gave every aid and comfort to the prisoners and
proved of invaluable assistance.

After parting from the *Amazon* Preble sailed directly to
Malta, which is nearly one-hundred miles closer to Tripoli than
Syracuse, arriving there some three days later, on the twenty-
seventh. There he paused only long enough to confirm the report he had just heard, after which he hastened on to Syracuse
where he expected that some more official word would be awaiting him. Even as he sailed, the weather must have been making
up for a storm, but the big *Constitution* took little notice of it
apparently, for they arrived at Syracuse on the twenty-eighth.
The little *Vixen*, however, which had been doing her best to
catch up with him, had no such luck. Lieutenant Smith brought
his ship into Malta the next day, only to find that the commodore had gone on to Syracuse. Not to be deterred, Smith took
aboard water and provisions and promptly struck out once
more in pursuit. It is an interesting commentary on the hazards
of the seas in those days that, though it took the *Constitution* only a single day to make the passage between the two
ports, it took the *Vixen*, following close behind, exactly *thirty*
days to cover the same distance!

Apparently some time during the voyage from Gibraltar,
the *Constitution* and the little *Enterprise* had parted company,
possibly from stress of weather, possibly for purposes of convoy duty. Whatever the reason, it is unimportant. What is im-

portant is that somewhere in the short voyage from Malta the *Enterprise* rejoined the big frigate, and they were together when they came to anchor at Syracuse. Probably the most important point of all is that the *Enterprise* was commanded by a young lieutenant named Stephen Decatur, who had already drawn some attention to himself in those waters.

In the meantime Captain Bainbridge was not just sitting despondent in the dungeons of Tripoli twiddling his thumbs. Bainbridge was no stranger to misfortune, for it was he who had commanded the *Retaliation*, 14—formerly the French *Croyable*—when she was recaptured by the French frigates *Insurgente*, 36, and *Volontaire*, 44, in the West Indies during the French War. He tasted the brutality of French dungeons in the West Indies, and had had the humiliation of commanding the frigate *George Washington* in 1800 when she carried the annual American tribute to Algiers and then been forced into Algerian service to convey the Algerian tribute of money and females, as well as upward of two hundred envoys, to the court of the Grand Turk at Constantinople. Now his grim luck seemed to be running true to form. But he was never a man to knuckle under. From his cell he had watched the salvaging of the *Philadelphia*, and as he did so a vague scrap of a plan came to him. If America was not destined to benefit by her services, perhaps the Tripolines were not either.

He had already received the assurances of several neutral consuls that they stood ready to forward his official communications to his superiors. The privilege, of course, had required his own parole, as well as those of his officers, not to attempt to escape. Nothing, however, had been said about sending out information. On the fifth of December Bainbridge wrote a letter to Preble which he forwarded by the regular channels. Ostensibly it was simply a routine report as to their conditions and situation. Between the lines, however, he wrote another letter in lemon juice, which is invisible when dry but which turns black when heated.

In this letter he described the position of the *Philadelphia* and then went on to say that from her current anchorage it would hardly be possible to rescue her. However, he suggested, a small party, adequately disguised, in what would appear to be an innocent merchantman, might under cover of darkness be able to slip up alongside and destroy her. It would be risky and daring, but it might be done.

Commodore Preble found this, among other letters, awaiting him on his arrival at Syracuse. As soon as he had read it he summoned a council of his officers and presented the idea to them. They responded enthusiastically, and Lieutenant Decatur was especially keen for it. He promptly volunteered to undertake the duty, and even went so far as to beg Preble's permission to try it without delay.

But Preble was not a man to be rushed. Nor was he one to act without first considering every possible chance of success or failure, or taking a close look at the means in hand. In the first place, he pointed out, they had no vessel at their disposal whose rig would not give them away as Americans even before they had entered the harbor. Secondly, they must reconnoiter the harbor and defenses as closely as possible before they could hope for success in such a night foray. Thirdly, they must be absolutely sure of their plans and their timing. Too often such daring undertakings had failed for want of careful preparation, he reminded them, and he went on to add that success would be a feather in their caps, individually and collectively, and well worth the risk, but that failure would be simply one ignominious disaster piled upon another, and those who had run the risk would get no thanks for it.

Lieutenant Decatur was inclined to persist in urging the project, but the commodore curtly replied that at the moment it was too hazardous to attempt. However, he added more kindly, if and when the time came to put the scheme into effect he would see to it that command of the party would be given to Decatur—provided, of course, that the lieutenant's duties did not demand his presence elsewhere at the crucial moment.

Preble and the *Constitution* lay at Syracuse, taking in

water, stores, and provisions, until the seventeenth of December, when they sailed in company with the *Enterprise* and *Vixen* on what was to be merely a routine cruise of reconnaissance.

Actually their original date of sailing had been set for the twelfth, but they had been held landlocked by contrary winds, and it was only when the commodore's patience finally wore thin and he ordered the vessels towed out by the squadron's boats that they finally got to sea.

That cruise, as it happened, turned out to be something more than routine. To be sure they put into Malta for dispatches and then stood across to the coast of Tripoli, where they took soundings and made note of the reefs and channels outside the harbor. At the same time they marked well the outer defenses of the Castle and the city, the stout walls—upon which even then Bainbridge and his men were laboring under the watchful eyes of their captors—and the chain of forts and batteries both above and below the town.

Thus far everything had been little more than ordinary procedure. On the twenty-third of December, however, a small Tripolitan ketch was sighted attempting to slip out of the harbor. Preble immediately ordered British colors to be flown throughout the little squadron—a stratagem that was considered quite legitimate in those days, provided one's true colors were shown before any attack was made—and signaled Decatur, in the *Enterprise*, to stand by to intercept the stranger if he could be lured within range.

The Tripolitan apparently took the bait and continued serenely on his course, never dreaming that these strangers were other than the Englishmen they pretended to be. Only when the English colors came down and were replaced by the Stars and Stripes did they seem to realize how neatly they had been trapped. They attempted to escape by running inshore, but Decatur was prepared for such a move and had little difficulty in heading them off and forcing a quick surrender.

The prize proved to be the *Mastico*, carrying a present of

"female slaves" to the sultan of Turkey. Apparently there were other passengers as well, for one record says that "Several officers of distinction were taken to the Commodore's table." The Tripolitan crew, of course, was taken out and a prize crew sent on board and all together they turned about and headed back toward Tripoli, where it may be that Preble had some intention of using the ketch, her cargo, and his prisoners as bargaining cards. They arrived off the city on the twenty-fourth, but before any move could be made a heavy gale came down on them out of the northeast, and after beating against it for four days the *Constitution* took the prize into tow and the entire squadron bore up for Syracuse. There they found further letters from Captain Bainbridge reiterating his suggestion regarding the destruction of the *Philadelphia*. At the same time Decatur was not backward in pointing out that they were now in possession of a small, native-rigged vessel, ideal for the purpose, and begged to be allowed to make the attempt. Lieutenant Stewart of the brig *Siren* also asked for the place. Commodore Preble must have been pleased and gratified at such evidence of an aggressive spirit among his junior officers. In any event he finally agreed and placed Decatur in command.

But there was yet much to be done before the attempt could actually be made. First, after the removal of her crew, cargo, and passengers, the prize had to be scrubbed and fumigated from truck to keelson, for she was filthy and alive with vermin. This done, she must be first formally labeled as a prize, judged and condemned; then, with equal formality, taken into the naval service. Even then there was a good deal of red tape involved in such a transaction, though not as much as there would be today. Eventually it was done. The *Mastico* became the U.S.S. *Intrepid* and lay ready to be armed and manned.

Arming presented little problem since, for her special mission, she could carry nothing but cutlasses and small arms such as could be concealed below decks. Any carriage guns, however light, would be sure to arouse suspicion if seen. Indeed, the greatest part of her armament was composed of combustibles:

shavings, tar, shredded lint, turpentine, and the like. Manning her, however, was a different matter. In the first place secrecy was essential to success. To call for volunteers would not only reveal the purpose—or at least enough of it to alert the enemy —it would also create a problem of selection and rejection which could lead to a certain amount of resentment on the part of those not chosen, for there was little doubt but that such a call would bring forth a practically unanimous clamor for inclusion. All hands were tired of inaction. Everyone wanted to go. Accordingly, the problem was solved by allowing Decatur to hand-pick his own officers and crew. Just before sailing additional volunteers, up to the capacity of the little ketch to accommodate them, would be accepted. Lieutenant Stewart seems to have been the sole exception. By Commodore Preble's especial order he was barred from volunteering, and it is more than likely that the fiery Stewart went about for some time with a "long lip." But the reason for the commodore's injunction was forthcoming in good time, and once it was understood perhaps the lieutenant was somewhat mollified. Someone, it seemed, had to command the *Siren*, which was to support the *Intrepid* in the mission. And Preble had already decided on the man.

All of these preparations, of course, took some time, and it was well into February before they were done. But the day came at last when they were ready, and on the ninth of February, 1804, they cleared from Syracuse and stood southward toward Tripoli, brig and ketch in company. Aboard the *Intrepid* was a crew made up largely of men from the *Enterprise* —some sixty-two in all. Besides Decatur there were ten officers, among them James Lawrence, who in the *Chesapeake* was later to fight the British *Shannon* off Boston Harbor during the War of 1812 and gain immortal fame with his dying words: "Don't give up the ship!" There were also Thomas Macdonough, who would become equally renowned as the victor of Lake Champlain in the same war; Joseph Bainbridge, the brother of the captive captain of the *Philadelphia;* Jonathan Thorn, who would later command John Jacob Astor's ship *Tonquin* at

Astoria and meet death at the hands of savage Indians in Nootka Sound, off Vancouver Island; five midshipmen from the *Constitution;* and Dr. Heerman, surgeon, from the *Enterprise.* They also carried a Maltese or Sicilian—the records differ as to his origin—pilot, Salvatore Catalano, who afterwards became a sailing master in the United States Navy.

At the outset, at least, the weather was favorable enough, and the two small vessels made the crossing to Tripoli in good time, according to schedule, arriving off the port after nightfall. But even as they dropped anchor outside the reefs the weather was turning threatening and the wind rose to such a pitch that the pilot declared it would be impossible for the ketch to get in through the passage. Through the night the gale increased in intensity until at length, before dawn lest they be seen from ashore, they were forced to slip their cables and run out northeastward to sea to ride it out.

It was Decatur's and Stewart's hope that the gale would blow itself out in the course of the day, and that they would be able to beat back at nightfall and resume their undertaking. But, as it proved, this was no mere puff and catspaw. For nearly a week the storm raged savagely, and the two tiny vessels suffered severely, especially the ketch *Intrepid*, which was not much larger than a fair sized yacht, thirty to forty tons burden, and which was several times in serious danger of foundering. They had been provisioned for only a few days, and to make matters worse, when they came to broach the casks it was found that the salt meat was spoiled. Commodore Charles Morris, then a midshipman aboard the *Intrepid*, gives some description of their situation in his autobiography:

The commander three lieutenants and the surgeon occupied the very small cabin. Six midshipmen and the pilot had a platform laid on the water casks, the surface of which they covered when they lay down to sleep, and at so small a distance below the deck that their heads would reach it when seated on the platform. The marines had corresponding accomodations on the opposite side, and the sailors had only the surface of the casks in the hold. To these inconveniences were added the want of any room on the deck for exercise and the attack of innumerable vermin, which our predecessors, the slaves, had left behind them.

Operation Fumigation, it would appear, had not been as effective as it was hoped!

But even the longest storm cannot last forever. By the fifteenth the weather began to moderate, and by nightfall it had calmed sufficiently for them to begin to work their way back toward the city. Since they could not risk being seen, however, they were forced to remain well offshore throughout the sixteenth, and as if by way of reward for their patience the night at last came on with smooth seas and a pale moon that every now and again hid its face behind wispy clouds. With an inrunning tide the conditions could not have been more favorable, and they slipped back to their original positions under cover of darkness. Just before starting their final venture a boat with six men from the *Siren* joined them, bringing the total aboard the *Intrepid* to eighty.

It was full dark when they finally reached the point of departure, still well out where there was little likelihood of being seen. There the *Siren* rounded to while the *Intrepid* continued on her way toward the port calmly as if she were no more than an ordinary trader. At the start of the run-in it was quickly evident that what with the sweep of the tide and the wind at her heels she was likely to gain the harbor too soon unless something were done. Accordingly Decatur ordered buckets and drags lowered astern to check her way, which by this means was effectively reduced to about two knots. Meantime every officer and man on board had been assigned a special station and a particular duty to perform. One group was to stand by the ketch. The boarders were to secure the spar deck first, after which selected parties were to clear the big frigate below decks. All was to be carried out in complete silence, with no firearms to be used except in the event of absolute necessity, and the *Siren*'s cutter was to secure all boats lying alongside the *Philadelphia* and prevent any swimmers from escaping to shore if possible. As soon as the frigate's decks had been cleared the crew of the cutter was to come on board and assist with the combustibles. It is said that it might have been possible for Decatur to bring the ship out, though this is highly doubtful, and in any case his orders were specific and rigid on that point. He was to destroy her where she lay, and make no attempt to rescue her.

By nine o'clock they had reached the channel where the *Philadelphia* had been lost and were in full sight of the city and the Castle as well as the frigate herself, moored close under the guns of the fort. Here Decatur took in the drags and buckets, the breeze having dropped to a mere whisper. At the same time he sent all but six of the ship's company into hiding, some below deck and others in the shadow of the bulwarks, behind barrels and mast and in various dark corners so that their unusual numbers might not forewarn the enemy. Those who remained purposely in the moonlight were disguised as simple Maltese sailors.

It was nearly ten o'clock when they finally came within hailing distance of the *Philadelphia*. Through the open ports they could see the lights below decks and even make out the figures of the full crew with which the frigate had been manned by the Tripolitans as they passed to and fro. They seemed to be awake, if not quite as alert as they should have been. Apparently, however, at least one guard stood watch, for as the ketch continued to head directly for the frigate he hailed, challenging in guttural Arabic, demanding to know their identity. As he had been ordered by Decatur, the pilot replied that they were only a simple Maltese trader who had managed to survive the recent terrific gale only with the loss of her anchors, and he begged permission to make fast to the frigate until morning, when another might be brought from shore.

While this exchange was going on another man appeared beside the sentry at the *Philadelphia*'s rail, and the pilot recognized him as the Tripolitan captain. He seemed quite unsuspicious and readily gave permission for the ketch to lie alongside for the rest of the night. In fact he even sent some of his men in a small boat with a line to help make the *Intrepid* fast astern. The situation called for quick thinking, but Decatur was up to it. He in turn sent out a boat with his own bow line. The two boats met before the Tripolitans could draw near enough to the ketch to see the hidden sailors, the lines were exchanged, and the Americans returned to the *Intrepid* with the stern line, while the Tripolitans went back to the *Philadelphia* with the bow spring. Another ticklish moment came when the Tripolitan captain called to ask what brig that was in the offing, so that it was at once abundantly clear that, for all their elaborate precautions, the *Siren* had been noticed. But once again Decatur was equal to the occasion, and he ordered the pilot, Catalano, to reply that she was the former British man-of-war *Transfer*, which he knew had been bought at Malta for the Tripolitans and which was even then eagerly awaited in the city.

For the moment this appeared to allay all suspicion, but the moment remained tense nonetheless. On the one hand, less than forty yards away, loomed the big guns of the shore batteries and the fort; 32- and 42-pounders in the main. On the other hand, about fifty yards distant the frigate's loaded, shotted broadside loomed ominously, while all around them Tripolitan gunboats lay moored. Had anything gone wrong at that moment and caused the Tripolitans to open fire upon them, at that pointblank range they would have been mashed to a pulp in the twinkling of an eye.

As soon as the lines had been made fast aboard the *Philadelphia,* the men showing on deck began to haul in on them, so that the ketch was slowly warped in toward the larger vessel. As much as possible the men on the forward line kept close to the rail, so that those who were hidden there could help and thus drag the smaller ship more swiftly in against the other's hull. By this means they got within some thirty feet before an observant guard aboard the frigate noticed that the ketch still carried an anchor. He loudly announced his discovery and, cursing the supposed Maltese for his deceit, started to scramble down the chains to cut away the ketch's line. By this time, however, the ketch was fairly alongside the frigate and needed only one more stout tug to bring the two ships into contact. By the same token they were close enough so that the Tripolitans, from their higher vantage point, could look down and see the men swarming against the *Intrepid*'s bulwarks. At once the cry went up:

"AMIRIKANI! AMIRIK——"

But by then it was too late. The Americans had already given that final, desperate haul. The hulls scraped and the grapnels flew, and even before they had caught, even before the cry of warning could be heard across the frigate's deck, the Yankee sailors were scrambling up, swarming over the side, cutlasses and pistols in their teeth or at their belts, and the belated shout died in a bloody gurgle.

So swift and unexpected was the attack that those Tripolitans above deck were either cut down where they stood or swept over the side. There was a brief, swift, savage melee, and then the Tripolitans broke and fled. A few managed to find their way below, but the Americans were at their heels and their only accomplishment was to show the way to their pursuers. Not a shot was fired. Not a prisoner was taken. Too many of the Tripolitans leapt overboard and tried to swim to safety for the one lone cutter from the ketch to intercept them all, so that many of them ultimately managed to reach either the shore or the gunboats, but none of them were swift swimmers by any standard, and while they were in the water, and before they could raise an alarm the Americans were going systematically about their appointed tasks.

As soon as the decks had been cleared a rocket was sent up to notify the *Siren* that the *Philadelphia* had been taken. At the same time those in the ketch began passing up the combustible material to the deck above. As each group received its allotted portion, it went at once to its appointed station and began to spread the materials at strategic points. Lint, tinder, and shavings were spread in the cockpit, on the berth deck, in the wardroom, on the gun deck, and heaped against the bases of the masts on the spar deck, and the whole was everywhere doused with a mixture of pitch and turpentine.

At a prearranged signal from Decatur the whole mass was touched off, and so swiftly did the flames spread that the party in the cockpit was very nearly trapped below and only with the greatest difficulty and danger were they able to make their way forward and escape to the spar deck through the fore hatch. As they gained the deck the flames were already climbing up the shrouds and they wasted no time in standing around "on the burning deck, whence all but they had fled," but hastily joined their companions in tumbling over the side into the waiting ketch. Lieutenant Decatur was the last to leave the burning frigate, and even as he leapt from above, the bows of the *Intrepid* had begun to swing clear, and it was only with difficulty that he was able to reach her shrouds and make his way forward and down to the deck. The entire operation had taken no more than twenty-five minutes!

By this time the *Philadelphia* was well ablaze. The flames were spurting higher and higher in her rigging and licking out through her portholes and gun ports, and there was very grave danger of her guns firing into the ketch as their charges exploded from the heat, not to mention the detonation of her magazines as the flames reached them. In that dilemma it is not difficult to imagine the overwhelming sense of urgency that gripped the little party on board the ketch. Frantic efforts were made to shove clear of the burning ship and make sail so as to get as far away from her as possible before either she blew up or the shore batteries should open fire. At one instant her boom fouled and her jigger flapped against the blazing vessel's quarter gallery, but fortunately so fleetingly that it did not take fire. At another spine chilling moment the flames from the frigate puffed in through the *Intrepid*'s cabin, where all of their powder and ammunition had been stored, covered only by a tarpaulin. But once again the dragon's breath of fire was of such flickering duration that the half-expected explosion did not come.

In the midst of so much tension it was momentarily forgotten that the Tripolitans themselves had made the little vessel's stern fast to the frigate. Who was the first to remember the fact is not recorded. Perhaps several thought of it at the same instant. In any case, it was no sooner recalled than a dozen cutlasses hacked at the rope, which parted with a crack like that of a small cannon, and the ketch lurched clear.

But all danger was not yet past. By now the light from the blazing ship illuminated the bay for hundreds of yards around, and the little ketch could not have presented a more visible or vulnerable target to the gunners in the shore batteries in broad daylight. Fortunately the Tripolitans themselves had not yet recovered from their abrupt surprise, and for several moments not a gun was fired. In the meantime the Americans did not stand idly by. With all haste they got out their sweeps— eight to a side—and bent their backs with a right good will to help pull the *Intrepid* out of that dazzling circle and into the sheltering shadows beyond. Even as they drew clear of the blazing frigate the Tripolitan gunboats first opened fire upon them, closely followed by the huge guns ashore. For a few moments the shots whistled close, and all around them tall white fountains spouted from the surface of the water, while between them and the burning vessel sprang up a handsome but harmless display of rainbow spray. Apparently the American seamen were justified in their scorn for Tripolitan gunnery, for not a single shot came close enough to do any damage.

It is entirely possible, of course, that had the furious cannonade continued long some chance shot might have found its mark, but before that could happen there came a welcome diversion. On board the *Philadelphia* the shotted guns, red hot now from the raging fires on the gun deck, began to go off, and even without being manned and aimed apparently did greater damage in the city and amid the gunboats and fortifications than did all the concentrated fire of the Tripolitans upon the one small ketch below. Ashore and in the gunboats gunners and crews scrambled for safety, and those aboard the *Intrepid* could hear the crash of the balls against the wall and the rattle of shattering tiles.

Then, all at once, the climax came in a single thunderous explosion as the licking flames at last found their way into the frigate's magazines. Masts and spars and bits of blazing plank and rigging soared aloft and then began raining down in a shower of flame and sparks and billowing smoke. And then, almost as suddenly as the night had been shattered by the blinding flash, pitch darkness clapped down across the harbor like a blanketing hand, leaving the little *Intrepid* to feel her way out in complete safety.

As they drew near the harbor's mouth they met the *Siren*'s boats, which had been sent to cover their retreat. But as there was no pursuit and they were by now well out of range, the boats' help, though appreciated, was unnecessary. Accordingly the escort turned about and, all together, they headed out to join the waiting brig. As soon as they were well outside, Lieutenant Decatur went ahead in one of the *Siren*'s boats to report the details of the affair to Lieutenant Commandant Stewart. For an hour or more after the *Intrepid* had come up with her consort, the two small vessels lay close together, unscrambling officers and crews and exchanging mutual congratulations and toasts. Then finally, toward midnight, a good wind springing up, they filled away and stood off northward for Syracuse, where they arrived on the nineteenth of February and immediately reported their mission successfully accomplished to Commodore Preble. The *Constitution*'s log for that day reads:

Sunday, Feby. 19.—A.M. At 10 appeared in the offing the United States Brig *Syren* and the *Intrepid*. The wind being light we sent boats out to assist towing in. At ½ past 10 they passed through our squadron in triumph receiving three cheers as they passed. Lieutenant Stewart of the *Syren* and Lieutenant Decatur of the *In-*

trepid waited on the Commodore and informed him they had passed
into the harbor of Tripoli agreeably to his orders, burnt and totally destroyed the late United States Frigate *Philadelphia*. The
business being so well planned not a man was killed or wounded on
our side. The Tripolitans had 20 killed, the others made their escape by jumping overboard after the ship was afire.

9

ACTION IN THE
MEDITERRANEAN

T H E R E is no question but that the destruction of the *Philadelphia,* and the dash and spirit of Decatur and his men in accomplishing it, went far toward improving American prestige
in the Mediterranean, and for that matter throughout Europe.
Even Lord Nelson, who was then commanding the British fleet
in those waters, called it "the most bold and daring act of the
age"—somewhat grudgingly, no doubt, since Nelson was never
known for his admiration of the American upstarts.

More practically the exploit had the dual result of prevent-
ing the Tripolitans from getting the frigate to sea against her
former masters and of removing the most formidable auxiliary
battery from the harbor, which was no small achievement since
it left the way open for further attacks upon the shore installations and the city itself.

The results of the adventure were not all to the good, however. The pasha was of course furious at such brazen temerity,
and he took out his wrath on the hapless prisoners. The officers
were promptly removed from the comparatively comfortable
quarters which the Swedish and Danish consuls had wheedled
for them and cast once more into the dank dungeons beneath
the Castle, while the seamen and lower rates were driven to even
harder and harsher labors on the walls and fortifications. More
broadly he exhibited his pique by refusing to entertain any

proposal for an exchange of prisoners and increasing the ransom demanded for the captives in his hand. Clearly there was nothing to be gained at that point by negotiation, and Commodore Preble began to clear his decks for action of a more decisive nature.

At that time the "amphibious assault" as it is known today, had not yet been invented. Even if it had been Preble did not have a sufficient force at his command to carry it out. Consequently his best strategy appeared to lie in a tightening of the blockade and as frequent and continuous bombardment of the city as it was possible to deliver. As a first step in this program he sent out the *Siren*, in command of Stewart, now a master commandant (a rank no longer in existence in the navy), and the *Nautilus*, Master Commandant Somers, to take station off the port while he himself began to gather his forces together for a full-strength attack.

Such preparations, however, needed time, and in the meanwhile he was not idle in other directions. Early in March he crossed to Tripoli in the *Constitution* for further reconnaissance and to support the *Siren* and the *Nautilus* with a show of force. At this time, apparently, there was no opportunity for any other action, so after parading off the port for several days and serving out supplies to the other two vessels, the *Constitution* withdrew to Syracuse for additional supplies and dispatches. Shortly after her withdrawal a brig was seen attempting to slip out to sea under the escort of several Tripolitan gunboats. As soon as the American cruisers were made out both the brig and the gunboats endeavored to beat back into the harbor. But the *Nautilus* went in pursuit of the gunboats, while the *Siren* bore down directly on the brig. The gunboats were already far enough inshore to escape to the shelter of the forts. But the brig was overhauled and surrendered without resistance. She proved to be that very *Transfer* which had been so eagerly awaited at Tripoli at the time of the *Philadelphia*'s destruction. She carried sixteen carronades and a crew of eighty, and although she claimed to be a British privateer, out of

Malta, and exhibited a somewhat dubious British commission in support of the claim, there was strong evidence that she actually belonged to the bashaw of Tripoli. Accordingly she was detained as a violator of the blockade and sent prize into Syracuse. There she was appraised and condemned, manned and taken into the United States' service as the U.S. brig of war *Scourge*. Lieutenant Commandant John H. Dent, who had been acting captain of the *Constitution* under Preble, was given command of her.

As soon as she was ready for service the *Scourge* was sent to assist in the blockade, and in the course of the next several weeks the *Enterprise* and the *Vixen* were added to the blockading force, while on the fifteenth of April Preble, returning to Syracuse from Tripoli in the *Constitution,* found the brig *Argus*, Lieutenant Commandant Hull, waiting for him, having escorted the American supply ship up the Mediterranean from Gibraltar. Instead of sending her back to Gibraltar, Commodore Preble sent her also to duty on the Tripolitan station.

In this way the blockading force was gradually strengthened and the cordon of ships before the port of Tripoli drawn tighter and ever tighter. As often as possible the *Constitution* joined them, prodding, feeling the enemy out for weak spots and possible points of attack. But administrative duties required Preble to spend much of his time at Syracuse, and there were yet other important matters which demanded his attention, so that the *Constitution*'s log reads something like a ferry schedule between Tripoli, Malta, and Syracuse for the next several weeks. Most of this, of course, was strictly routine and needs no elaboration. But at least twice she turned aside from her beaten path, and both digressions are worth mentioning.

It was after the *Argus* had been sent to join the blockade before Tripoli that Commodore Preble took the *Constitution* into Naples, apparently with his own plans in mind. It was the first time that one of the big, new American frigates—let alone an American commodore—had been seen in that port, and their visit aroused a good deal of curiosity and enthusiasm among the Neapolitans, and a cordiality which has survived to this day.

There was good reason why this should have been especially so at that moment, for the United States and the Kingdom of the Two Sicilies—of which Naples was the capital—had much in common just then. Both were at war with Tripoli. And that one point was as much as Preble needed. He paid a diplomatic visit to the king of the Two Sicilies, and came away with a reinforcement of six gunboats and two bomb ketches. True, they were not large vessels, nor were they ever intended by their builders to go to sea. They were flat bottomed, clumsy craft that sailed indifferently and were even difficult to manage under oars. The gunboats weighed twenty-five tons and carried a single long iron 14-pounder in the bows and a crew of thirty-five men. The bomb ketches were about thirty tons and were armed with a single 13-inch brass sea mortar. They were manned by some forty men. In order to get them to the scene of action it was necessary to tow them first across the Tyrrhenian Sea and through the Straits to Messina, and thence along the southern coast of Sicily to Syracuse, where they joined the rest of the American squadron not actively on duty off Tripoli. There he left them to be armed and fitted out in preparation for the forthcoming attack, and himself, in the *Constitution*, crossed to Tripoli by way of Malta to see how the blockade was being maintained.

The force which he had left on station there consisted of the *Siren*, Stewart; *Argus*, Hull; *Enterprise*, Decatur; *Vixen*, Smith; and *Scourge*, Dent; and on his arrival he found that they had not been idle during his absence. They had bombarded the forts ashore several times, probably accomplishing little against the thick walls, but at least they had served notice of their alertness and their readiness to match gun for gun with any opponent who cared to come out and fight. Shortly after that they had sighted a Tripolitan felucca attempting to get into port under the cover of a heavy fog. The *Siren* immediately went in pursuit, and the enemy promptly ran their craft ashore about ten miles to the west of Tripoli. Stewart at once ordered the *Siren*'s boats away in chase under command of Lieutenant James Caldwell, while the boats from the other vessels followed as the ships came up. Unfortunately Lieutenant Caldwell's launch got hung up on a rock not far from shore, where they were virtually sitting ducks for the massed Arabs on the beach, who were now being rapidly reinforced by several bodies of cavalry. The Americans returned their fire with spirit, and the other boats of the squadron joined in as they came up, but one American was killed, and by the time they were able to free the *Siren*'s boat from the rock the Arabs were too strong and too well posted among the rocks ashore for such a small force to dislodge them. Accordingly Caldwell ordered all boats to return to their ships. The *Argus* and the other smaller vessels then took station where they could fire into the stranded and abandoned felucca, quickly battering her to pieces so that she was rendered useless, while in the meantime the *Siren* ran down along the shore and opened fire on a ravine in which the Tripolitans had hidden and with a few rounds of grape soon dislodged them. The felucca, which was completely destroyed, proved to have been carrying a full cargo of salt, an item much in demand at that time in Tripoli.

Not long afterward Lieutenant Commandant Hull, in the *Argus*, came across a sloop anchored close inshore. He sent Lieutenant Blake with several boats to cut her out, which was done without much difficulty. She proved to be a Tunisian sloop laden with earthenware pots and jugs. But Hull suspected her of running arms and ammunition to Tripoli and accordingly sent her prize into Malta. Still later he intercepted a Spanish ketch leaving Tripoli under an American passport and ostensibly bound for Malta. She had been stopped by other American cruisers and allowed to pass, but Hull counted noses and discovered that she was carrying more passengers than her captain could account for. The fact seemed suspicious to Hull, so he seized her also and sent her in under a prize crew.

As a result of Hull's capture of the Tunisian sloop, by the

time Preble and the *Constitution* arrived off Tripoli the bey of Tunis was breathing fire and brimstone and threatening reprisals upon a number of American merchantmen lying in his harbor as well as demanding restitution of the sloop and damages for her seizure. Preble heard out Hull's report and snorted that the "Bey complains of trifles" and that "The boat and cargo was not worth $100, and if she had been worth ten thousand she would have been a good prize!"

However, to keep the record straight he ordered Hull, in the *Argus*, and Decatur, in the *Enterprise* to accompany him, with the *Constitution*, to Tunis. Apparently this bristling display of force appearing suddenly under his nose had a salutary effect on the belligerent bey, for he quickly changed his tune, and when Preble left a few days later he carried with him the bey's full assurances of peace and friendship.

With his rear thus secured, Preble now felt free to get on with the business in hand. Accordingly he sent the *Argus* and *Enterprise* back to their station and himself returned in the *Constitution* to Syracuse to gather up the gunboats and the other vessels remaining there. By the twenty-fifth of July he had gathered together off Tripoli his total force, consisting of the frigate *Constitution*, 44; the brigs *Argus*, 18, *Siren*, 16, and *Scourge*, 16; the schooners *Nautilus*, *Vixen*, and *Enterprise*, of 12 guns each; the six borrowed gunboats, each armed with a single long 24; and the two bomb ketches, each carrying a long 32-pounder brass bombard—fifteen vessels in all armed with 138 guns and manned by some 1,060 officers and men. Opposed to this force, which was, of course, mobile, the Tripolitans had some two hundred guns, most of them heavy and two thirds of them mounted in fixed positions behind stout fortifications. To man them they had about 25,000 men—scarcely even odds, but the factor of mobility gave the Americans a certain slight counterbalance. At least they could dodge.

At this point the weather took a hand in the game. The wind freshened shortly after Preble's arrival on the twenty-fifth, just as they were all ready, victualled, watered, and armed, and they were forced to fill away and stand out to sea to ride out the gale. By the twenty-eighth the wind and sea seemed to have blown itself out, and they approached for the attack once more. But they had scarcely regained their former positions before the storm burst out again with redoubled fury from the west-northwest, and blew with such violence that they were forced to beat a second retreat.

This time it lasted for several days, swinging gradually around to the south as it blew, a fact which undoubtedly saved some of the smaller vessels, especially the gunboats and bomb barges, from foundering or being towed under since it gave them the protection of a weather shore. Such protection, however, was of slight advantage to the larger ships, for the wind lashed at them with hurricane force, and the *Constitution's* close-reefed foresail and main topsail was blown from the bolt ropes in ribbons.

Not until August 3 were they able to get within striking distance under anything like favorable conditions. On that day, however, at 12:30 P.M. Commodore Preble finally advanced to the attack.

With the wind east by south, the entire fleet stood in to within point-blank range of the batteries on shore and the shipping within the harbor, their position then being just outside the barrier reef and nearly due north of the two westernmost entrances to the harbor. There Preble noted that the Tripolitans had formed their gunboats in three divisions: five at the northerly entrance, nine at the east, and seven in reserve inside the reef, and he decided to begin the action with them. At his signal the six gunboats and two bomb vessels were cast off.

Here the sluggish sailing quality of the gunboats was quickly apparent. Of the six only three were able to weather the point. These, however, dashed in boldly to attack the nine Tripolitans at the easterly entrance. The number four boat, under Stephen Decatur, headed straight for the first of the Tripolitans, withholding fire until within point-blank range. Inside a dozen yards Decatur opened with everything he had, and instead of round shot he had loaded his one long gun with several bags each containing a thousand musket balls. Under that withering hail the Tripolitan crew went down like tenpins, and those that were left fled aft. Within seconds Decatur laid them alongside, and with Midshipmen Thorn and Macdonough and twenty-two of his seamen, he boarded and made short work of the survivors. Hauling down the Tripolitan colors, he quickly returned to the gunboat and started to tow his prize to a place of safety.

While this was happening Decatur's younger brother James, in gunboat number two, following his brother's example, drew close alongside the second Tripolitan boat. There he, too, loosed a withering fire with such effect that the Tripolitans promptly hauled down their flag and surrendered. The younger Decatur lost no time in closing, and was in the act of stepping aboard the prize when the Tripolitan captain treacherously shot him through the head with a double-shotted pistol and, running up his colors once more, resumed the fight

From his position not far off, the elder Decatur witnessed the entire proceeding and without hesitation he cast off his prize and went in pursuit of the now fleeing enemy. They were fairly alongside before the Tripolitan could get under way, and after pouring in a smashing fire of grape and musketry boarded furiously through the smoke. Captain Decatur singled out the Tripolitan commander, a huge Turk, for his own personal vengeance, and lunged for him with a boarding pike. The Turk parried the blow and wrenched the weapon from Decatur's grip, at the same time striking at the American with his own pike. Decatur managed to parry that thrust with his sword, which broke off short at the hilt. Immediately the Tripolitan struck again and managed to wound Decatur severely in the chest and arm. But before he could strike again Decatur closed with him and the pair went down in a struggling tangle on the deck. As they went down both crews rushed to their assistance and instantly the two leaders became the center of a fierce hand-to-hand battle which, surging to and fro over them, tripped, stumbled, and fell on top of them in a piled-up mass of arms and legs and bodies.

Thus pinned, their desperate struggles were hampered. But the Turk managed to get one of his yataghans free and was probing for a vital spot with the short sword when Decatur, with a similar effort, managed to draw a small pistol from his pocket. Before the Turk had a chance to strike, Decatur pressed the muzzle of his gun against his enemy's chest and pulled the trigger, sending the ball through the other man's heart.

The death of their leader apparently demoralized the Tripolitans, most of whom leaped overboard, and Decatur lost no time in making the vessel his second prize of that day. But he was not a lone hero. There is a legend in naval annals that at the height of the hand-to-hand scuffle one of the Tripolitan crew aimed a slashing blow at Decatur's head with a razor-sharp scimitar. There was no time for anyone else near to parry the stroke, but a young seaman named Reuben James, both of whose arms had been disabled, was able to fling himself forward and catch the blow intended for Decatur on his own skull, thus suffering a severe gash that bit deep into the bone. Whether or not the wound was sustained in exactly that manner seems to be uncertain. But it is a matter of record that Reuben James was there, that he was terribly wounded, and that he did become a rather special protégé of Decatur, whom he served until the former's death in 1820. It is also recorded that he was a "two-fisted" drinking man. He used to boast that he had been in "ten fights and as many skrimmedges," and it was his custom in later years to celebrate each one appropriately on its anniversary. Whatever the truth, it makes a fine story.

While the gunboats commanded by the two Decaturs were so engaged, the others were not entirely idle. Gunboats numbers three and five were unable to close. Number three, under Lieutenant Joshua Blake, responded to a signal of recall that was mistakenly bent for a moment aboard the *Constitution*.

Gunboat number five, under Midshipman Joseph Bainbridge, lost her lateen yard while still under tow of the *Siren* but managed to get within range of the shore and continued to pour a heavy fire into the batteries until she touched on the rocks and was obliged to haul off.

Gunboat number six, commanded by Sailing Master John Trippe, followed the Decaturs' example and closed with one of the nine Tripolitans at the eastern entrance. As it happened, Trippe led the boarding party, followed by Midshipman Henley and nine of his crew. But before the rest could join him a freak of wind separated the two vessels and Trippe found himself and his little party cut off from both retreat and support and faced with some four-to-one odds.

In such a situation it would have been understandable if the American boarders had retreated. It would have been simple to jump overboard and swim to the safety of their own boat, which could not have been far away. Instead, however, they charged impetuously and engaged the Tripolitans savagely at close quarters. During the melee Trippe received eleven saber wounds before he managed to strike down the Turks' commander with a boarding pike. At almost the same instant the American gunboat was again brought alongside, and the rest of the crew poured on board to the support of Trippe and his handful of supporters. Their arrival, coupled with the loss of their commander, took the starch out of the remaining Tripolitans, and those who could flung themselves over the side, while the remainder surrendered.

While this was happening at the easterly passage, Lieutenant Somers, in the number one gunboat, unable to join with the others, had made for the northerly entrance, where five more of the enemy's gunboats waited. As he drew in he kept up a heavy fire of grape and round shot so effectively that all five of the Tripolitans turned and scurried for shelter. Somers followed them doggedly and three fled to shelter behind the rocks while the other two were disabled. By this time, however, Somers was within a hundred yards of a battery of twelve guns on the mole behind which the wounded Tripolitan vessels had sought shelter, and since it was impossible to pursue them further Somers turned to retreat. In doing so he had momentarily to expose his entire defenseless flank to the full point-blank fire of the battery.

Hitherto the battery had not dared to open fire on him for fear of hitting one of their own ships. Now that they were clear, however, and Somers was alone and defenseless, it seemed inevitable that gunboat number one would be shortly blown into matchwood. But just at that instant a lucky shot from one of the gunboats lobbed a heavy shell squarely into the battery, blew up the platform, and drove the Tripolitan gunners to cover. Before the Tripolitan guns could be manned again one of the schooners had darted in and taken Somers and his gunboat in tow and drawn them well away to safety.

But the action was not confined to the gunboats. They were smartly supported by the brigs and schooners and other small vessels, which kept up a steady fire on the harbor, the town, and the batteries. Twice the enemy's reserves attempted to sortie and separate the American gunboats from their prizes. But each time they were driven back. Besides the three vessels captured, three others were sunk and the decks of most of the others cleared of men. At the same time the shore batteries were severely battered with round shot and much damage was done to the shipping in the harbor, while a number of shells were thrown into the city itself and a minaret was knocked down.

Nor was the *Constitution* idle. Because of her greater draft she could not run in as close against the rocks as the smaller vessels. But she did enter the harbor and, sailing close under the Tripolitan guns, poured broadside after broadside into the town, the castle, and the batteries at close range. With her heavy long guns in constant action she did great damage, firing parts of the city with red-hot shot and silencing several batteries during the two hours that she was engaged at close quarters. She herself did not escape without injuries in this, her first serious engagement in the near seven years since her launching. But even those were minor. Only one man aboard was wounded and none were killed. One 24-pound shot went through her mainmast, and another smashed one of her quarterdeck guns. Her main royal yard was shot away and her upper rigging much cut up. One shot came in aft, hit one of her guns, and smashed in many flying pieces. Commodore Preble was in the direct line of fire, but though his uniform was torn in several places and he sustained some minor cuts, he was not seriously hurt, though one of the fragments hit a marine who was standing near him, taking off the tip of his elbow. After some two hours, the wind rising from the northeast and threatening, the *Constitution* drew off and signaled the rest of the squadron to follow.

The figures as to casualties and prisoners are far from accurate. During the fighting aboard the gunboats many of the enemy leapt overboard. Many of these doubtless escaped, but some were cut down while swimming while others were drowned, so that no true count is possible. By the same token, since the Tripolitans made no report of them, it is impossible to estimate the casualties in town resulting from the bombardment. It is known, however, that the Tripolitans suffered at least seventy-seven killed and some forty-four wounded. Twenty-seven were brought in prisoners, but many of these were severely wounded and died after being taken on board the *Constitution*. The Americans had only one—James Decatur—killed and nine wounded.

This was by way of being the *Constitution*'s baptism of fire. To be sure she had seen service during the quasi-French War in the West Indies, but the extent of her activities there had been confined to patrol duty, the capture of a few small privateers, and stand-by service while her boats cut out pirates and privateers close inshore. At Tripoli, however, for the first time she engaged in a full scale action, using both broadsides and all her batteries, and proved herself a capable and efficient fighting machine of her class.

But the action off Tripoli was more than a mere test of the

Constitution's fighting qualities. For the first time since hostilities had begun, the Americans served notice that they did not
intend simply to sit outside and wait for the Tripolitans to
come to terms. Before that bloody afternoon in August 1804,
the Tripolitans had been inclined to regard the fighting qualities of Americans rather lightly. It needed the action of August
3 to teach the Tripolitans how wrong they were. For centuries
they had been accustomed to having their own way in the central Mediterranean. Throughout Barbary there were no fiercer
or more feared rovers. Even in Roman times these Libyan corsairs had the respect, if not the admiration, of the proconsuls.
In more modern times—meaning the late eighteenth and early
nineteenth centuries—"peace at any price" had been a general
policy, European as well as American, toward them. And it
must be said that it was the British and the French who first
bought them off. In paying tribute to Tripoli and her barbaric
sisters the United States was merely following the example set
by much older and presumably wiser powers.

Hitherto it had been the Tripolitan custom to attack swiftly
and savagely, closing as quickly as possible and then carrying
the fight to their victims' decks with knife, pistol, and scimitar.
Seen in time they might be held off by gunfire, for their own
gunnery was notoriously bad. But once they had closed and
swarmed aboard there was not a force in the world that could
stand against them—so thought the Tripolitans, at any rate,
and because the rest of the world seemed willing to accept them
at their own valuation it had been many a year since anyone
had dared to stand against them.

On this occasion, however, they suddenly found themselves
faced by a foe not only willing to meet them on their own terms,
but eager to carry the fight to their own decks. The Americans
had not attempted to hold them at a distance. Instead, despite
the Tripolitans' numerical superiority, they had driven ahead
and closed and boarded and fought it out with pike, pistol, and
cutlass until the crews of those Tripolitan vessels boarded were
driven to surrender or into the sea. Three of the Tripolitan

gunboats were taken and three sunk, while the remainder were
forced to do what Tripolitans had never done before—retreat.
Ignominiously they had fled to the shelter of the rocks and the
shore batteries, and there they had been pinned by the accurate
gunnery of the Americans.

If nothing else, the attack taught them a sanguine lesson,
for never again were they quite so willing to come to grips at
close quarters.

10

CHANGE OF COMMAND

E v e n as he was putting a set of teeth into the war with
Tripoli such as never before had been displayed, Commodore
Preble was being superseded. This was the result of ignorance
rather than politics, though there is always a certain shadow
lurking in the background. Preble was a state of Maine man, a
New Englander. The Barrons, Samuel and James, were
Virginians—and one wonders. Preble was hurt, as his journals
show. Officially he never complained. But it is significant that
he did not serve again. The Barrons skimmed the cream. But it
is curious that the cream should be so often close to sour.

What happened three thousand miles away, in a day when a
dispatch or a letter was lucky to travel at twelve miles an hour,
is a matter of pure speculation. Congress knew nothing of
Preble's assumption of the offensive until long after it was
done. They voted him a commemorative sword when they found
out.

In the meantime they had only just heard of the loss of the
Philadelphia, and their minds were fixed upon vengeance.
Preble was there, to be sure, but he needed help—or even replacement. What mattered which? For once Congress recognized the fact that the United States must take its place—must
make its place—in the eyes of the world. And if Preble could
not do it, someone else must. So much for official confidence.
Even as the attack of August 3 was under way, Samuel Barron, one of the navy's most ineffectual captains, was already at

sea, en route to relieve the fighting Preble. Fortunately he brought with him, as his second in command, the able Captain John Rodgers, then in command of the frigate *Congress*, 36.

Following the bombardment of August 3 the *Constitution* and her consorts lay offshore, well out of gunshot range but still in a position to maintain an effective blockade, while they effected repairs and the smaller vessels replenished their supplies of food and water from the flagship. The three gunboats taken from the Tripolitans were refitted and manned and added to the squadron, and a French privateer came out from the port, where she had lain at anchor throughout the engagement, with a letter from the French consul reporting that since the attack the pasha was inclined to be more reasonable, and suggesting that Preble send in a flag of truce to discuss terms. Preble persuaded the privateersman to carry back fourteen badly wounded Tripolitans so that they might be properly cared for by their friends. But no responding exchange came back, and when Preble's flag of truce was not answered from the castle all decks were immediately cleared for action and the American crews called to quarters.

No time was lost. Preble moved in at once, but the wind and current being what they were the *Constitution* was unable to close with the batteries. As a result Preble lay off in directing range while the smaller vessels, under the *Constitution*'s signals, moved into the attack. The bomb ships were placed beyond range of the batteries, at a point from which they could throw their shells into the city. The gunboats, under oars and sails, drove against the western batteries. About 548 rounds were fired and some damage was done in the town. The Tripolitans remained at anchor behind the shelter of the rocks and did not attempt to come out. On the American side one of the prize gunboats was blown up by a lucky hit with a red-hot shot from one of the shore batteries. The shot slashed into the magazine and Lieutenant Caldwell and Midshipman Dorsey and eight others were killed in the explosion aft. Forward Midshipman Spence heroically stayed by his gun as the ship was struck.

Even as the vessel was sinking under him he and his crew completed the loading, fired, and dove over the side. Spence, who did not know how to swim, was lucky enough to find a floating oar to which he clung until he was picked up.

At six o'clock the squadron hauled off as a strange sail had been sighted heading offshore but evidently waiting. Hull in the *Argus* was sent to investigate, and the newcomer proved to be the frigate *John Adams*, Captain Chauncey, the forerunner of the new fleet bringing the word that Samuel Barron was on his way to replace Preble. The *John Adams*—not to be confused with the *Adams*—was in no shape to take part in the forthcoming attack. Evidently it was a piece of congressional policy to send out ships that were unready for combat, as was presently to be shown in the case of the *Chesapeake*. At any rate, though the *John Adams* carried a full crew and provisions and was pierced for her full rate of 28 guns, her carriages had not been mounted and she was as useless as a ferryboat on a mud flat at low tide.

Preble was a dyspeptic and scarcely known for his patience. His plans were laid and he had no intention of waiting for the rest of the reinforcements beyond any reasonable time. As it was he waited for some eleven days, meantime distributing the guns and crew of the *John Adams* among the other vessels of the squadron. When the looked-for successor did not arrive within eleven days he made up his mind to move in, but still another lashing gale drove him to seaward. When the blow eased the fleet stood back in and anchored within six miles of the shore, leaving no question of his intent.

The arrival of a supply ship from Malta with water and provisions went far to boost morale, and the transfer of livestock brought fresh meat, which at that moment was even more welcome than an extra ration of rum. In the meantime an attempt at negotiations was going forward ashore. On the tenth of August the pasha indicated a willingness to talk by hoisting a white flag of truce upon the French consul's flagstaff. Preble sent off a boat with an answering flag and a query as to terms.

In lieu of tribute, the pasha demanded a ransom of $500 for each captive and for terminating the war—a sum amounting to some $200,000. This was not satisfactory to the commodore, though it was a considerable reduction from previous demands. Preble's response was to authorize the French consul to offer a lump sum of $100,000 as the price of prisoners and future peace, but this, in turn, was sniffed at by Yussuf, the Tripolitan pasha.

Accordingly, on the twenty-fourth Preble moved in close to the harbor with the intention of a night attack. They were not yet in position at midnight when it fell calm and the smaller vessels had to be towed into position just outside the rocks. At two o'clock in the morning the signal was given for a general bombardment, which lasted until daylight. Little real damage was done beyond a few shots which fell into the town and on the castle, one in particular nearly finishing the luckless Captain Bainbridge as it smashed through a wall under which he was sleeping and sending rocks and mortar tumbling down all around him. Fortunately his companions pulled him out of the rubble unhurt save for a few minor cuts and bruises. But the moral effect of the attack was evidenced by the number of refugees that fled from the city the next day and refused to return. It is said that all business came to a virtual standstill inside the town and remained so as long as the American fleet remained offshore.

The winds off Tripoli shifted as capriciously as ever with the dawn and for three days blew with such force that it was out of the question to follow up the attack. By the twenty-eighth, however, it had come around to the proper point, and they prepared for another early-morning strike. Under cover of darkness the smaller vessels, including the *Argus*, moved in with the gunboats to anchor so close to shore that they were within range of the shore batteries. Just before daybreak, at 4 A.M., the signal to cast off was given by the *Constitution*, and at 4:30 they began a heavy fire on the town. The Tripolitans returned the fire with spirit, and for an hour the exchange was heavy. At

5:30 the gunboats and other vessels were recalled while the *Constitution* stood in to cover their retreat. According to Preble's subsequent report to the secretary of the navy:

We continued running in, until we were within musket shot of the Crown and Mole batteries, when we brought to, and fired upwards of three hundred round shot, besides grape and canister, into the town, Bashaw's Castle, and batteries. We silenced the castle and two of the batteries for some time. At a quarter past six, the gunboats being all out of shot and in tow, I hauled off, after having been three quarters of an hour in close action. The gunboats fired upwards of four hundred round shot, besides grape and canister, with good effect. A large Tunisian galliot was sunk in the mole— a Spanish Seignior received considerable damage. The Tripoline galleys and gunboats lost many men and were much out.

The *Constitution* herself was also much cut in her rigging, and some grapeshot was found sticking in her hull. But not one of her men was hurt, the only casualty aboard the *Constitution* occurring about a week after the engagement when one of her staysails was loosened and a large grapeshot caught in the folds fell to the deck and injured a seaman's foot.

One other sharp bombardment followed this attack, but it was inconclusive and was quickly overshadowed by an event that matched Decatur's destruction of the *Philadelphia*. For some time it had been Commodore Preble's most cherished hope to send a fire ship into Tripoli's cramped and crowded harbor with the intention of destroying the crowded shipping and harbor works and possibly even doing considerable damage to the town and castle itself. So far the only thing that had prevented him from doing so had been the awful risk to which the move would expose the officers and men who undertook the task. With a new commander on the way, however, it became painfully clear that now was the time to do it if it were ever to be done at all. Accordingly, on the afternoon of September 3, 1804, he summoned the officers of his squadron to council on board the *Constitution* to explain the details of his plan and ask for volunteers.

He had already had the ketch *Intrepid* prepared for the attempt. One hundred barrels of powder had been stowed below decks, just forward of the mainmast. On top of this were stowed a hundred 13-inch shells and fifty 9-inch shells, all solidly packed together with several tons of solid shot and kentledge. Holes were bored through the bulkheads, both fore and aft, and a train of powder laid from them to the forward scuttle and the after companionway where they terminated in boxes filled with a highly inflammable mixture of shavings, waste, and lint soaked in turpentine and pitch. Each fuse was calculated carefully to burn for fifteen minutes, which would allow ample time for the crew to escape in the two small boats that would be towed unobtrusively overside.

Thus prepared, the plan was that the ketch should slip into the harbor under cover of darkness. Once they were well inside, the fuses would be lit below decks and the crew would immediately take to the boats and pull as far toward the entrance as possible. Once the fire found the loaded magazine, it was hoped, the resulting explosion would so distract the attention of the Tripolitan guards that the Americans would be able to continue to pull away to safety unnoticed.

After describing the scheme, Preble pointed out the very real risks involved and called for volunteers. He might have saved himself that one step. Every man present wanted to go, and in the end he had to choose from among them all just as if he had not troubled to consult them. His choice finally fell upon Lieutenant Richard Somers to command and Midshipman Henry Wadsworth to act as second. Another midshipman from the *Constitution*, Joseph Israel, was so determined to go too that though he had been refused permission he stowed away anyway. He was discovered at the last moment, but apparently it was then too late to send him back so he was allowed to remain. Of the ten seamen aboard, four—James Simms, Thomas Tompline, James Harris, and William Keith—were from the *Nautilus*. William Harrison, Robert Clark, Hugh McCormick, Jacob Williams, Peter Penner, and Isaac W. Downes were all from the *Constitution*.

September 4 had been bright and pleasant, with a cloudless

sky and a fair breeze. As the night came on a thick mist gathered over the water between the ship and the shore, partially blocking off the view of the coast itself though the minarets of the mosques and the tops of the taller buildings of the city could be seen and the stars were bright overhead. At dusk the *Intrepid* warped in alongside the *Constitution,* and the officers and men who had volunteered for the duty went aboard her. Since everything necessary for the brief task had already been sent on board and placed, there was little left to do but make a final inspection and say a few brief farewells. Just before dark the lookout aboard the *Constitution* reported that three of the largest Tripolitan gunboats had moved from the harbor and come to anchor just inside the western entrance through the rocks—the very route that had been chosen for the *Intrepid*'s passage. Decatur passed the word to Somers and warned him to keep a sharp watch out for them lest they should attempt to board him before he reached the harbor. But Somers laughed, and replied confidently that recently the Tripolitans had grown so gun-shy that if they saw him coming they were more likely to slip their cables and run than to come out to meet him.

About eight in the evening the *Intrepid* cast off from the *Constitution* and got under way. She was accompanied by the *Argus,* the *Vixen,* and the *Nautilus,* Somers' regular command. Not long afterward, under special orders from Preble, the *Siren* also weighed and stood in after them to assist in picking up the returning boats, should they come out by the northern pass. The *Constitution* was the last to get under way, trimming her sails to the minimum and standing off-and-on as close as sounding would permit in order to observe as closely as the night and the mist would permit the outcome of the undertaking.

The *Nautilus,* however, was the last to communicate with the ketch. Running in as close to the entrance as its crew dared, the little schooner finally sheered off. First Lieutenant George Read leaned over the rail as they passed close astern and waved silently in a gesture of wish-you-luck. On the deck of the *In-*

trepid Somers waved back, and in the next moment the details of the scene faded and the ketch became only a black blob in the murk and haze. Presently she seemed to disappear entirely.

Only young Midshipman Ridgely of the *Nautilus*, watching from the schooner's rigging through night glasses, was able to follow her to the end, and then he could make out no more than her outline. At his last clear view of her she was standing in toward the harbor, about a musket shot from the mole.

After that, for a time, through minutes that must have ticked by like hours, there was nothing, not a sight or a sound, though throughout the fleet eyes and ears were strained by everyone for the slightest sign of what might be happening. The crash of the first alarm gun must have made them jump, but there was no indication that the ketch had been hit, and the instant echoing fusillade of random shots from the shore batteries was ample proof that the gunners had no idea of what they were shooting at. They were simply firing blind in the hope of hitting something—anything—whatever it might be that was out there.

In the darkness the stabbing lights might have thrown some reflection on her sails or for an instant otherwise have outlined the *Intrepid*'s position. But they did not. It was something quite different. Ridgely, in the ratlines, saw it. So did Lieutenant Carrol standing by Master Commandant Stewart's elbow and staring intently out into the darkness through the *Siren*'s gangway. Carrol grasped Stewart's elbow almost fiercely and stabbed the night with his other hand.

"Look there! See? The light!"

Stewart saw it too then, for an instant—a dim, waving, wavering line, moving unsteadily as if someone were running along a vessel's deck with a lantern. Scarcely had they seen it when it stopped, hesitating, then dropped abruptly out of sight as if whoever had been carrying it had dropped down a hatchway. For an instant there was complete and total darkness. Then the night was abruptly ripped apart by a tremendous explosion that lit the shores and shipping and seas for

miles around, and even at that distance thudded against the
vessels of the fleet outside as if with a giant, invisible hammer.

For a moment the watchers in the fleet were too stunned to
speak. Then as they began to regain their faculties they turned
to one another to ask what in the world had happened. What
had gone wrong?

To be sure the ketch had blown up most satisfactorily, just
as she was supposed to do. But it had not been right. She had
been still far from her goal. Something unexpected had happened. But what? All night long the smaller vessels of the fleet
prowled back and forth, just outside the reef, hoping against
dwindling hope that at least one small boat might come out to
them with an answer. But none ever appeared, and to this day
her premature loss remains a mystery. There are two schools of
thought in the matter. The first simply contends that a red-hot
shot from the shore batteries found her magazines and touched
off the blast. The second, and easily as plausible considering
the reports of a running light glimpsed just before the explosion, is based on a remark made by Somers to the effect that he
would not be taken alive. Boarded unexpectedly by boats from
the Tripolitan galleys, either Somers or someone under his command had deliberately set off the charges in preference to capture and exposure of the plan.

Whatever the cause, the results of the blast were evident at
dawn the following day, when the *Constitution* stood in as close
as possible to the reef. From the quarterdeck Preble could see
the wreck of a mast and a tangle of cordage and canvas on the
rocks at the northern entrance, and on the other side and along
the shore were the fragments of other vessels. One of the largest
of the Tripolitan galleys was missing entirely, while two more
were being hauled up on shore in a badly shattered state. Of
the three gunboats that had been stationed at the entrance
crowded with soldiers one appeared to have been sunk and the
other two had been run aground to prevent their sinking. But
of the ketch itself there remained not a vestige.

Later it was learned that two bodies, mangled beyond hope

of recognition, had been found in the bottom of the wreckage of the ketch. Four more were discovered on the sixth of September and six the day after, drifting in the harbor or cast up on the rocks. A final body had drifted ashore in the *Constitution*'s gig, which had been sent in with the *Intrepid*. All thirteen, the exact number of the ketch's crew, were laid out on the beach and Captain Bainbridge and some of the American officers prisoner in the city were allowed to see them, but all were so badly burned, mangled, and disfigured that it was impossible to identify any of them—"or even to distinguish an officer from a seaman," Bainbridge wrote. One of the bodies is said to have had on the remnants of a pair of nankeen breeches, and the hair of its head was black. Since Somers was the only one of the group on board who fitted even this meager description it is believed that the body was his.

This was the final action and virtually ended the war with Tripoli, for there were no further attacks and the Tripolitans showed no disposition to sortie. Foul weather forced the fleet offshore the next day, and on the seventh, in the face of the increasingly threatening weather plus the fact that he had expended most of his ammunition, Preble decided to send the *John Adams* and the smaller vessels, including the gunboats and bombards, back to Syracuse. He himself remained in the *Constitution*, with the *Argus* and the *Vixen*, to maintain the blockade and await the arrival of his successor.

He had not long to wait. Three days later, on the ninth, the new squadron commander, Samuel Barron, arrived with the frigates *President*, 44, and *Constellation*, 36. Preble hauled down his broad pendant and turned over the squadron command, though he remained aboard the *Constitution* until she reached Malta on the fourteenth. There he left her and returned to the United States on the *John Adams*.

11

INTERIM

ALTHOUGH Commodore Preble went home soon after the bombardment of Tripoli, it was to be some time yet before the *Constitution* followed him. Stephen Decatur, who had been promoted to the rank of captain following his exploit on the *Philadelphia*, took his place, but at this time his tenure was short lived. He was still at Malta on November 7 when by order of Commodore Samuel Barron he exchanged places with Captain John Rodgers, taking command of the *Congress* while Rodgers moved into the great cabin aboard the *Constitution*.

Rodgers went on to Syracuse where he found Commodore Barron, in the *President*, already before him. Since the *Constitution* was in need of men and repairs, it was considered advisable to send her to Lisbon. She sailed in the face of buffeting headwinds toward the end of the month and only arrived in the Tagus after Christmas. On the way her bowsprit was badly damaged and both sails and rigging needed replacement. This, of course, took time, but by the end of February they were back at Malta, armed and ready for another round at Tripoli.

At this time, the beginning of 1805, the American naval force in the Mediterranean was the strongest and most impressive yet gathered in those waters. It consisted of the frigates *President*, 44 (flag), Master Commandant George Cox commanding; *Constitution*, 44, Captain John Rodgers; *Congress*, 36, Captain Stephen Decatur; *Constellation*, 36, Captain Hugh G. Campbell; *Essex*, 32, Captain James Barron—

brother of the commodore; the 16-gun brigs *Siren,* Master Commandant Charles Stewart, and *Argus,* Master Commandant Isaac Hull; the 12-gun schooners *Vixen,* Master Commandant John Smith, *Nautilus,* Master Commandant John H. Dent, and *Enterprise,* Master Commandant Thomas Robinson; and the sloop *Hornet,* 10, Lieutenant Samuel Evans. In addition there were a number of gunboats and bombards already on hand and at least eight more of the former already en route from the United States. Moreover, the past two years of continuous service had shaken both ships and men together into an efficient, well-coordinated fighting unit, alive and alert and ready for action.

With such a force at his command the commodore had little choice but to announce publicly his intention to carry on the aggressive policies of Preble, though privately he must have had some doubts as to his own ability to do so. Probably there was no man in his entire command less ready or fitted for the task, for besides his almost chronic ill health he seems to have suffered from a lack of decision quite foreign to one in his position and thoroughly incompatible with the duty he now faced. Perhaps it is only fair to assume that his physical condition affected his judgment and made him subject to fits of procrastination and indecision.

Under the circumstances he was fortunate to have such a man as Captain John Rodgers as his second in command. Rodgers was as close to being an old-timer as it was possible to be in the young navy. Born near Havre de Grace, in Harford County, Maryland, in 1773, he had gone to sea as an apprentice—which is one degree lower than a cabin-boy—and within five years had risen to command of his own ship. In the merchant service he had gained familiarity with European and West Indian waters as well as American, and had won the full confidence of his owners. With the outbreak of the naval war with France, he had been commissioned a lieutenant in the navy and assigned to the frigate *Constellation,* under Truxtun. In that capacity he proved himself in the fight with the French frigate *Vengeance*, and was given command of that vessel after the battle. Following the Peace Establishment Act of 1801 he was retained on the list of captains, but in an inactive capacity. For more than a year he commanded a merchant ship—of which he was also the owner—trading to the West Indies where he had rendered important assistance to his fellow countrymen trapped at Cap François, in Santo Domingo, between the rebel blacks and the French invaders. At the outbreak of the war with Tripoli he was recalled to active service and given command of the Frigate *John Adams*, on which he saw duty under Commodore Morris in the Mediterranean. He had returned to the United States in 1803, soon after Preble's arrival, but as we have seen had been sent back to the Mediterranean in command of the *Congress* the next year.

In brief, Captain Rodgers was a seaman of broad experience and exceptional ability. He was also a man of quick decision, sound judgment, and prompt action; an officer who was respected and admired by everyone who served under him. Although he was a strict disciplinarian he was no martinet. He trusted his men, and they trusted him.

Throughout that long and often frustrating winter it was Rodgers who maintained the efficiency of the blockade while Barron lay sick abed. As Yankee power grew in the Mediterranean, there were those who pressed for another quick attack. And as the Yankee power grew, so did the Barbary bluster diminish. Some peace feelers found their way to Malta and Syracuse, and Barron was plainly tempted. But Rodgers was opposed.

As second in command, of course, he was not in a position to say what would or would not be done. He could only recommend. Though Rodgers was in active command, the passive—and telling—decisions were Barron's; the last word was his. Consequently, for the moment at least, Rodgers could do no more than hold the line, and he did that superbly well.

While Rodgers was blockading Tripoli, a curious diversion took place to the eastward. It was responsible for a number of

United States "firsts" and plays an important part in the traditions of the United States Marine Corps, and as such is celebrated in song and story to this day. One of Barron's passengers on the journey out to the Mediterranean was William Eaton, who had previously been the American consul general at Tunis. Eaton's knowledge of North African politics was excellent. He was aware, for instance, that the then ruler of Tripoli, Yussuf Karamanli—or Caramanli, as he has been called—had usurped the power in that country by driving his elder brother, Hamet, from the throne. Hamet had fled, leaving his wives and children in Yussuf's hands, and had taken refuge in Egypt. Tripoli still contained many dissatisfied elements who would have been glad to see Yussuf ousted and Hamet returned to power. Accordingly Eaton had proposed that with the help of the United States, Hamet be encouraged to raise an army and invade Tripoli from the east. Congress had approved the plan, provided the necessary appropriation to finance the venture, and named Eaton commissioner to contact Hamet and set the action afoot. For his immediate assistance in the undertaking Eaton was given the services of Lieutenant Presley N. O'Bannon, a sergeant, and six privates, of the marines. This was the American "army" which spearheaded the attack that resulted in the capture of Derna; the first action of the United States Marines in the Old World, and the first unfurling of the American flag in conquest of foreign soil.

This handful of Americans, with their supporting ragtag and bobtail army of several thousand "Arabs and Levantines," were successful in their immediate objective. But the action was of small consequence militarily. However it did have important effects politically and psychologically in Tripoli itself. With his richest province and its one good seaport east of Tripoli in the hands of rebels, and with the American fleet swarming in increasing strength before his very gates, Yussuf began to grow somewhat uneasy. He was on the horns of a dilemma. If he turned his attention to the rebels the Americans would batter down his walls. If he ignored the threat from the east and sought only to drive away the Yankee pests, the rebels with Hamet at their head might swarm over his back, and he had not sufficient force at his command to face both ways at once.

At the same time Yussuf was well aware that it would be useless to attempt to deal with his brother. Hamet had suffered such indignities at his hands that he would be satisfied with nothing less than Yussuf's complete removal, preferably with the assistance of the court's high executioner. Accordingly Yussuf decided to put out peace feelers to the Americans. His offer was made toward the end of April to Commodore Barron, as commander in chief of the United States' naval forces in the Mediterranean, and to Colonel Lear, at Algiers, as the ranking American diplomat in the area.

The bashaw opened negotiations with roughly the same offer he had made to Preble. He demanded a lump payment of $200,000 as the price of peace and as a ransom for Bainbridge and his comrades who were still in captivity in Tripoli. Immediate restoration of all property, ships, and cargoes to their original Tripolitan owners and the return to Tripoli of all Tripolitans held captive by the United States was a further condition of the proposed agreement. Nothing was said at the time of any further tribute to be paid annually to Tripoli, but the tone of the communications left little doubt that the matter would be discussed and settled on terms agreeable to Yussuf before any final treaty would be signed.

At the time Rodgers was in the *Constitution* commanding the blockading squadron off Tripoli. Naturally, since he was not in chief command, he was not consulted by the pasha. His duty was simply to send on the offer to Barron at headquarters at Syracuse and Lear at Algiers. Nothing, however, prevented him from expressing his opinion, and he did not hesitate to do so. Any such terms, he stated flatly, were ridiculous and were important only because they suggested that Yussuf was ready to consider the question at all. Doubtless they could be whittled down by shrewd bargaining, but the extent to which they might be so reduced would depend entirely upon Yussuf's respect for and fear of American sea power. Accordingly it was Rodger's conviction that no terms whatever should be discussed or even entertained until the full weight of the now powerful American squadron was arrayed before Tripoli and the city subjected to at least one more punishing bombardment. Only so would the pasha be made to understand that the United States could now apply enough power to support its own demands.

At first Commodore Barron seemed inclined to agree with Rodgers that at least one more attack should be made upon Tripoli before any negotiations were begun, and from one of his letters to Rodgers, written on May 1, it would appear that he intended to take active command of the fleet before Tripoli some time that month and commence offensive operations.

Barron's health, however, instead of improving as he had hoped, took a severe turn for the worse, and when it appeared certain that the full strength of the fleet could not be mustered before Tripoli before mid-June or early July, he simply bowed to the inevitable. In his current condition he could not hope to hang on that long, let alone assume an active status. As a result he decided to turn in his resignation as commodore and hand over the reins to Rodgers.

On the twenty-second of May, 1805, Colonel Lear, the United States representative in the Mediterranean, arrived at Malta. Later that same day, Barron penned his resignation and turned over the Mediterranean command to Rodgers—who was at the time on duty off Tripoli. In his instructions to his successor Barron directed Rodgers to cooperate with Lear in securing for the United States as honorable a peace as possible. Not until five days later, on the twenty-seventh, did the frigate *Essex*—Captain James Barron, brother of the former commodore, commanding—deliver Colonel Lear and his new orders to Rodgers aboard the *Constitution* before the blockaded port!

Rodgers was not disconcerted by the unlooked-for turn of events. His first move was to hoist his flag as commodore aboard the *Constitution*, designating her as his flagship. His next move was to send the *Essex* in toward Tripoli under a flag of

truce, with Colonel Lear aboard. The castle responded with an
acknowledgment of the signal and a boat carrying the Spanish consul, as a disinterested neutral, and a representative of
the bashaw came out. Thus the negotiations were begun. Colonel Lear objected to the Spaniard as an intermediary, and his
place was taken by Nicholas Nissen, the Danish consul, and in
due time the articles were drawn up. Yussuf's original demands
were scaled down very considerably. In the end it was agreed
that the United States should no longer pay tribute to Tripoli,
peace was declared without indemnity and the captives held by
each belligerent were to be exchanged. The United States held
few prisoners, but Tripoli still held Captain Bainbridge and
the rest of the crew of the *Philadelphia*—a considerably larger
number. For this excess the United States agreed to pay a ransom of $60,000, and in future American vessels were to be un-
molested by Tripolitans or their allies or overlords.

At home there were some who objected to the payment of any
ransom for Bainbridge and his companions, but the fact remains that the terms were far short of the original demands,
and that thenceforward Tripoli ceased to be a piratical menace
not only to American shipping but to that of other nations as
well. Nothing was to disturb the peace in that quarter, so far as
the United States was concerned, for many a year to come.
Samuel Barron returned home in the *President*, 44, commanded by his brother Captain James Barron.

So the war with Tripoli came to an end. But the *Constitution*'s tour of duty in the Mediterranean was still far from
finished. As the Tripolitan venture was drawing to a close the
neighboring bey of Tunis, apparently laboring under the mis-
taken notion that Tripoli was reaping a handsome profit from
the war and hoping to gain a little something on his own account, began to show signs of truculence. In April a Tunisian
corsair with two prizes had been taken while trying to slip into
the harbor of Tripoli during the blockade. Now the bey began
to bluster and threaten the United States with war unless the

three vessels were returned to him and damages paid for their detention.

He could scarcely have picked a less auspicious moment. Every man in the American fleet, from Rodgers on down, had been primed for action, and with the abrupt collapse of Tripolitan resistance they felt cheated. They were spoiling for a fight, and if the bey of Tunis insisted on one they would be only too glad to oblige. As soon as the treaty with Tripoli had been drawn and signed and Bainbridge and his companions released, Rodgers turned his attention to Tunis, and late in July he sailed in the *Constitution*, accompanied by some seventeen other vessels of the squadron—the largest fleet yet sent out against a single objective by the United States—and on August 1 came to anchor off Goleta within plain sight of the city.

The totally unexpected appearance of the American fleet, and Commodore Rodgers' quite obvious willingness to fight if the Tunisians insisted, apparently rocked the bellicose bey back on his heels and caused him to pause and think. To cover his hesitancy he took refuge in bombast and evasion. But however he squirmed it became increasingly evident that not only did Rodgers mean what he said, but that he also had the means at hand to make good his threat. As a result, toward the end of August the bey finally recognized the hopelessness of his position and agreed to a new treaty under which an ambassador was sent to the United States to discuss the matter of the captured vessels, and the payment of annual tribute by the United States to Tunis was ended forever.

With this satisfactory conclusion of the Tunisian dispute peace came at last to the Mediterranean—at least so far as the United States was concerned—and there was no longer much need for a large American force to be kept in those waters. It was not possible, however, just to turn around and go home. So far as the action went, it was all over. Still it was necessary to wait for confirmation of the treaty and its acceptance by Congress. Any departure prior to that would be premature, and in the event of congressional objection might even be disastrous. And even after Congress accepted the treaty, it would be wise to maintain a token force in the area; to "show the flag" and keep the nation's late enemies aware of continued United States vigilance.

In carrying out this policy, Commodore Rodgers continued for something more than a year cruising the Mediterranean in the *Constitution*. Much of the fleet, however, was dispersed. In September the *Congress*, Captain Stephen Decatur, left Tunis for Washington with Suleiman Melli-Melli, the Tunisian ambassador, aboard. The vessel was accompanied by the *Constellation*, the *John Adams*, and the supply brig *Franklin*. The *Essex* and the *Vixen* were sent to Gibraltar to keep an eye on American interests in those waters. His own headquarters Rodgers maintained at Syracuse, though he was a frequent visitor at Malta and Messina, Naples and Leghorn, while the other vessels of the fleet were in equally constant motion.

Not until May 1806 did Rodgers receive final and peremptory orders to turn over his command and return home— "peremptory" because it was some time since he had received the first suggestion that he take such a course. At that time, however, he had appeared twice at Algiers and once at Leghorn and had been able to observe at first hand the salutary effects of those visits. He had bluntly protested the move and begged that the force then at hand be properly maintained. But President Jefferson had never been a staunch navy man. In fact, he had been inclined to look upon the naval service with a suspicious eye, considering it a potential threat to democratic principles. Furthermore, he considered the maintenance of a strong naval force abroad a possible source of involvement in Europe's endless quarrels. He wanted no part of any foreign entanglements, and considered American isolation behind its broad Atlantic barrier the nation's best line of defense. In his opinion all that the United States needed was a force of small gunboats, capable of patrolling its harbors and coastal waters, and unfortunately the experience of the navy off Tripoli, where only small vessels of shallow draft were able to operate successfully, seemed to bear out his theory. What Jefferson apparently did not understand was that a score of gunboats could not hope to stand up to a full sized ship of the line or even a big frigate on the open sea, and that there were several European nations with fleets strong enough to support an invasion of the United States or a blockade of its coast. Only with capital ships could the nation hope to keep open the lines of its rapidly expanding commerce, and instead of maintaining the fleet Jefferson was laying up the heaviest ships in ordinary and turning the most experienced officers and men out to grass. He was already committed to the "gunboat policy" and from his point of view it was imperative that the Mediterranean command be reduced as speedily as possible.

So it was that on May 28, 1806, Commodore Rodgers reluctantly removed his flag to the *Essex* and turned over command of the *Constitution* and the Mediterranean squadron—such as it now remained—to Captain Hugh G. Campbell. On May 28 the *Argus* and the *Siren* cleared for America. Not until June 3 did Rodgers in the *Essex*, accompanied by the *Vixen*, the *Vengeance* and the *Hornet*, get to sea, followed shortly afterward by the *Nautilus*.

Why Rodgers chose to leave the *Constitution* on station remains a mystery, unless perhaps he had been deliberately ordered to do so as a sort of backhanded reprimand, the *Essex* being a smaller ship. Certainly the *Constitution* should have had the priority, for of all the ships that had served abroad she had been longest away from home, and subsequent events were to show that those who had served so long and well in her were only too ready to return "stateside."

The *Constitution*, alone of all the navy's frigates, remained another year on the Mediterranean station. Indeed, but for the "lucky little" *Enterprise*, which had been built on the eastern shore of Maryland, she was the only "home grown" vessel in those waters. It is not too difficult to understand the forces of discontent that were building up during that year of idleness. A round of social gaiety at a half a score of Mediterranean ports might be all very well to maintain the officer morale and keep the young midshipmen happy, but for the men below decks and before the mast it was just another senseless period of drudgery and wasted time. Most of them—indeed, all who had come out from home—had already served longer than their enlistments required. Their time was up. They had done their duty. But still the ship was kept abroad, and the same articles of enlistment required that they continue to serve aboard until the ship could be brought into a home port. It was obviously a clause that was simply intended to cover the "safety of the vessel." That is to say, it meant that if a man's time expired while the ship was still at sea he was not to lie back and refuse to help fetch her home, but must continue to work until she got back. But it was equally obvious that it was a clause that could be stretched, and in the case of the *Constitution*, was being stretched to the utmost. And there was nothing in the law to say that the men so imposed upon could not resent it.

Almost miraculously the year passed without untoward event. The men of the *Constitution* took a reef in their patience and waited, sure that before too much longer they would be relieved.

Not until late in the following spring of 1807, however, did the word arrive that they were to be relieved by the frigate *Chesapeake*, 36, with the newly appointed commodore, James Barron. In cheerful anticipation of her arrival the *Constitution* moved up to Gibraltar where she waited—and waited— and waited, for a ship that never came.

12

FREE TRADE AND SAILORS' RIGHTS

T H E end of the Revolutionary War had brought freedom and political independence to the American colonies. But that freedom evidently did not include the freedom of the seas. As a rather small island nation England had always found it necessary to depend on her far-flung overseas trade and the might of her great fleet to maintain her position of world supremacy. She did not idly boast that "Britannia Rules the Waves!" for not since the days of the Spanish Armada had any other nation seriously dared to challenge her dominion of the seas. To her the oceans of the world were simply an extension of her own shores, and she did not take kindly to interlopers who sought equal rights upon them.

So long as Britain held to this attitude, additional clashes between her and the fledgling United States were practically inevitable. The undeclared naval war with France had diverted American attention from the British problem, temporarily postponing a showdown. Preoccupation with the Barbary corsairs delayed it somewhat further, but the time of reckoning was approaching quickly.

The *Constitution* had already been waiting for some time when, on June 22, 1807, the 36-gun frigate *Chesapeake*, Commodore James Barron, her decks still cluttered with last-minute gear and few of her guns yet mounted in their carriages, cleared from Hampton Roads to relieve her at the Mediterranean station. The *Chesapeake* was followed to sea by the British frigate *Leopard*, 50, which had been lying at anchor in Lynnhaven Bay for some days. They were fifty miles at sea and well out of sight of the land before the Englishman hove alongside and requested that she carry a packet of dispatches for him to Europe.

There was nothing out of the ordinary in the request since public vessels frequently extended such courtesies to one another in those days. Accordingly Barron hove to and a few moments later the *Leopard* lowered a boat and sent an officer across to the American. When the officer stepped on board, however, he brought with him no dispatches for Europe. That apparently had been only a subterfuge to bring the *Chesapeake* to. Instead he handed Barron an order, dated June 1 and signed by Vice-Admiral Berkeley, commanding on the North American station, directing the commanders of all British men-of-war to halt and board the *Chesapeake* wherever she might be found upon the high seas and search her for deserters.

It is true that among the *Chesapeake*'s crew were four men known to have deserted from the British frigate *Melampus*. But these men had all been pressed into the royal navy from an American merchant ship. Three were known definitely to be Americans, while the fourth, though he was unable to prove it, swore that he had been born in this country and there was no evidence to the contrary. Accordingly the United States government had refused the demand of the British minister that they be given up and had retained them.

This was obviously the basis for Berkeley's order. Nevertheless the point-blank order was presumptuous and high-handed; an affront to the sovereignty of the United States. That the admiral was well aware of it is borne out by the fact that he added, as a slight sop, that Commodore Barron or other American officers might avail themselves of the same privilege when searching for deserters.

Commodore Barron quite properly sent the British officer

packing back to the *Leopard* with the message that, since the *Chesapeake* was a public armed vessel representing the government of the United States, he could not permit her to be so searched. At the same time he called his crew to quarters, but as we have already seen, her decks were in a state of complete disorder and few of her guns were even mounted for action. Indeed, rammers, wads, matches, gunlocks, linstocks, and even powder horns could not be found amid the confusion. As soon as Barron's message had been received on board the *Leopard*, her commander, Captain Humphreys, hailed the *Chesapeake*. But Barron was unable to understand what was said. By this time the *Chesapeake* was resuming her course, and without warning the *Leopard* threw at least one shot—some say three —across the *Chesapeake*'s bow. Before Barron had time to heed this peremptory signal to heave to, even if he wanted to, the *Leopard* ranged alongside and from a distance of about two hundred feet poured a full broadside into the hapless American!

For fifteen minutes the Englishman continued to pour in broadside after broadside, while the *Chesapeake* lay helpless to return the fire. Indeed, the only gun fired from the American was discharged by a Lieutenant Allen, commanding the second division, who fetched a live coal from the ship's galley in his bare hands and applied it to the touch hole of one of the few available pieces.

That shot hulled the *Leopard*, even fired at random as it was. But the *Chesapeake* had suffered far more. All three of her masts were damaged and her sails and rigging much cut. Three men had been killed outright, eight more were badly wounded, and ten, including the commodore himself, were slightly wounded. When Barron struck his colors the action ended, and several British officers boarded the *Chesapeake*, mustered the crew, and impressed into the British service the four seamen they had been seeking. Commodore Barron informed Captain Humphreys that he considered the *Chesapeake* the Englishman's prize, but Humphreys refused to accept his sword in token of surrender, and the *Chesapeake* was forced to limp back to Norfolk without even the solace of an honorable capitulation.

The effect of the event upon the nation was swift and violent. At Norfolk and Hampton aroused mobs destroyed the casks sent ashore to procure water for the British squadron and chased the boats' crews back to their ships. Elsewhere in the nation public meetings were held to denounce the attack, and even among staunch Federalists who had hitherto supported if not favored the cause of Anglo-American amity, there were many voices raised for war. Indeed, so great was the clamor that even Jefferson, who hoped desperately to avoid a war, felt constrained to issue an order closing American seaports to British armed vessels, and those vessels that were still left in the Mediterranean were recalled, while officers on inactive duty were recalled to service.

It was midsummer before the report of the outrage reached Gibraltar, where the *Constitution* lay impatiently awaiting her relief. Under the circumstances one can understand why Commodore Campbell felt it might be wise to leave Gibraltar. Indignation ran high among both officers and men toward the British navy, and Gibraltar was an English naval base. The slightest incident ashore might easily explode into a very disagreeable and potentially dangerous situation. At the same time he felt that men who were kept busy would have less time to brood upon their discontent. Accordingly orders were sent down to prepare the ship for sea.

But it was already too late. If there is anything that spreads faster than fire in a wooden ship it is scuttlebutt. News of the *Chesapeake* leaked out before the order, and the crew leaped to the conclusion that the disablement of the relief ship would postpone their return. From the oldest hand before the mast to the smallest powder monkey they stood shoulder to shoulder and flatly refused to work the ship unless the sailing orders were for home.

It was mutiny, of course, any way one chooses to look at it, even though there was some degree of extenuation in the fact that most of the men's enlistments had long since expired, and they were long overdue for discharge. Even Commodore Campbell understood and was sympathetic. But he could not let the insubordination pass without notice. Fortunately what action he intended to take will never be known, for at the very height of the tension the orders arrived to return home, and this was the one command that no one was in any mood to dispute. Early in the fall of 1807 the *Constitution* arrived at Boston, and from there was ordered to New York where her crew was paid off and she was laid up for repairs.

In view of the naval policy then being stubbornly pursued by the Jeffersonian administration, it is scarcely surprising that the *Constitution*'s "repairs" should take nearly two years to complete. Shocking as the *Chesapeake* affair had been, it apparently had little effect upon the thinking of the President or his most trusted advisers. They had already committed themselves to the wasteful and utterly ineffectual gunboat policy, and there was no turning them back from it. By the end of 1807 the construction of 278 of the tiny mosquito craft had been authorized by Congress, and in the end some 176 of them were built at a cost of $1,500,000—a sum that would have launched and equipped at least five 74-gun ships of the line, or eight to ten frigates similar to those already in service. The capital ships would have nearly doubled the strength of the existing fleet and greatly enhanced the nation's ability to meet an enemy at sea in any ship-to-ship engagement. As it was, few of the little one-gun gunboats saw any serious duty at all. They could scarcely hold their own against a well-armed sloop or schooner, let alone face a frigate, and when the War of 1812 finally broke out all but a small handful around New Orleans were sent far up the smaller creeks and rivers, well out of reach of the enemy, where they were left to rot.

But the gunboat policy was not the only reason for the neglect of the *Constitution*'s repairs. In conformity with the administration's policy of strict isolation and his own determined insistence on noninvolvement in any form, late in 1807 President Jefferson called for and Congress passed the Embargo Act, which forbade American ships to sail for foreign ports, forbade the exportation of American goods and products in foreign bottoms, and required all coastal vessels to post bond of double the value of ship and cargo to insure that the goods would be relanded at an American port.

Within a month American trade was at a standstill. American shipping lay rotting in the harbors, and American seamen stood stranded on the beach. As for the principal combatants at whom the measures were leveled, the American action was little more than the plaguy bite of a pestiferous mosquito. As for the navy, there was no point wasting time and expense in repairing ships to protect our commerce when there was no commerce to protect.

It was a situation, to be sure, which cured itself—in time. But from 1807 to 1809 the *Constitution* lay at New York and felt the tap of hammers now and then, when the work of gunboat-building could spare the time. No one, apparently, thought to look below the waterline.

By election time, 1808, the fallacy of the embargo policy was already painfully apparent, and grave doubts were felt as to the wisdom of the gunboat theory. Jefferson gave way to Madison. Robert Smith was supplanted by Paul Hamilton as secretary of the navy. Smith did remain in the government as secretary of state, but at least he was out of the navy's—and the *Constitution*'s—top hamper. The embargo gave way to the Nonintercourse Act, which allowed American vessels to take to the seas again and trade with all nations as they would—*except* Great Britain and France.

To enforce this act, it was obvious that the major ships of the navy must be put back into action. The "cockboats or whirligigs of the sage of Monticello," as the little gunboats have been called, were sent into mothballs and the *Constitution, President, Constellation, Essex, United States, Chesapeake, John Adams* were called into service.

Throughout the interval John Rodgers had been in command of the Navy Yard at New York, principally employed in the irksome task of building and commanding the gunboat squadron there. In February 1809 he received orders to make the *Constitution* ready for sea. The clatter of hammers took on an increased tempo and a more purposeful sound, but it was not until the middle of August that the *Constitution* finally took to sea. She made a "cruise of observation and instruction" at that time, paused at Newport and New London, and again put to sea in company with the *Essex* and the *Argus*. Forty-eight hours out, in a calm sea, the fore and main, with accompanying yards, went by the board, carrying one of her seamen to death. Obviously, the accident was not the result of wind and weather, but of the poor quality of timber used. The *Constitution* went back to port for repairs again, but by the spring of 1810 she was once more at sea, capturing ships like the *Golconda* of New York, and the *Rose* of Philadelphia, for violation of the Nonintercourse Act. For the ship it was sea service. For the officers and men it was hardly inspiring duty!

But better days were coming. Rodgers had not been happy with the *Constitution*'s sailing qualities, and he considered her over-sparred. But there was another captain to whom the ship was home. This was Isaac Hull, whose career had been intertwined with hers since the French War. In 1810 Hull commanded the *President*. Rodgers had the *Constitution*. Rodgers suggested, and Congress approved, an exchange, which was made at Hampton Roads on June 17, 1810. Rodgers took command of the *President*, taking with him his officers and crew, while Hull took command of the *Constitution*, taking with him *his* officers and crew.

Apparently there was a sympathetic bond between the man and the ship. Where Rodgers had been only dissatisfied with the sailing qualities of the *Constitution*, Hull seemed to sense the trouble. His first orders were to Boston for water and provisions, after which he was to rejoin Rodgers and the northern squadron. But on the way the ship sailed so poorly that he was late in port. From Boston he reported that it would not be possible for him to be back in the Chesapeake at the time due. Before he left Boston he wrote to Hamilton: "I have no hopes of her sailing any better than she did coming here—I fear she will never sail as she has done until she goes into fresh water."

What he meant was that her bottom was fouled with salt water growth—mussels, barnacles, oysters. These would only be killed by taking her into fresh water. He did not add that they could not be altogether removed except by careening and scraping. Even then a seagoing man apparently understood that in dealing with political bureaucrats one went only one step at a time.

By midsummer he was back at Hampton Roads where, in an interval of calm, he sent divers overboard to examine the ship's bottom. The result confirmed his hazarded opinion. The divers reported that the bivalves were hung all over the ship below the waterline "like bunches of grapes," so thick that it was difficult to pry them apart, and they managed to bring up some ten bushel basketfuls as samples. By their estimate there were at least ten wagon loads encrusted on the ship. To prove his point and to indicate the need for cleaning the ship's bottom, Captain Hull is said to have forwarded several bushels of the bivalves—doubtless including many choice Mediterranean specimens—to Washington to grace the secretary's table. No doubt they were the most desirable of epicurean delicacies when they were brought up, and Hull may have made more than one meal of them himself, but considering the climate of Chesapeake Bay in midsummer and the lack of refrigeration at that time, it seems likely that Secretary Hamilton got the message through his nose rather than his palate by the time they arrived!

In the meantime Hull did not waste time waiting for orders. He stood at once up the bay in order to get as far into fresh water as possible. Since he was unable to careen the ship and set men to chop the growth away and scrape the copper clean as such work was usually done, Hull devised an iron rack, something on the order of a modern peg-tooth harrow, which was dragged back and forth across the bottom of the ship so that it scratched off the barnacles that were dead or dying. But even with this ingenious arrangement and the brackish waters of the upper bay, it was impossible to dislodge all of the crustaceans. By the end of August, Hull felt that the ship was as ready for sea as she ever would be, short of being hove down, so he stood back down the bay, and by early September rejoined Rodgers off Sandy Hook. From there he wrote to Hamilton that the ship sailed much better than she had before, but added that she still left much to be desired. But nothing more could be done until she could be hauled in and hove down for a thorough going over. In the meantime he would make the most of it.

The rest of that summer and early fall was almost in the nature of a schoolboy cruise. There were new men and officers aboard, especially among the midshipmen, and these as well as the ship had to be whipped into shape. In that day and age the term was meant quite literally. During that period Hull cruised between Boston and the Virginia Capes, trying out both and occasionally lying off Sandy Hook as a gentle hint to such Englishmen as might be prowling in the vicinity that their presence was unwelcome. On one such pause, off the Jersey shore, Midshipmen Charles M. Morgan and Richard Rodgers requested permission to take a boat on shore "to shoot." They did not specify what sort of shooting they had in mind, and the permission was granted without question.

It was a period in which a gentleman's honor was particularly sensitive, and satisfaction for an affront, real of fancied, was only to be had by resort to arms. When men—or boys who considered themselves men, which especially in the case of midshipmen meant anyone from the age of eight upward— quarreled, the only proper way of settling the matter was by means of the code duello, with swords or pistols or whatever other deadly weapon the challenged party chose to name.

"The Code," of course, was not recognized by the authorities. Murder was murder, even then—in most instances. But when gentlemen met on the "field of honor" the results were often as not regarded by the police and the courts as a private matter. The classic example is, of course, the meeting at Weehawken, New Jersey, in 1804 in which Aaron Burr shot and killed Alexander Hamilton. Less well known is the fact that Hamilton's son Philip died on the exact same "field of honor" as his father three years earlier! Equally well remembered is the duel between James Barron and Stephen Decatur, at Bladensburg, Maryland, where Decatur fell mortally wounded.

With such an example set them by their elders, it is scarcely surprising that the youngsters should be ready and willing to fight at the slightest provocation. The navy did not encourage the practice, but there is little doubt that it generally left such matters to be settled between the officers involved in their own way. There is a record that a Midshipman Redick fought a Midshipman Barrymore over the matter of a hat worn in the wardroom. The meeting took place in an orchard about a mile from the New York Navy Yard, in Brooklyn, but the record does not name the winner. Again, Midshipman Danielson, a stepson of General Eaton, faced Midshipman Schuyler, antecedents not mentioned, over the pistols at ten paces for no reason that has ever been given. Danielson died with a bullet through his heart, and as the record quaintly states, Midshipman Schuyler "absconded" into New Jersey.

In the case of Morgan and Rodgers, the "permission to shoot" had nothing to do with shore birds. The two young officers shot at one another, with the result that Midshipman Rodgers returned to the *Constitution* feet first. Morgan was seriously wounded, and both he and his second were placed under arrest. But the fact that one of the seconds was named Hamilton, and that his father was the secretary of the navy, may account for the fact that nothing more was heard of the matter.

Nor were duels Hull's only problem during this period. Another midshipman, Sylvanus Sprogell, was lost when he fell out of the main chains and was drowned. Another, whose name is

The *Constitution* fought her last battle against the British frigate *Cyane* and sloop of war *Levant* near the Madeira Islands off the African coast in February, 1815. The *Cyane* surrendered 40 minutes after the engagement opened; the *Levant* shortly after.

The *Constitution* towing the *Cyane* to a neutral port on the African coast. Upon reaching there she sighted three British ships and so cut anchor and fled to sea. A chase ensued but the *Constitution* eluded them.

In 1834 a political controversy broke out over the *Constitution's* figure-head. Jacksonian Democrats replaced "Old Ironsides'" insignia with a statue of the incumbent President Jackson. Anti-Federalist Bostonians cried out in protest. One Cape Cod merchant stole out to the ship one stormy night and sawed off the head of the emblem. The figurehead was eventually restored and adorned the ship's prow for many years.

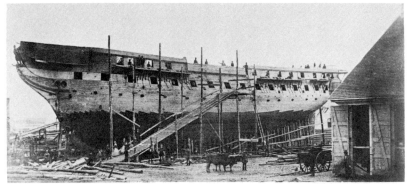

In 1855 the *Constitution,* badly in need of repair, entered drydock in Portsmouth, N.H. Above, she is shown ready for launching in 1858. An appeal for her repair had been eloquently voiced twenty-five years earlier by Oliver Wendell Holmes, a Harvard law student who had glorified the "shattered hulk" in a stirring poem, "Old Ironsides."

In 1860 the *Constitution* was used as a training ship for the Naval Academy at Annapolis. Shortly after the Civil War began, she was spirited from Annapolis to New York in fear for her safety.

In 1861 both the *Constitution* and the Naval Academy moved to Newport, R.I., where they remained for the duration of the Civil War. There she was anchored off Fort Adams, at the entrance to the harbor. To her stern, in this picture, is a steamboat—symbol of a new age of sea power.

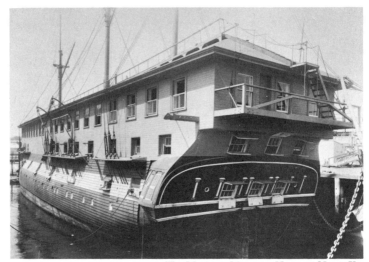

"Old Ironsides" celebrated her 100th anniversary in 1898 in the Portsmouth, N.H., harbor as a barracks ship for sailors coming into port, her hull all but hidden under the barracks. John F. Fitzgerald, grandfather of President Kennedy and then congressman from Massachusetts, investigated reports that the vessel was sinking at the pier and urged her repair.

The *Constitution,* once again in need of repair, as she appeared in 1907 just before Congress appropriated $100,000 for a much-needed restoration.

After nearly a quarter of a century of inactivity, the *Constitution* sailed away in 1931 on one of the longest voyages of her career, in the course of which millions of visitors came aboard. She visited ninety of the nation's ports, as far east as Bar Harbor, Maine, west to Bellingham, Wash., and south to Balboa in the Canal Zone. Above, she enters New York Harbor.

"Old Ironsides" traveled nearly 22,000 sea miles in her three-year cruise. Commander Louis J. Gulliver called it "the longest and most hazardous towing cruise in history." It was not marred by a single accident.

The *Constitution* now rests in the Boston navy yard. Hundreds of thousands of people come each year to pay tribute.

The *Constitution's* spar deck. Carronades are on either side, the mizzenmast and wheel in center. Although designed as a 44-gun frigate, the *Constitution* ofter carried more. In the battles with the *Guerriere* and the *Java* she carried 55 guns.

Each year, in an attempt to minimize the effects of weather caused by staying in one position, the *Constitution* turns around. She presents alternately her port and starboard sides to the sun. At left, midshipmen and navy tugboats lead "Old Ironsides" away from the pier in her annual turnaround.

U.S. Navy

U.S. Navy

The U.S.S. *Constitution*, world's oldest warship in commission afloat, is a symbol of the nation's sea power. This painting, now in the possession of the government, hangs in the study of the President of the United States in the White House.

not revealed, was sent ashore on indefinite leave with an illness
which Hull reported to the secretary "is not a very gentle-
manly one," though he does not specify whether it was of the
Bostonian or Baltimorean variety, these being the only two
ports of call at which the ship had paused long enough for a
young officer to have contracted such an ailment.

The interval, however, was not entirely devoted to the adventures and misadventures of the *Constitution*'s younger set. Far
more serious, if somewhat monotonous, was the constant prowl
and search up and down the coast on the endless lookout for
violators of the Nonintercourse Act and of Macon's Bill No. 2,
which closed American territorial waters to all French and
British armed vessels except those on special, official missions,
packets, and such others as might be forced into port by dis-
tress or accident. Other duties included the apprehension of
private armed vessels illegally fitted out in American waters,
and the reporting of all American citizens who assisted or sup-
plied foreign armed ships. At the same time American vessels
legitimately engaged in trade were to be given every assistance, and all American commanders were to be particularly
vigilant in an effort to prevent further impressment of American seamen from American ships.

Throughout the summer and into the fall scarcely a day
passed without one or more of the American squadron chasing,
halting, and examining an inbound or outbound vessel. In the
main the ships stopped were peacefully engaged about their
proper business, in which case they were allowed to proceed
without further hindrance. But there were some incidents that
were indicative of the underlying state of affairs. In June the
President caught the French privateer *Revanche du Cerf* at
Hampton Roads. In the Gulf of Mexico, Lieutenant Trippe, in
the *Vixen,* was fired upon by the British brig *Moselle.* The shot
passed over the *Vixen*'s quarterdeck and carried away the main
boom, but Trippe did not return the fire and the Englishman
apologized, saying that he mistook the American for a Frenchman, and Trippe accepted the explanation. Further north the

British royal schooner *Vesta* flitted in and out of American waters, each time she was stopped reporting simply that she was "on a cruise." At length, however, she was found within sight of Sandy Hook in the act of boarding a ship and was chased. But she was faster than her larger pursuer and escaped. The ship she had halted proved to be the Spanish ship *Oceana*, and at the time of discovery the *Vesta* had been in the act of impressing a seaman from her victim despite ample proof of the man's Spanish birth.

The event was eloquent of England's attitude toward the rights of other nations' territorial waters. Clearly it would need more than diplomatic protest or congressional legislation to teach the royal navy a lesson.

13

THIN ICE

THE *Constitution* spent the winter of 1801–11 at Newport, Rhode Island, with the rest of Rodgers' squadron. As soon as possible in the spring they got to sea, Hull and the *Constitution* standing up the New England coast as far as Maine and then swinging in to Boston to recruit, while Rodgers and the *President* stood for New York, where the British were reported to be making trouble in the bay.

Neither cruise produced anything of startling note, unless it was the recruit who was lured on board the *Constitution* at Boston, according to report, to serve as "the captain's gardener"! Apparently he was still wobbling from the effects of the recruiting officer's generosity when he came on deck and called for his shovel and hoe. But a touch of the cat, which was as much a cure-all in the American navy in those days as it was in the British, it is said, convinced him that there had been some mistake, and in the end he was satisfied to settle for a carpenter's hammer and chisel.

At Boston, Hull received orders to proceed to Annapolis, where he was to prepare his ship for foreign service of an unspecified nature. He reached Annapolis late in May and at once asked to be enlightened. While he waited for an answer events of importance were taking place offshore.

In point of action the *Constitution* was not involved, yet the events were to affect her future. The first occurred on the first of May, when the British frigate *Guerriere*, 38, under the command of Captain Samuel John Pechell, brought to and boarded the American merchant brig *Spitfire* from Falmouth (now Portland), Maine, for New York, within sight of Sandy Hook. The British boarding party seized and impressed a passenger, a John Diggio or Deguyo of Maine, a native-born American citizen, and carried him aboard the frigate where he was forced to serve.

Well knowing the furor that the act would raise in the United States, Captain Pechell had the name of his ship—*Guerriere*—painted in huge black letters across his topsail, thus advertising his identity, while he continued to prowl the forbidden seas. Pechell apparently was spoiling for a fight. The sensation he obviously hoped to create was as nothing compared to the outraged clamor that arose from the Atlantic seaboard. Hull, of course, was still awaiting orders and could not move. But Rodgers, in the *President*, put to sea at once and prowled back and forth in search of the offending *Guerriere*. A passing merchant ship reported having sighted the *Guerriere* off Cape Henry, and Rodgers turned in that direction. Shortly after noon on the sixteenth of May he sighted what was evidently an English man-of-war and went in chase. Both vessels beat to quarters and hoisted their signals, but neither seems to have been intelligible to the other. Not until dusk did the American overhaul the Englishman, and then—Rodgers feeling sure that the other was the sought-for *Guerriere*—fire was begun.

The details of the fight that followed differ considerably, depending on the reporter's point of view. All accounts agree, however, that it was dark when it started, and that it was impossible for either ship to identify positively the other's exact character. It is further agreed that both ships stood cleared for action, and that both commanders hailed simultaneously at close range with the identical words: "*What ship is that?*" But from that point on, the stories disagree, both as to who fired the first shot and how long the engagement lasted.

What does matter here is that a battle did take place, and that when the smoke cleared and the next day dawned the

stranger proved to be, not the anticipated *Guerriere*, but his
Britannic majesty's sloop of war *Little Belt*, 20, Captain
Arthur Batt Bingham—which incidentally had no more right
to be in those waters than did the *Guerriere*. During the engagement the *President* suffered little damage. One boy was
wounded and one 32-pound shot struck the ship's mainmast
while another lodged in the foremast. Beyond that her hurts
were superficial. The Englishman, on the other hand, was
badly mauled. Her spars, rigging, and sails were heavily damaged and one of her pumps shot away, while she took many
shots between wind and water which passed completely through
her from side to side, raising havoc below decks. At the same
time her casualties were heavy, numbering thirteen dead, including a midshipman and a lieutenant of marines, and nineteen wounded, among whom were the acting master and another lieutenant of marines.

As soon as he discovered his adversary's identity in the morning, of course, Commodore Rodgers sent a boat aboard with
proper regrets and an offer of assistance in repairing the
damage. The offer was "politely declined" by Captain Bingham, and the *President* squared away for New York, leaving
the *Little Belt* to limp off northward for Halifax.

As may be imagined the event had loud repercussions on
both sides of the Atlantic. In America the general reaction was
one of jubilation. For once, it was felt, the tables had been
turned. British arrogance had been humbled. The long list of
intolerable insults had been partially avenged and the *Leopard*'s unprovoked attack on the *Chesapeake* had at last been
answered in kind; indeed in the only language that the British
could seem to understand! In England, understandably, quite
the opposite reaction was the result. There were, of course, all
the customary official exchanges on the diplomatic level, which,
as usual, came to nothing. But the fact remained that on both
sides of the ocean the popular temper was wearing thin.

Meanwhile, the *Constitution* still lay at Annapolis awaiting
orders. Though it was less than forty miles to Washington by

the Post Road, it was not until after the *President*'s encounter
with the *Little Belt* that the *Constitution*'s orders finally arrived. When at last they did turn up Captain Hull might possibly have indulged in a bit of quiet gloating—not to mention
the reflection that everything comes to him who waits! For this
was to be no routine cruise, patrolling offshore waters. On the
contrary, it was to be a voyage that would take him and the
Constitution straight into the lion's den.

It is true that the principal object was diplomatic rather
than belligerent. But Isaac Hull was a fighting man. He had
often expressed his views on the subject, and there could be no
doubt in anyone's mind that he would accept no insult at anyone's hands, even in their own home waters.

Specifically, wind and weather permitting, the *Constitution*
was to carry out several duties. First, she was to convey the new
American minister, Joel Barlow, and his family to France,
landing them at Cherbourg. Next, Hull was to proceed to
Texel, where he would deliver the interest due on the United
States Revolutionary War debt to the Dutch—some $28,000
in gold specie. When this had been accomplished, the ship
would return to Cherbourg to pick up Jonathan Russell, late
chargé d'affaires at Paris, and convey him to England, where
Russell would assume his new duties as chargé at London. Considering that, in addition to their resentment of the *Little Belt*
affair and their contempt for American naval power, England
was locked in a bitter struggle with France, some inkling of the
delicacy of the task will begin to be clear. Add to this the facts
that (a) Napoleon was gathering his strength for an invasion
of Great Britain; (b) the British had strung an iron blockade
along the French coast, while the sails of the home fleet
whitened the waters of the English Channel; and (c) the recent annexation of Holland by France raised some question as
to whom the interest should be paid to; and it becomes even
clearer—if that is quite the word!

Mr. Barlow, however, was apparently in no haste to assume
his new duties at Paris. The *Constitution* lay at Annapolis

from May until August waiting for him. In the meantime his preparations went forward somewhat ponderously. At one point, it is reported, he expressed his desire to take his carriage, along with a vast mountain of personal luggage. But at this Hull put his foot down. The luggage could be safely stowed below, but the carriage would have to be lashed on deck, and Hull pointed out that there it would be in danger of serious damage from the salt spray—which was no lie. At the same time, he advised Mrs. Barlow and her sister, who were to sail with them, to be prepared for a passage of sixty days. However, he did everything he could to make things comfortable for the ladies. He even moved out of his own after quarters and took space with the rest of the officers. At the last moment a marine was discovered to have smallpox. He was promptly sent ashore and the rest of the crew inoculated after the crude fashion of the day. Hull wrote fervently that he "hoped none took it the natural way."

Fortunately none did, and by the first of August they were ready to sail. Shortly after, their passengers came on board and they dropped down to Hampton Roads. It was the fifth of the month when they were finally able to clear away and stand out between the Virginia Capes under a fair wind for France.

Barring the presence of ladies aboard, and the social clutter that always follows the sex, there was nothing unusual in the outward passage. For all his thirty-eight years Hull was still the senior bachelor aboard, and as such was responsible for the social tone aboard, just as, as captain, he was in supreme command of the ship. In his capable hands there was no room for error on either score. As for the weather, it was generally fine and favoring, save for a brief, violent blow that struck them between Hatteras and the Bermudas and sent the ladies below for several days.

But it was not all beer and skittles, for they were not half way across when the plague broke out forward, among the crew. Every precaution was taken to keep it from spreading to the after cabin, not that Hull feared for himself or his fellow officers, but he regarded his passengers as a sacred trust, to be guarded from harm at all costs. At one point it was proposed to seal off the after cabins and fumigate the rest of the ship at sea by burning sulphur candles below sealed decks. But as any seaman knows, this is a fearful remedy even in a modern vessel snugly anchored in port, and the plan was abandoned as being worse than the disease.

In spite of all this—and although Captain Hull had warned the ladies to be prepared for a passage of sixty days—the *Constitution* arrived in the English Channel by September 1. On the fifth, exactly a month after their departure from Hampton Roads, they came in sight of Cherbourg—and of the English fleet blockading it at that moment.

Every way they looked, it seemed, there was an English sail in sight. But Hull had no intention of letting himself be intimidated. He sent his men to battle stations and resolutely maintained his course. One of the English frigates, apparently the flagship of the blockading fleet, ranged alongside, signals snapping at her halyards:

"Permission to come aboard?"

The man might be an Englishman, but at least he seemed to know his sea manners. Hull eased way slightly, permitting the other frigate to send a boat. In a few moments a British lieutenant was conveying the British commander's compliments and would the American commander be so good as to step aboard the British flag?

Hull, who had no intention of knuckling under, declined.

A second English frigate ranged up on the opposite side. The gun ports might not be open, but the threat was there.

The English lieutenant returned.

If Captain Hull would not deign to come aboard his majesty's frigate, would he at least delay his entry into Cherbourg until—say—tomorrow afternoon?

Hull's exact reply has not come down in history. But it was probably saltier than that generally reported:

"My compliments to your commander, Lieutenant, and will

you inform him that the *Constitution* is a ship of the United
States Navy, carrying the flag not only of the commander-in-
chief in European waters but also the diplomatic flag, which is
presumed to cover every movement of a non-belligerent vessel
on a presumably co-friendly mission."

Such might be the law—or usage, since there is no true valid-
ity in international law. As a matter of courtesy the *Constitution* hove to and waited—but with her gun ports open and men
at battle stations.

A midshipman from the British frigate finally waited on the
captain of the United States Navy. He asked that the American captain come on board the British flagship. Hull's reply
was to put the *Constitution* back on her course into port. The
record shows that there was still another visit from the British
fleet—a lieutenant, this time—demanding that the American
frigate wait until it was convenient for the English to allow her
passage. Captain Hull simply returned his previous response
and continued in to his expected anchorage.

His resolute attitude, bluff or not, had its expected effect.
The sun was not far over the yardarm when the *Constitution*
came to anchor in Cherbourg harbor, and her passengers, female and otherwise, set on shore.

Since Jonathan Russell, who had been chargé d'affaires in
Paris and was to assume similar duties in London, was still in
the French capital, Hull sailed on the twelfth for Holland.

But bad weather delayed him in the Channel, and to avoid
the blow he put into Deal. Today the little Channel port is
hardly more than an excursion point for London's Sunday
trippers. But in those days it was an important stage on the
London-Paris route. It was not the first time that Hull had
been there. He had friends ashore, and he went into town just
long enough to doff his hat and take a cup of cheer.

The next day, however, the weather had cleared enough for
him to get away. Accordingly he stood over and up, past the
Hook of Holland to Texel, where he delivered his specie. That
done, and the weather again turning up blustery from the

south, he cut across to Portsmouth, where he went ashore and
went up to London to see his friends. Hull had scarcely departed the vessel, when the *Constitution* became involved in a
minor dispute that threatened to have major repercussions.

Then, as now, Portsmouth was to the royal navy much as
Norfolk is to the United States Navy today. When the *Constitution* came to anchor she found herself surrounded on all sides
by British ships of the line and lesser sails of the royal navy.
Especially close was the frigate *Havanna*, 50, which was anchored just astern of the *Constitution*.

It happened that in the crew of the *Constitution* there was
one seaman who, on enlisting, had given his name as Thomas
Holland and sworn that he was an American born. It did not
occur to anyone to question his word, for he appeared to be a
good hand who was reasonably well liked by all. On the night of
November 13, however, while the *Constitution* lay at anchor,
not far from the British frigate *Havanna*, he either acciden-
tally fell overboard or managed to slip down the chains and
swam to the British frigate, where he was picked up in a condition too exhausted to speak coherently, for the water that night
was very cold.

The following morning, the *Havanna* sent a boat to the *Constitution* to inform the acting captain, Lieutenant Charles
Morris, that one of his crew had "fallen overboard" during the
night and had been picked up by the *Havanna* and was being
held aboard her for the Americans. When a boat from the *Constitution* went to pick up the sailor, however, the officer in
charge was blandly informed that it had since been learned
that the man who had called himself Thomas Holland, an
American, had been discovered to be one Charles Davis, an
Irishman by birth, and therefore a British subject. The English captain added that he could not surrender the man without
an order from Sir Roger Curtis, the British admiral commanding at that port. As for Holland—or Davis, whichever his
name may have been—he had already been sent to the guard

ship, where he was being held pending Sir Roger's decision.

Lieutenant Morris was scarcely a man to shrug off his responsibilities indifferently and simply sit back and wait for Hull to return from London. So far as he knew Hull might not be back for weeks. That would depend upon what orders—or lack of them—he found there. Morris was no newcomer to the fleet. He had signed on as midshipman in 1799, and he had particularly distinguished himself before Tripoli, having been first over the side of the *Philadelphia* when Decatur had so daringly destroyed that vessel. In fact he had been in command of the party designated to fire the cockpit and lower decks nearest the magazines and had come near to being blown up with her himself.

Accordingly, Morris went on shore to demand of the British admiral that he either return the man, as had been previously promised, or give a proper explanation for keeping him. Sir Roger, however, merely passed the buck, replying that since Holland-Davis had been sent to the guardship the matter was now one which rested with the admiralty board alone.

Within a few days Hull returned from London and received a report of the incident from Lieutenant Morris. Apparently Captain Hull was in none too good a humor about such matters, two of his gig's crew having slipped away ashore the moment his back was turned, and accordingly he sat himself down to write a sharp official letter to Admiral Sir Roger Curtis, Bart., summarizing the entire case in all it details and demanding the man's return.

Hull was no fool. He was perfectly well aware of the usual fate of official correspondence. However, he was also aware of the fact that all such official correspondence must eventually find its way to the Board of Admiralty—and thence, perhaps —to the floor of Parliament. There, at least, it might have some effect, if only as a pawn in some political game. However, he had no illusions as to Sir Roger's reaction. He explained that he was accountable to his government for the crew under his command, and courteously requested that Sir Roger "be pleased to order the said Thomas Holland returned to this ship."

As he suspected, Sir Roger was of no such pleasing a mind. Holland-Davis stayed where he was, and that night Hull ordered extra marine guards posted on all decks of the *Constitution* for the duration of their stay in Portsmouth—which was to be short—with explicit orders to fire at anything that might be seen moving in the water near the ship.

The "night was but a pup," as the saying went, when several muskets blasted from the *Constitution,* and Hull was informed that there was a man in the water close alongside. The firing was stopped and ropes lowered, a boat sent out to assist, and presently, uniform and all, a dripping seaman from the *Havanna* was brought on board. The record does not give his name, but he claimed to be an American.

On the following day a boat came down from the *Havanna* and named the man and demanded that he be returned to them as a deserter. Now it was the *Constitution*'s turn to blandly inform the British that they could scarcely expect the Americans to return one of their own countrymen to the *Havanna.*

The British did not take kindly to this turn of events. The *Havanna* moved closer to the *Constitution,* and another unnamed frigate came up on the other side, so that there was some question of whether the *Constitution* would be able to go clear of them when she sailed, as she was due to do that very night. Hull ordered the *Constitution* to drop back about a mile to seaward, and the pilot—an Englishman, of course—expressed a fear that he might not be able to clear one or the other of the close lying warships. He might foul one or the other of them, he said. Hull directed the pilot to proceed anyway, and the *Constitution* managed to move to the new anchorage without incident, save that one of the frigates followed and dropped anchor not far away. Hull still was not at all sure whether he would be able to leave port without a fight.

At dusk all hands were beat to quarters, and the drums—in

those days taking the place of current day bugles and bull horns—rattled off anchors aweigh. The decks were cleared. Marines manned the fighting tops. Gun crews stood by their guns with taut lanyards. Seamen swarmed aloft to loosen sail, and the boatswain's pipes summoned the capstans' crews to the bars. The sails dropped from the yards, and the anchors came up from the bottom, dripping with mud. This was the time when a strike would come, if it were coming. But not another ship moved or even shortened her cables. With a proper dip of the colors and a salute for the admiral of the port the *Constitution* came about and stood away to sea.

The British flagship returned her salute while the frigates dipped their colors, but no vessel followed her. The guns were run in and gun ports closed, carriages made fast and anchors stowed and everything made shipshape.

It took them two days to beat across the Channel, and scarcely ever were they out of sight of a British sail, but none ever challenged them. By the twenty-second she was snugly moored at Cherbourg. While Lieutenant Morris went to Paris to pick up dispatches from Barlow for the home government, Hull exercised the ship and the crew in the Channel.

They based at Cherbourg from November 22 until January 10, 1812. It was a cold winter, and probably the most notable and frequently repeated entry in the log was: "Extremely cold. Carpenters employed all day making coffins."

On his mission to Paris, Lieutenant Morris saw Napoleon and met Lafayette and Kosciusko, as well as many survivors of the French Revolution. But it was probably Barlow's dilatoriness in getting his dispatches ready for home that delayed him until January. It was not until the tenth of that month that they were finally able to sail.

The homeward voyage was cold and stormy, and it was forty days before they dropped their hook off Old Point Comfort. In spite of her very thorough going-over before going aboard, Hull had found the vessel's sailing qualities almost worse than before. Obviously something needed correcting. Accordingly

late in March, Hull took her up the Potomac to the navy yard
at Washington where he requested the Navy Department to
have her hove down for examination and repair of the timber
and copper of her bottom. Fortunately Congress acceded to the
request, and so she was moved into shallow water and all her
stores and ballast, top hamper, guns and ammunition, removed,
and then she was hauled over on her side so that she lay exposed
from keel to waterline. As luck would have it, her old sailing
master, "Jumping Billy" Haraden, was master of the yard at
the time, and for him it was a labor of love. Furthermore, he
was determined there should be no more errors in her repairs. It
is said that she received practically a whole new set of bottom
planking and a complete new copper sheathing, together with
certain alterations in rigging and spars, so that her sailing
qualities were phenomenally improved. It was doubtless the extreme care with which this work was done that enabled her to
escape from what seemed almost certain destruction by the
guns of five British frigates, shortly afterward, as well as giving her a great advantage in her famous encounter with the
Guerriere.

14

CRY HAVOC

"CRY 'HAVOCK' and let slip the dogs of war. . . ."
So runs Shakespeare's well remembered line from *Julius Caesar*.
It might almost as well have applied to the Anglo-American situation at this moment, save that the year was 1812 instead of 44
B.C., and "Caesar's spirit, ranging for revenge," applied rather to the bitter mood of American merchants and seamen
against the high-handed British attitude at sea.

That, at least, was the major cause of the War of 1812. Another was British encroachment on the western frontiers of the
United States. At that time actual settlements did not extend
much beyond the Alleghenies, but the United States claimed all
the territory westward between the Ohio River and the Great
Lakes. The British had acknowledged American sovereignty
there after the Revolution, but now they were creeping in and
pushing Americans out. Certainly the United States could not
accept that treatment. Nor could it accept continued British
provocations at sea. Whenever the commander of a royal navy
vessel felt that he needed another hand before the mast he had
no hesitation about stopping any American ship he met and
pressing such men of her crew as he needed on the pretext that
they were really Englishmen sailing under false passports.
When one stops to recall that Ireland was British at that time,
as were Quebec and Nova Scotia, Prince Edward Island and
Newfoundland, it is obvious that they had plenty of places

where a man might have been born, and it was up to him to prove otherwise.

Naturally, Americans resented this attitude and did not hesitate to say so. As a result the British finally revoked the orders in council which had permitted such action on June 16, 1812. But it was too late. Congress, spurred on by a group of warhawks who felt this would provide an opportunity for an easy conquest of Canada, declared war two days later—long before report of the revocation of the orders in council reached America. Ships of the United States Navy were ordered to sea immediately.

News of the United States declaration of war, in turn, did not reach England for several weeks, and it was several weeks more before it came back from London to Halifax and thence filtered out to the various ships on station. As a result when the first action of the war took place, about 120 miles southwest of Nantucket Shoals, between the United States frigate *President*, 44, Captain John Rodgers, and the British frigate *Belvidera*, 36, Captain Richard Byron, Captain Rodgers knew very well that a state of war existed but Captain Byron had no idea of the situation. As it happened the *Belvidera*, which was a much lighter ship but one of the best in the British navy, defended herself in a masterly fashion and was able to escape with very minor damage.

Rodgers, who is always considered one of America's naval greats, did not come off so well. The *President* herself suffered only minor damage, but an "officer and a gentleman," even if only such by act of Congress, should first have found out whether or not his opponent knew what it was all about before beginning his attack.

The *Constitution* was lying at anchor off Annapolis on the eighteenth of June, 1812, when war was officially declared. But though it was only forty miles from Washington, it was two full days before she received the official word. The entry in her log for June 20, 1812 reads:

. . . The Commanding Officer, Lieutenant Read, had the crew turned up, and read to them the declaration of war between the United States and the United Kingdoms of Great Britain and Ireland that had passed the senate and authorizing President James Madison to employ the Armies and Navy of the United States against the above written powers. The Crew manifested their Zeal in support of the Honor of the United States Flagg by requesting leave to Cheer on the occasion (granted them). Crew returned to their duty, light airs from the Southward and Eastward.

Isaac Hull was not on board at the moment, which accounts for the message being read to the men by Read, who was acting captain in his absence. He had been in Washington completing his report on his recent European cruise, but he had left for Annapolis before the actual declaration of war was announced, though there is little doubt that he was well aware of its inevitability. On his arrival on board the *Constitution* his fears were confirmed by the letter from Secretary of the Navy Paul Hamilton, which he found waiting for him there. It was dated the eighteenth of June:

SIR: This day war was declared between the 'United Empire of Great Britain, Ireland and their dependencies, and the United States and their territories,' and you are, with the force under your command, entitled to every belligerent right to attack and capture and to defend. You will use the utmost dispatch to reach New York, after you have made up your complement of men, &c., at Annapolis. In your way from thence you will not fail to notice the British flag, should it present itself. I am informed that the *Belvidera* is on our coast, but you are not to understand me as impelling you to battle previously to your having confidence in your crew, unless attacked, or with a reasonable prospect of success, of which you are to be, at your discretion, the judge. You are to reply to this and inform me of your progress.

Clearly it was not Secretary Hamilton's intention to get the fighting ships to sea where they could fight, as Rodgers had so

naturally assumed, but rather to send them scurrying to
safety. Once they reached New York they were to be laid up in
the harbor, their guns removed from one side to the other, as
the position of their anchorage might demand, and there they
would lie throughout the war, mere floating batteries, useful
only for defense from a fixed position! That they would be
commanded by their regular captains while so laid up must
have been pure gall and wormwood to such officers as Hull and
Decatur, Bainbridge, Stewart, Porter, and Macdonough, to
mention only a few. It seems incredible that any responsible
official could have been so blind to the inevitable result of such a
policy and at the same time so spineless as to advocate the total
withdrawal of this nation's most effective fighting force from
any possible scene of action. Yet that is exactly what happened. Albert Gallatin, a holdover from Jefferson's administration, was still secretary of the treasury and exercised great
influence upon the President. Paul Hamilton, the secretary of
the navy, was a more recent appointee and it is understandable
that he would place great faith in the judgment of the elder
statesman. But it was Gallatin who was most strongly opposed
to sending the navy to sea to do the work for which it had been
expressly created, and it would seem that Hamilton must have
been equally at fault to have allowed his department to be so
misused. Fortunately, there were such men as Bainbridge and
and Stewart and Hull at hand to protest such a fainthearted
course. Bainbridge and Stewart, the ranking officers then in
Washington, waited upon Hamilton in an effort to save the navy
from such a disgraceful course. To their amazement they learned
that there had already been one cabinet meeting to discuss the
matter, and it had been decided then that this was the proper
course. At their insistence another meeting was called, but to
their chagrin it was decided to make no change of plan. Still
they persisted and a third protest brought them to a meeting
with President Madison. He heard them out, noted their
enthusiasm, and at length decided to override the decision of
the cabinet and issued the order for the ships to put to sea.

In the meantime, the *Constitution* sailed on June 21, three days after the declaration of war, with orders to proceed to New York where she was to join the squadron commanded by Commodore Rodgers. At that time her complement was only partially filled, many of her officers and men had not returned from their shore leave, and in any case she was short-handed, a number of Englishmen in her crew having been released from sea service. Only a few of her guns were mounted, and it was rumored that she was woefully short of powder and ammunition. Fortunately, thanks to "Jumping Billy" Haraden, she was well prepared for sea otherwise, for she was newly coppered, rotten timbers had been replaced, and her rigging was as taut and shipshape as it was possible to make it. On her way down the bay she must have performed wonders of training and recruitment, for when she passed out to sea between the Virginia Capes, on the twelfth of July, her crew was nearly complete, her guns were mounted and were already being exercised, her officers were apparently all present, and she was well found and equipped, both as to stores and ammunition.

It was an auspicious start. In two weeks' time she had shipped an almost full crew, green hands for the most part, to be sure, some of whom had never been aboard ship before. But Isaac Hull was her captain. Her first lieutenant was Charles Morris. And the rest of her officers, even down to her midshipmen, were good, capable men. They knew how to make sailors out of farm boys, and their ability in this respect was amply demonstrated within a very few days.

After clearing Cape Charles, the *Constitution* bore northeastward to allow ample room to clear the central Jersey capes. Thence, off Barnegat she came up almost to true north, which in the course of time would bring her to a point almost exactly forty miles to the eastward of Sandy Hook, the area where British ships of war had been reported to be patrolling. This report had been sent to Hull, but he failed to receive it before sailing. At the same time he was under the impression that Commodore Rodgers, with the northern portion of the Ameri-

can fleet, still lay at New York, and it was his intention to join
forces there. What he also did not know was that Rodgers had
sailed from New York, as soon as he had heard of the declaration of war and without waiting for orders from Washington,
taking with him four other ships of his squadron. Rodgers had
hoped to intercept a large and very rich convoy of British
merchantmen which was presumed to be en route from the West
Indies for England, but his delay in turning aside to chase the
Belvidera enabled the Jamaica fleet to escape. The *Belvidera*
put into Halifax with the first news of the outbreak of war and
the exact whereabouts of the American fleet.

Vice-Admiral Sawyer, commanding all British forces on the
American station, at once ordered out a squadron from Halifax, under the command of Captain Sir Philip Broke, in the
Shannon, 38. With him when he sailed were the *Belvidera*, 36,
Byron; the *Aeolus*, 36, Captain Townsend; and the 64-gun
razee *Africa*, Captain John Bastard. These were later joined
by the *Guerriere*, Captain James Richard Dacres, off Nantucket. Thus even as Hull was heading northward for New
York, hoping to join the American squadron which had already left, a British squadron of even greater force than the
Americans was heading southward from Nantucket to blockade
that port. That they should meet was virtually inevitable. Only
the results were at all surprising.

The weather was hot and sultry, still, almost airless, as it
often is off the coasts of New Jersey and Long Island in July
and August. This was not so in the morning and early afternoon, for the *Constitution*'s log at noon on July 17 records
clear weather with fresh breezes from the north and east. But
the breezes must have dropped off sharply, for at 2 P.M. when
the masthead lookout cried out: "Sail ho-o-o-ooo!" the wind
was reported as very light.

The lookout had sighted four ships, all bearing north-
northwest on the starboard tack, heading westward. At this
point they were about twelve miles off Barnegat. At 3 P.M. the
Constitution's lead showed 18½ fathoms—about 110 feet—and

Hull, feeling that he was being drawn too close inshore to maneuver properly, brought his head about on the opposite tack and steered due east. At 4 P.M. a fifth ship was sighted from the masthead bearing about northeast and standing toward the *Constitution* under all sail.

By this time, although he could not identify the ships individually, Captain Hull was convinced that all five were British men-of-war, and in this he was quite correct, for the four first sighted were the *Shannon, Africa, Aeolus,* and *Belvidera,* while the fifth was the *Guerriere,* Captain Dacres.

The wind held light from the northeast until 6:30 P.M., when it shifted around to the southeast, giving Hull the weather gauge. Taking advantage of this, he brought the *Constitution* up and bore down on the *Guerriere,* keeping her just off his port bow, and within an hour, having come just within gunshot of her, he cleared his ship for action and beat the crew to quarters.

The two frigates converged gradually in the growing darkness, neither one as yet being prepared to open fire, either for fear of firing on a friend or from a lingering suspicion of the identity of the other five vessels in the distant background—the *Nautilus,* an American vessel just captured by the British, also having hove in sight by nightfall. Thus they kept pace with one another for three hours more, still drawing cautiously together.

Finally, at 10:30 P.M. Hull ran up the private recognition signals and kept them aloft for nearly an hour. But the other ship failed to return them, and Hull was then certain that the other was a British ship. However the other vessels, which were still trailing him at a distance, were also English. Finally, at 3:30 the following morning—July 18—the *Guerriere,* then only about half a mile to leeward, fired two guns and sent up a rocket, evidently some sort of signal to the other vessels. But again they failed to answer, and Dacres later reported that since they neither responded or seemed to understand his signals he came to the conclusion that they were the rest of

Rodgers' squadron, and accordingly he immediately wore 'round and stood away from the *Constitution*.

As may be imagined, Hull was not a little perplexed by this maneuver, yet he could not go in chase because at that moment the airs fell away almost entirely, and when daybreak came the *Guerriere* was nearly two miles away to the northward.

Daylight also brought with it another dismaying development, for now all of the strangers ran up their colors and revealed their true character. Until then Hull had more than half suspected why Dacres had turned tail and run away, and although his judgment had told him better he had clung to the faint hope that the morning would prove him wrong and that the strangers would turn out to be Americans after all. But now there could no longer be any question as to his situation. He was, indeed, in the dangerous neighborhood of a very superior enemy force. He had no choice but to sheer off, crowd on as much sail as his ship would carry and try to put as much distance as possible between himself and them.

Unhappily for Hull now, however, there was no wind whatever—and a sailing vessel without a breeze is about as helpless as a raft of logs. At this moment their position in relation to one another gave all the advantage to the English. The *Constitution* was in the lead, to be sure, but with only enough steerage way to be able to keep her head to the eastward. *Belvidera* and *Guerriere*, in that order, lay about four or five miles away on his lee quarter—that is, diagonally astern, but bearing up toward him. The other ships—the *Shannon*, *Africa*, *Aeolus*, and the captured *Nautilus*, which by now, of course, was manned by a British crew—were strung out almost dead astern at distances varying from seven to twelve miles.

This scarcely enviable position soon was made worse by the fact that as the breeze died away for the *Constitution*, it continued to blow, even though lightly, for her pursuers. At the same time, inexplicably, as the wind died and she lost steerage way the *Constitution* tended to come around slightly, so that eventually instead of heading southward toward the open sea and safety she would be lying flatly becalmed and heading northward almost directly toward her onrushing enemies.

But Hull had no intention of giving up, even in the face of such disastrous circumstances. Without hesitation he ordered out the ship's small boats to tow her around to the south, at the same time putting the sweeps—great long oars carried by all ships that depended on the weather—to help. At the same time what breeze the British had been able to whistle up died away for them as completely as it had for him.

For a time after that the *Constitution* managed to widen the distance between them. But the advantage proved only temporary. It took the English about half an hour to figure out the reason for this sudden spurt on the part of the Americans; then they put their small boats to work, too. In the meantime the crew of the *Constitution*, green though it may have been, was far from idle. In addition to taking turns at rowing and wetting down the sails with sea water passed aloft in buckets in order to close the pores of the canvas and take advantage of every breath of air, they cut away a section of the taffrail aft and whipped two long 24's up from the gun deck, mounting them at the openings so that they would bear upon their pursuers. Two other guns were run out of the after cabin windows, but these proved to be useless because of the lightness of the deck under them and the overhang of the stern. At the same time some 2,300 gallons of fresh water was pumped over the side to lighten the ship as much as possible. Seeing their quarry begin to creep away so maddened the English that they opened fire with their bow chasers, but the range was too great for accurate firing, though it is said that some of the British shot passed *over* the *Constitution*. The Americans, of course, replied through their improvised gun ports. Whether any of these shots took effect is not reported.

For a time, the race continued in this manner. Then the *Shannon*, which was now leading the pursuers, thought of a way to improve its speed. All the boats of all the British ships were brought forward to help tow that frigate, and once again the gap began to close. But just as it began to look dark for the Americans, a sudden whiff of wind sprang up. The *Constitution*'s sails were still set. But the British, in order to make the labor of towing lighter, had furled theirs, and before they could take advantage of the opportunity the Americans had again drawn ahead some distance.

But once again the advantage was only temporary. As soon as the British sails were set again, they began once more to overhaul. It was Lieutenant Morris who at this moment remembered that he had once served aboard a merchantman which had managed to get into port by means of "kedging" while a dozen other ships lay outside in a flat calm waiting for a wind to carry them in.

Now "kedging" in a sailing ship means that an anchor is bent to as long and stout a hawser as can be put together. A boat's crew then carries the anchor as far ahead as the length of line will allow and drops it there. As soon as the anchor finds holding on bottom, the crew aboard mans the capstan bars and literally walks the ship up to where the anchor was dropped. In the meantime a second kedge is rigged and carried ahead and dropped. As soon as the first kedge is brought, dripping, to the surface the boat carries it forward once more and drops it well beyond the second anchor. The action is repeated over and over as long as necessary.

The maneuver is obviously a shallow-water one, intended mainly for entering or leaving a harbor or clawing along a shallow shore when there is no wind. But the last sounding, made only a few moments before, showed them to be in only 18½ fathoms of water, and it was undoubtedly this that prompted Morris to recall the event. He promptly suggested the procedure to Hull, who felt it worth at least a try. All the hands that could be spared for the task were accordingly set to rigging two kedges, with the result that they were soon ready and the first anchor was sent out and dropped when the British were almost within range, and by this means the *Constitution* was literally walked away from the sweating British, who were still trying to overtake them by towing!

Thus once again the British were outwitted by Yankee ingenuity. But the trick was not a new one and nearly every experienced seaman was more or less familiar with it. Ordinarily the sails were clewed up during the maneuver to allow the seamen at the capstans to bring the ship along more easily. In this case, however, Hull kept all sails set in order to be able to take advantage of every stray breeze that might come his way. Perhaps it was this fact that so perplexed the British commanders as they watched the American, apparently as windbound as they, seem to glide out of their clutches, for it was some time before they could understand what was happening. But at length Captain Byron, in the *Belvidera*, decided to try the same thing, and once again the British ships came on, more scattered now since the heavier *Africa* could not move as quickly as her lighter consorts.

Now, for a time, the ships continued to move at an equal pace. Then the British decided to double up on their small boats again. Boats from the *Aeolus* and the *Africa* were sent to help tow the *Belvidera* and the *Shannon*, which now began to creep closer. Indeed, at one point they seemed close enough for the *Shannon* to risk a broadside. But it still fell far short, and the bark of the American stern chasers was really only a snort of derision. Then a breeze came on that lasted for several hours, and since the *Constitution*'s sails were already set she was able to widen the gap by several miles before the British could get their boats aboard and loosen their sails.

But the wind did not last, and soon they were at it again, rowing and kedging, rowing and kedging. In this manner the chase continued for three days and two nights, or 66 hours and 30 minutes in all. Finally, late in the afternoon of the nineteenth, a black squall was seen approaching from windward. Hull, who was thoroughly familiar with the weather in that area, saw that it would be a stiff blow but of very short duration. Nevertheless it was a chance to play one more Yankee trick on his pursuers. At once he sent all hands aloft and shortened sail just as the wind struck.

To leeward the pursuing British had watched all this with

interest, and thought that Hull had been caught off guard and
nearly laid on his beam ends. The squall had not yet struck
them, however, and to avoid a similar experience they at once
fell to shortening sail, though the teeming rain hid the American from view. But Hull had anticipated this, and as soon as
the rain had blotted out their view he set all sail again quickly,
cut his course to the set of the wind, and ran before it for as
long as it blew. All night long they held their course with a
good breeze, and by daylight the British were scattered and far
behind, being visible only from the masthead, and even there
only hull down. For a time they continued to chase, evidently in
the faint hope that they might somehow be able to regain their
lost advantage. But the breeze held, and Hull kept the crew at
work wetting down the sails to make them draw better, so that
the *Constitution* continued to widen the already large gap.
Finally, about mid-morning, the last of the British pursuers
hauled their wind and stood away to the northward, probably
to take up their belated stations off New York, leaving the
Constitution free to follow her own course.

That course had been originally for New York, though Hull
had even then had his doubts as to the wisdom of going there.
Now, however, it was clearly impossible, and Hull decided to go
up around Cape Cod and in to Boston, where the *Constitution*
could replenish stores and replace the water it had been forced
to dump over the side. As they bore around Nantucket Island
and Cape Cod, nothing of further interest occurred save the
halting of two American merchantmen, whom he warned of the
presence of the British off New York and possibly off the Delaware Capes and the Virginia Capes. Accordingly they altered
their courses for Charleston, South Carolina, which might have
been out of their way but where, at least, both they and their
cargoes would be safe. Meantime the *Constitution* continued on
her way, arriving in Boston on Sunday, July 26.

15

A RMS AND THE M AN

T H E A R R I V A L of Hull and the *Constitution* at Boston at
this moment was auspicious in more ways than one. Most of
New England had been and still was bitterly opposed to the
war, and no place was more so than Boston. Trading with the
enemy was common, and there was a faction which spoke
openly of secession and a separate peace, while in Vermont
there was even talk of going over to the British and becoming a
part of Canada. It was twenty-two days since the *Constitution*
had cleared from the Chesapeake, and not a word had been
heard of her since. The opposition press had made the most of
all this, reporting that she had been sent to sea with an inade-
quate crew and without shot or powder for her guns. Others
claimed that even were she adequately armed she was a poor
sailer and would be no match for a single British ship of a
lesser rating and would be captured without difficulty.

Consequently the *Constitution*'s appearance in President
Roads, just below Boston Harbor was a relief to some, a matter
of chagrin to others. Not only had she proven her sailing qualities during her chase and escape; her officers had also proven
their abilities. As for her hands—those green farmer boys—
they had proved their mettle as well as their adaptability, and
as they swaggered through the streets of the city they were
regarded—and acted—as seasoned tars, quite capable of taking care of themselves and their ship. Captain Hull himself
proved his diplomacy as well as his right to command by the

following notice, which he caused to be inserted in the Exchange Coffee House books:

Captain Hull, finding his friends in Boston are correctly informed of his situation when chased by the British squadron off New York, and that they are good enough to give him more credit by escaping them than he ought to claim, takes this opportunity of requesting them to make a transfer of a great part of their good wishes to Lt. Morris, and the other brave officers, and the crew under his command, for their very great exertions and prompt attention to orders while the enemy were in chase. Captain Hull has great pleasure in saying, that notwithstanding the length of the chase, and the officers and crew being deprived of sleep, and allowed but little refreshment during the time, not a murmur was heard to escape them.

At the same time he reported his safe arrival at Boston to the navy department, as well as to New York, where he thought Commodore Rodgers might have left orders for him. After that he waited impatiently for further instructions. But when word came from New York that no letters had been left there for him he put to sea again on August 2.

But for the event that lay in store for him and the *Constitution*, which he could not possibly have foreseen, his impetuousness might well have cost him dear, for on the day after he sailed, the waited orders arrived from Washington. According to them he was to exchange vessels with Commodore Bainbridge, turning over command of the *Constitution* to the latter, while Hull was to be given a smaller frigate.

Hull had his own excellent reasons for leaving when he did. Every vessel that entered the port, down to the most insignificant wood, hay, and cod monger, brought tales of increasingly bold British activity off the New England coast. The *Guerriere*, and the *Spartan*, 36, Captain Brenton, seemed to be the two chief offenders in those waters—the *Spartan* by far the worst since scarcely a day went by but what she captured and burned some American vessel. But there was still a third, and even more important reason for his anxiety to be away. That was the danger of being blockaded in port, unable to get away to sea, to simply lie and rot and chew his nails.

Government funds were not forthcoming to furnish the $17,000 in supplies that the *Constitution* needed, since Colonel Binney, the navy agent at Boston, had already exhausted his regular allotment and gone heavily in debt to keep what forces he could at sea. He could do no more. The Federalist merchants of Boston were ready enough to shout "Huzza!" when it cost nothing, but otherwise they could only shrug and say they were "sorry"! But there was one man—he deserved the fortune he made in the China trade after the war—William Gray, who was ready to dig down into his pocket and advance the necessary sum on Hull's signature alone. His name should be remembered beside Isaac Hull's and that of the *Constitution* herself, for it was he who made it all possible!

From Boston the *Constitution* stood eastward for two days, but finding nothing of interest in that quarter she turned northwestward and looked into the Bay of Fundy. But the enemy raiders, which had reportedly been active in the area, had apparently been forewarned and gone to ground. From there Hull bore southeast, standing just far enough off to clear the treacherous shoals around Cape Sable. Thence he turned northwestward again to skirt the coast of Nova Scotia and crossed the mouth of the St. Lawrence River to the latitude of Cape Race, at the southeastern tip of Newfoundland. Here Hull took up his first station, hoping for a chance to intercept some of the traffic that passed this way between England and Quebec or Halifax.

The comparative lack of excitement was quite satisfactory to Hull. A large part of his old crew had been paid off and discharged in Boston, their terms of enlistment having expired, and it had been necessary to replace them with new hands. Unlike his former men, most of these were experienced seamen, but it was necessary to weld them into a fighting team and to exercise them at the guns, and most of the first fortnight had been devoted to that. On August 10 they had intercepted a light

British brig from Newfoundland bound for Halifax. Since she was of so little value that it was not worth sending her in as a prize, Hull followed the example set by the British themselves, removed her crew and burned her. The next day the small British ship *Adiona*, out of Nova Scotia for England, met a like fate at his hands. Her cargo was entirely composed of spruce and pine ship timbers. Apparently the British meant to try out a few "fir-built frigates" themselves. With all that pitch on board she burned merrily.

At daybreak on the fifteenth, something more promising hove in view. Through the thinning mists five sails were sighted, and on chase proved to be four merchantmen under convoy of a small ship of war. As the *Constitution* swiftly bore down upon them they scattered like a covey of frightened quail. The man-of-war, which proved to be towing a brig, cast loose and left the brig in flames, making all sail to windward as fast as she could go. This was not cowardice on the man-of-war's part, for she was plainly no match for the *Constitution*. Hull later learned that she was the British ship-sloop *Avenger*, 15, a very fast sailer.

Turning his attention to the other vessels, Hull went first after the largest. It turned out to be a British vessel which had been taken by an American privateer and had been en route to an American port with an American prize crew. She had just been met by the *Avenger* when Hull appeared, and his arrival on the scene undoubtedly saved her from recapture by the British. The second of the convoy turned out to be the American brig *Adeline*, which had been captured while en route from Liverpool to Boston. Hull took out the British prize master and his crew and sent his own prize crew on board with instructions to take her into the nearest available United States port.

All this, of course, was mere flexing of the muscles fore and aft for the *Constitution*, which by this time they had worked so far to the eastward that Hull, who was stalking larger game, decided to change his cruising grounds and turned down toward Bermuda. The deciding factor in this decision was the in-

formation gleaned from some of the prisoners he had taken
that the squadron which had chased him off New York was then
working at the western edge of the Grand Bank and could not
be far away.

He saw nothing more until late in the evening of the eighteenth when he sighted a large brig, which he chased and
brought to. She proved to be the American privateer *Decatur*,
14. When her captain came on board he told Hull that on first
sighting the *Constitution* he had taken her for a British
frigate—a natural enough error since at that time it was not
customary for ships at sea to show their colors until overtaken
or at least until they were certain that the other ship was
friendly. In this case the *Decatur* had fled, and during the
chase had thrown overboard 12 of her 14 guns in order to
lighten ship. Hull was unable to replace the jettisoned guns,
but he sympathized with the American captain and was able to
advise him to head for Charleston since both Boston and New
York were under British blockade. In return he learned that
only the day before the *Decatur* had outrun a large British
frigate.

This was welcome news, for it not only gave him the approximate position of the English frigate but also told him that the
Constitution was faster than the Englishman, for the *Decatur*
had been able to run away from her but had been unable to outrun the *Constitution*. As soon as he had sent the *Decatur* on her
way, he went in search of the British man-of-war. He did not
have far to go, for at 2 P.M. the following afternoon a large sail
was sighted from the masthead bearing about east-southeast
and the *Constitution* immediately bore off with all sails set to
intercept her. The breeze was good on the starboard quarter,
and within an hour they were close enough to recognize her as
the British frigate *Guerriere*, one of the ships that had chased
her only a few weeks before.

The *Guerriere* had left the British squadron before New
York and was on her way to Halifax for equipment and repairs,
but she showed no inclination to run. On the contrary, she

showed every intention to stand and fight. When sighted she was standing by the starboard tack, under easy canvas. She hauled up her courses and took in her topgallant sails, and at 4:30 backed her main topsail, so that she came practically motionless, waiting. Very deliberately then Hull began to shorten sail. He took in the topgallants, staysails and flying jib, sent down the royal yards, and put another reef in the topsails. All was made snug below and presently the rolling drums beat out the call to quarters. This was the moment for which the frigate had been built, and on her action now depended all of her excuse for being. Also, whether or not they were aware of it, upon these men and their behavior and that of the ship as well depended to a great extent the fate of the nation, for things had not been going well ashore and United States morale was at a low ebb.

It is doubtful if anyone among them, even Hull, thought of that as the two ships drew together. The one thought uppermost in their minds at that moment was that here at last was a ship to beat. This was the moment for which they had been drilled and trained incessantly for weeks, for months, some even for years, and every man aboard knew his exact place and just what was expected of him. They felt ready. They were ready.

Barefoot (for shod feet might slip on bloody decks), stripped to the waist (for lint might lodge in a wound and fester), they ran to their posts. By every gun stood a bucket of sand to be scattered on slippery gore, and the powder monkeys were busy scattering sand across the immaculate white decks. (In both the British and American navies the original practice had been to paint the decks and inner bulwarks red on the theory that it made the blood of battle less conspicuous, but that had been abandoned long since.) Orders and responses, such as were necessary, were given in low, even tones that spoke of self-control rather than in the shouts and yells that betokened hysteria.

It was two o'clock in the afternoon when the ships first

sighted one another from their respective mastheads. Then they had been mere specks of sail upon the distant horizon. But within an hour they were close enough to make out one another's manner of rigging. By four they could watch the activity taking place upon each other's decks, and by 4:45 they could almost hear what commands were being passed. Throughout this time the *Constitution* was bearing down directly on the starboard quarter—that is, diagonally from the side rear—of the *Guerriere* in such a way that as she drew within range she would be exposed to almost the full broadside of the Englishman, while at the same time the only guns she would be able to bring to bear would be her bow guns, which were probably long 24's.

At this time the *Constitution* carried thirty long 24-pounders, twenty-four 32-pound carronades, and one long 18. The *Guerriere*, on the other hand, carried thirty-two long 18-pounders, sixteen 32-pound carronades, and one 18-pound carronade. Thus the Yankee outgunned the Englishman, both in the number of guns he carried—55 to 49—and in the weight of metal he could throw. The reason for the disparity was that the best British naval opinion of the day held that 24-pounders were too heavy for a ship as lightly built as a frigate. And they were probably quite right insofar as their own vessels were concerned, for the British frigates were much more lightly built than the American ships of the same classification. So far as the range went, there was little, if any, difference between the batteries. It was simply that the Americans could throw a heavier shot and required a greater charge of powder. If it hit, the 24-pounder could do more damage. If it missed it cost more.

The crew of the *Constitution* numbered 468, including Captain Hull, while that of the Englishman was 263, though the actual number involved on each side was more or less immaterial as long as there were enough men to man the guns and sail the ship. Any greater number would simply get in one another's way.

This, then, was the general picture as the *Constitution* bore down and the *Guerriere* waited without flinching, welcoming the chance to come to grips. Oddly enough, the two commanders were acquaintances, if not indeed friends, of long standing. Just where they had met or under what circumstances the record does not say, but at least they did not meet this time as strangers. Nor, it might be added, did this encounter in any way seem to affect their regard for one another, for many years afterward they are reported to have been seen walking arm in arm down a street in Rome arguing the relative merits of Italian and Spanish wines. They were an oddly assorted pair, for Hull was short and stoutish—"chubby" might be the word—at the time of the battle, for he is said to have become so excited at the effect of the first broadside that he leapt upon an arms chest so violently that he split his breeches from crotch to waistband, to the vast amusement of the crew. Dacres, on the other hand, was tall and lean, almost gangling—"double-jointed" today's schoolboy would call him—one who could never get a uniform made to fit him in the snug fashion of the time; a dour man, yet one with his own peculiar sense of humor. Hull was excitable, but thoroughly capable and sound of judgment. Dacres appears to have been calm and calculating; a sailor "by the book" as it was written by the British Admiralty, but quite as able as his opponent in his own way. However, it is unlikely that either was aware of the identity of the commander aboard the other vessel as they closed at this time. Certainly if they were they did not let the acquaintanceship stand in the way of their conduct during the encounter. There is a story to the effect that some time before they had discussed the possibility of such a meeting, and on that occasion had each bet a hat upon the outcome.

It was the Englishman who fired first. Though the American had the weather gauge the *Guerriere* was in a position to fire his full starboard (right) broadside. As soon as Dacres judged the *Constitution* to be within range he did exactly that. But the seas were heavy and the *Guerriere* was rolling. Whether Dacres' judgment was in error or the British fire came on the down roll, the volley fell short. Geysers of white water spouted from the surface of the slaty seas, but none of the iron balls touched, or even fell near, the *Constitution*.

The *Constitution*'s only response was a few shots from her forward guns, which were apparently as ineffective as the British fire, though they seem to have passed over the Englishman rather than falling short. This, too, could have been due to the lift and roll of the seas. The *Constitution* may have similarly miscalculated and fired on the lift rather than at the crest, as intended. The wink of an eyelash could make that much difference.

The chase continued, the Englishman yawing now to bring his port battery to bear. Again he let go his full broadside, and again it fell mostly short, though closer. Spray fell on the *Constitution*'s decks and two shots actually hit: one snapped a brace as it passed over the ship; the other bounced off the stout, oaken side like a tennis ball but did not even spring the timber. It may have been from this that the *Constitution* earned her everlasting nickname: "*Old Ironsides.*"

This was the way it began, with the *Guerriere* yawing from side to side so as to bring first one broadside and then the other to bear. But each time she yawed the American followed suit, so that most of the British shots fell harmlessly into the sea, for by the time the lanyards were pulled on the British ship the Yankee was no longer where she had pointed. And all the while Hull continued to bore in, holding the full weight of his fire.

Perhaps it should be explained here that since the Revolution the Americans had striven to improve their weapons, so that they had a certain advantage of invention. One such was that while British ships still relied on the old, unsighted guns of Nelson's day, the Americans had adopted sights for even their heaviest guns, which permitted a far greater degree of accuracy, even in a heavy running sea, such as they were both now encountering. One by one the American guns spoke sporadically in response to the English broadsides. But where the British blasts were of a sort of birdshot nature, hoping that one or more would do some damage, nearly every carefully aimed shot of the Americans had some effect.

Just as they had been the first to open fire, the British were the first to show their colors. At ten minutes past four (some say five!) the British frigate hoisted the red ensign to each masthead. But Hull, still playing his waiting game, waited yet another three-quarters of an hour before setting his own colors—a jack at each masthead and a huge ensign at the mizzen peak.

Now the *Constitution* ran down with the wind nearly aft, ignoring the risk of yet another British broadside before she could get into position, and drew alongside almost within half pistol shot on the *Guerriere*'s port beam. Immediately a furious cannonade began, broadside to broadside, and the *Constitution*'s first blast sent a twenty-four-pound shot crashing through the heart of the *Guerriere*'s mizzenmast, which tottered and then fell crashing, with topmen and hands aloft, knocking a great hole in the Englishman's counter and acting as a sort of gigantic jury rudder, counteracting every effort of the regular helm.

Even at such close range the British fire was curiously ineffective. A number of shots from her first broadside hulled the *Constitution*, but not one of them penetrated the stout oak planking. They merely dented and then bounced back into the sea. Several men had been killed as they stood to their guns during the approach, but no one seems to have been hit by that first broadside exchange. Neither were any of the masts damaged. But the rigging and the sails suffered considerable damage, making the ship more difficult to manage. Ready hands, however, promptly leaped to repair the breaks.

On board the *Guerriere* it was a different story. The heavy 24-pounders, each double-shotted with one round shot and one canister of grape—musket balls which spread out scattergun fashion on discharge—smashed home a hail of blood and death and destruction that swept the English frigate from stem to stern.

But this was not all that first fire accomplished. The Americans' shot swept both the spar and gun decks of the Englishman. As they struck home, the splinters flew in a cloud as high as the mizzentop, and where only a moment before they had been able to hear the confident cheers and shouts of victory, the Americans now heard only the screams and cries of the wounded. Decks that had been holystoned white as a maiden's skin now were stained with gore and guts. The Americans had struck their first blow and it was a telling one. The Englishman staggered, reeled, and for a moment was unable to reply at all to the fire from the American, which was now practically constant, each gun firing "at will" after that first organized broadside.

In addition to the loss of her mizzenmast by that first broadside, the *Guerriere*'s mainyard was shot away in the slings, and her hull, rigging, and sails were badly mauled. Noting her enemy's crippled state the *Constitution* now put her helm hard to port, in order to rake, but the loss of some of her braces together with wounds in the spanker and mizzen topsails, prevented her from falling off as quickly as she might. Nonetheless she was able to get off two more raking broadsides before—at about 6:15 P.M.— the *Guerriere*'s jib-boom and bowsprit swung across the *Constitution*'s quarterdeck, and the two ships tangled and hung close together.

Fifth Lieutenant John Shubrick commanded the *Constitution*'s quarterdeck guns. He looked around for a bight of rope to pass around the spar and so fasten the two ships together, but like many another man before and since, in the midst of a tangle of ropes and cables he could see none to fit the purpose.

At this juncture there appears to have been some fear on each side that the other would avail himself of the opportunity to board. Lieutenant Morris clambered up on the spar and looked down upon the British deck, where he saw the English crew massing with pikes and cutlasses to board or repel as might be necessary. He passed the information along to Captain Hull, who at once ordered:

"Boarders away!"

The command was the signal for all hands save the few needed to work ship and hold in reserve to drop everything and seize pike and cutlass and race to the point of contact. Gunners and gun crews left their weapons, leaving only a few to fire occasional shots as might be offered by chance. For one breathless instant the two ships were so closely hung, "in irons" cheek by jowl, that an American seaman snapped his boarding pistol at the face of a British seaman not six feet away. When the gun missed fire the American, in complete disgust, flung it at the Englishman and hit him squarely between the eyes.

In the fighting tops the marines—seven to a top, six to load while the best sharpshooter in the group fired as rapidly as the guns, rifles for the Americans and muskets for the British, were handed to him—looked down upon a scene of milling uniforms such as seldom came to them, even in their wildest dreams; uniforms and officers and epaulettes all mixed up together! A man could close his eyes and just pull the trigger and know he had shot an enemy in such a mob.

Apparently they did not waste the opportunity, for although contact between the ships was fleeting, it was at this point that both suffered their heaviest casualties. Captain Dacres, hastening to lead his boarding party, took a ball in the back and for a moment was laid out for dead. Lieutenant Morris of the *Constitution* sprang onto the bulwarks only to receive a ball in the belly that blasted him to the deck below. First Lieutenant William Bush of the United States Marines had just called out to Hull, "Shall I board them?" when he took a ball between the eyes and fell dead. John Alwyn, the sailing master, had leaped to the bulwarks at the same time as Morris. A ball in the shoulder spun him back. Hull had seen Morris fall, and he ran to him, knowing that to lose this officer would be like living without an arm. Morris was unconscious for an instant, but then was able to smile and reassure his captain. Later he struggled to his feet and, literally holding in his entrails through his gaping wound with his hands, went about his duties and continued them until the end of the fight! A shot smashed home against the mast where Hull's head had been only an instant before. Hull was not aware of it, but others saw it and reported it.

This was obviously the work of well-stationed, well-trained marksmen. The story is told that when Hull saw Morris fall he rushed forward to lead the boarders himself, when a hand grasped his arm and held on tightly. Hull turned in indignation to see who, on his own ship, would dare to lay a hand upon him. To his astonishment he saw only an ordinary seaman, and the words of fury came bubbling to his lips—but he never spoke them.

"Don't go up there, cap'n," the man said simply, "leastways not till ye've taken off them swabs."

Meaning the great gold epaulettes of his rank that marked Hull out as captain.

Because the seas were heavy, the ships broke apart almost as soon as they touched. As they did, a burst from the *Guerriere*'s stern battery, still only a few feet from the *Constitution*, fired into Captain Hull's cabin, smashing everything within and setting curtains and hangings aflame. But this was quickly extinguished by Lieutenant Hoffman, who was in command in that area.

Already the Englishman was lost. The *Guerriere*'s two remaining masts were tottering, and with another broadside from the American they went by the board. Without a stick left even to hang a token of surrender upon, Dacres was forced to get a cabin boy to wave a white tablecloth to signal his submission. The firing ceased and the Englishman, utterly helpless, rolled heavily in the trough of the seas, dipping his open gun ports under at each succeeding sea and taking water heavily.

From the *Constitution*, which was practically untouched, a boat put out under Lieutenant Read to receive the Englishman's surrender, if that was what he intended. The boat pulled in close under the *Guerriere*'s quarter, where the following exchange is supposed to have taken place:

"Have you struck, sir?" demanded Read.

Dacres was evasive.

"I don't know that it would be prudent to continue the engagement any longer," he replied.

"Do I understand you to say that you have struck, then?" Lieutenant Read asked.

"Not precisely," replied the gangling Dacres, "But I don't know that it will be worthwhile to fight any longer."

"If you cannot decide I will return aboard my ship and we will resume the engagement," Lieutenant Read replied.

There was a moment of silence.

"Come about, boys," said Read in a tone that could be heard aboard both ships.

"Now, just a moment!" Captain Dacres is said to have called out somewhat excitedly. "You can see I am pretty much *hors de combat* already. I have hardly men enough left to work a single gun and my ship is in a sinking condition."

Read was unimpressed.

"I wish to know, sir," he responded peremptorily, "whether I am to consider you as a prisoner of war or an enemy. I have no time for further parley."

Captain Dacres' reply came with obvious reluctance.

"I—I'm sorry," he said, "but I believe now that there is no alternative. I—I would, with pleasure. But—I must—must surrender."

"Very good, sir," Read replied. "I will report your answer to Captain Hull. He will expect you on board as soon as possible. If you would care to come with me——?"

"Thank you, lieutenant," was Dacres' reply, "but I still have my own gig and enough hands to manage it. Please report to your captain that I will be on board as soon as I can have it swung over and manned."

"Very good, sir!" replied Read, in accord with naval usage, and returned to the *Constitution* to report.

A few moments later the English captain's gig came alongside the American. Hull stepped to the rail.

"Dacres, give me your hand," he called down. "I know you are hurt."

Dacres' response is not recorded, probably because it was not printable. After all, the man was suffering from a wound in the back and chest, and he had just lost his ship. He could hardly be expected to be happy about it.

The exchange as he came on board, however, has been recorded. As he came over the side Dacres offered his sword to Hull in the customary token of surrender.

"No, no!" Hull is reported to have said, "I will not take a sword from one who has shown that he knows so well how to use it. But I will trouble you for that hat!"

Which would seem to bear out the old legend of the prewar wager.

When the *Constitution*'s prize crew went on board the defeated British frigate they were startled with what they found. Apart from the guts and gore that spread over the *Guerriere*'s decks, there was plenty of other evidence of the damage done by the American frigate's guns. She had been hulled at least thirty times through her copper sheathing well below the waterline by American 24's. There were dead and wounded lying thick on the spar and gun decks, the living oblivious to the blood of the dead. A signal brought off the *Constitution*'s surgeon's mate and some of his assistants. Eventually all the wounded were transferred to the *Constitution*. When this was done, and every usable thing removed from the once proud British frigate, she was blown up and sunk, since there was no hope of getting her into port as a prize. The captain's report, the log books of the Englishman, which had been saved as a matter of routine, and the prisoners themselves would have to be witness to the victory.

But on the *Constitution*'s return nobody seemed to worry about such minor matters. The great point was that a Boston ship with a Yankee skipper had won the first great victory of the war at sea; the war of the youngest against the long mightiest sea power in the world. And it was important that this be told across the land: The British were not invincible, even at sea! Let Americans ashore take heart!

16

TWISTING THE
LION'S TAIL

H U L L shaped the *Constitution*'s course for Boston and arrived there some ten days after his victory, dropping anchor in Nantasket Roads, just inside Cape Pemberton, on August 30. The following day he moved up to the Long Wharf, not far from the place where the *Constitution* had been launched. There the ship's welcome was wildly tumultuous and enthusiastic.

This was the first real victory that American arms had won and it was a smashing one. Hitherto all the news had been bad, and it was scarcely surprising now that public enthusiasm ran high. As soon as the lines were fast and the gangplank down the people began to flock on board, and many a bewildered and bewhiskered jack-tar was soundly bussed by strange but pretty girls, who did not remain strange for long. Indeed, it is said that it was at this time that Isaac Hull met his bride-to-be.

Hull enjoyed only a brief moment of triumph aboard the *Constitution*. The long-awaited orders from Washington had arrived, and he exchanged commands with Commodore William Bainbridge and was presently transferred to command of the new Boston Navy Yard. Although he had proven himself one of the nation's greatest fighting sailors, Hull was destined never again to command a fighting ship at sea. Bainbridge, whose record hitherto—through no fault of his own—had been spotted with misfortune, took Hull's place aboard the *Constitution* and thereby was given the opportunity to gain his proper niche in history.

Clearly, the *Constitution* has always been a lucky ship for those who commanded her!

Bainbridge took command on September 15. Apparently he was not, at this time at least, very popular with the men. Perhaps he was something of a martinet, for the crew were so openly disgruntled that several had to be sent ashore and tried for mutiny. This might seem harsh indeed, but it was the only way of maintaining strict discipline and attention to routine, and only so could Bainbridge establish and maintain his authority at sea.

The *Constitution* remained in port for about six weeks, taking aboard supplies and ammunition, and repairing damages received in her recent fight. On the twenty-seventh of October she got to sea in company with the sloop of war *Hornet*, 20, Master-Commandant James Lawrence, intending to rendezvous with the frigate *Essex*, 36, Captain David Porter, in the south Atlantic. There they were to prey upon the heavy English convoys bound around the Cape of Good Hope for India and the Far East. But the *Essex* did not appear on time at the appointed spot, São Fernhão do Noronha, so Bainbridge and Lawrence paused long enough to take on water and fresh provisions and leave a letter for Captain Porter, then continued on the cruise according to their orders.

When Captain Porter arrived in December at São Fernhão and found the *Constitution* gone, he proceeded to the vicinity of Cabo Frio where he cruised for as long as he thought prudent. Again failing to make contact, with the other two ships, Porter fell away southward and slipped around Cape Horn, into the Pacific. No other American man-of-war had ever operated in those waters, and the appearance of the *Essex* there came as a complete surprise to the English. For months, before he was cornered near Valparaiso by the British and battered into surrender by the frigate *Phoebe* and her consort, Porter operated as a lone wolf in a flock of unguarded sheep, playing havoc with the British whalers and sealers who swarmed there. Today this might seem unimportant, but at that time the lamps of the world—and of England in particular—were fueled with whale oil, and the Pacific was the source of almost 80 per cent of that. Porter's raid was no small tour de force.

In the meantime the *Constitution* and the little *Hornet* had sailed westward. Were it not for the apparently endless troubles with the crew, the voyage as far as São Salvador—today's Bahia—in Brazil would be scarcely worth mentioning. The weather was fine, and in general the routine was perfect, but the ship's log for the period is remarkable, even for those days, for the number of punishments recorded. Looking a little between the lines Bainbridge must have been something of a "sundowner," for a crew is not usually so unruly, even for a skipper who is strict but just.

But open mutiny did not come. The *Constitution* and the *Hornet* reached the snout of South America, where it juts to the eastward, probably in the vicinity of Cabo São Roque, and thence swung southward toward Cabo Frio in the hope of falling in with the *Essex*. When they did not they put about and stood back northward to São Salvador, and there they found the British sloop of war *Bonne Citoyenne* at anchor and about to sail for England.

By tonnage and by gunnage the *Hornet* was just about the Englishman's equal, and Captain Lawrence was sure he could capture her. He requested permission to try, and Bainbridge granted his request. Accordingly he went outside the harbor mouth and patrolled just beyond sight in hope of catching the Englishman's topsails when they hove over the horizon.

But the *Bonne Citoyenne* had on board a large amount of specie, which her captain had no intention of risking, even though Lawrence taunted him with a challenge, and Bainbridge added his own message promising not to interfere in any battle between the *Hornet* and the *Citoyenne*. The presence of the Americans resulted in a good deal of correspondence be-

tween the captain of the *Bonne Citoyenne* and the British consul and the Portuguese governor of the province—Brazil being
then Portuguese—the latter claiming angrily that the presence
of the American cruisers off his coast was a violation of his
neutrality. However, he never once mentioned the fact that an
English man-of-war, certainly as much a belligerent as the
Americans, was actually at anchor inside his harbor.

Bainbridge finally left the *Hornet* to deal with the *Bonne
Citoyenne* and continued his cruise off the coast. It was just
after Christmas and before the New Year—on December 29,
1812, to be exact—that two sails were sighted about thirty
miles east of Bahia, coming down from the northeast, with the
wind on their heels. The *Constitution* was heading seaward on
her port tack, and she promptly came about to northwest to get
a better look at them. It needed an hour to get close enough to
be sure. Then one appeared to be a merchantman, now heading
in frantically toward shore; the other a large frigate, which
was heading directly toward the *Constitution*.

Watching her through his glass, Bainbridge judged her to
be a British frigate and he came about once more to draw her
away from her consort and out into open waters. He hoisted
private signals, but they were not answered, while the other
ship flew signals which he could not make out. It was a ticklish
situation, for in those waters the stranger might well be Portuguese, in which case he wanted no part of her. On the other
hand, if she was British, as he suspected, he would welcome a
fight. For nearly two hours they continued on parallel courses
to the eastward, the stranger gradually overhauling the *Constitution*. Once they were well outside territorial waters, however,
Bainbridge eased his canvas and waited for the other to come
up. She turned out to be the British frigate *Java*, from Spit-
head bound for the East Indies, while her companion was the
American merchantman *William*, captured only a few days before (and which, incidentally, was recaptured soon afterward
inshore by the *Hornet*).

Shortly past noon both ships ran up their true colors, and

about half past one Bainbridge, having gained what he felt was a safe distance from shore, came about and headed directly toward the *Java*. About twenty minutes later he wore around to avoid being raked, shortened sail, and beat to quarters. At two o'clock Bainbridge fired a shot across the *Java*'s bow, the Englishman being then about half a mile to windward, and immediately after he fired a full broadside and they then went at it hammer and tongs.

That first broadside apparently did little damage to the English ship, but they were fairly evenly matched except that the *Java* appeared to be much the swifter of the two in point of sailing; within minutes she was almost within half a pistol's shot away. The *Java*'s broadsides inflicted heavy damage, killed a number of men, and cut up the American's rigging badly. The *Constitution*'s wheel went by the board almost immediately, and Bainbridge had to handle his ship by means of orders shouted down through the grating to men at the haul ropes. But the American's 24's were too much for the Englishman's 18's. The *Constitution*'s second broadside carried away the *Java*'s jib boom and the end of her bowsprit, and left her headsails dangling, thus inflicting greater wounds than she had received. The American put two more raking broadsides into the Englishman's stern while the *Java*, with headsails gone, was unable to wear around. At the same time the British sailing master was brought down, and the only recourse left to Captain Lambert of the *Java* was to try to close and board and fight it out hand to hand on the American's decks.

Even as Lambert gave the order, however, the *Java*'s foremast toppled and went by the board, trailing by such slender ropes as had not been cut away by American shot. This slowed the Englishman's drive so that the stub of her bowsprit just scratched against the side of the *Constitution* as she passed, and she went on and around, just barely manageable, while the *Constitution* raked her again and then again, first across her bows and then across her stern at such close range that Captain Lambert himself fell, wounded by a musket shot from a rifleman in the *Constitution*'s tops. Then the *Java*'s main topmast fell, immediately followed by her mizzen, so that she was entirely dismasted. For a moment both ships lay cheek by jowl, so close that *Java*'s guns set her own trailing rigging afire.

Here again the vast superiority of the Americans' gunnery was dramatically evident. The *Constitution*'s fire was rapid and accurate, thanks to well-trained crews and those new-fangled sights. The *Java*'s guns were slow and ragged, and the death rate among her division officers—five midshipmen were killed and four wounded—was appalling.

It was obvious to Bainbridge that the Englishman were already beaten, and had been almost before the fight had really begun, so he ordered the *Constitution* to lay away from the crippled *Java* and took time out to make a few necessary repairs to his rigging.

The British also tried to put their ship to rights, but it was too much for them. They chopped away the trailing wreckage and under it they found a topgallant mast which they tried to rig as a jury foremast, the original having smashed down through the forecastle and main decks. But even as they were about this devil's labor the mainmast went over the lee side and had to be cut away, leaving them rolling helplessly in the trough of the seas. The *Constitution* chose this moment to return for the kill. Lieutenant Chads, who had succeeded to command when Lambert fell, sent his battered men back to such guns as could still be used, but there was no point in firing guns that would not bear on target. The *Constitution*'s bows were crossing those of the *Java*, and in an instant she would loose a raking fire to which there could be no possible chance of reply. They were within speaking-trumpet range and Chads hailed to say that he surrendered.

But the Americans had not gotten off without hurt. Bainbridge himself was twice wounded severely, and First Lieutenant John Alwyn, who had succeeded to command when Bainbridge was carried below, died a month later of his wounds. There are conflicting reports about the casualties. The total

American loss was apparently about 9 killed and 25 wounded, while the British had about 60 killed and 101 wounded.

Like the *Guerriere*, the *Java* was such a wreck that she was hardly worth saving. And there was no nearby port to which she could be taken since the governor of Bahia was definitely unfriendly to the Americans. Accordingly Bainbridge ordered the transfer of the British survivors to the *Constitution*. Only one of the Americans' small boats survived, while every boat aboard the Englishman was destroyed, so the transfer of the prisoners and their baggage was a back-breaking task. The Americans made no effort to take out the valuable stores on board the *Java*, but they did remove her wheel and fit it onto the *Constitution* to replace the one that had been shot away. On New Year's Day 1813, the Americans set fire to the wallowing hulk, thus celebrating the incoming year with a grand display of fireworks, for there was still plenty of powder left in the Englishman's magazines.

On January 2 Bainbridge set his prisoners ashore at São Salvador (Bahia) under parole, made a few quick repairs to his own vessel, and then sailed for Boston, where he arrived after a tedious voyage of nearly two months, on the twenty-seventh of February. There Bainbridge went ashore to receive a wild welcome and triumphal march up Tremont Street. Amid the celebration, however, he found time to sit down and write a letter to remind Congress that the $50,000 which it had appropriated for apportionment among the officers and men for the total destruction of the *Guerriere* had not yet been paid. Possibly as a result of his letter, an additional $50,000 was appropriated, and through Bainbridge's efforts the total of both sums was paid over to the men within six weeks.

But the war was not yet over, and the *Constitution* still had a few knots to tie in the lion's tail. Captain Bainbridge was transferred ashore, and his place was taken by Charles Stewart, who had until recently been in command of the *Constellation*. Stewart's ship had been blockaded in Norfolk, so that he had seen no action at all. As may be imagined Stewart was greatly pleased at this sudden change in his fortunes, and only too anxious to be away.

But it was not to be quite that simple. Shortly after her arrival, the *Constitution* was moved up to the Boston Navy Yard for a thorough overhaul, and it was found that some of her timbers and her masts had been seriously weakened in the fight with the *Java*. Moreover, the crew that had sailed with Bainbridge were almost all paid off, their time being up, and almost an entire crew had to be recruited to replace them. Fortunately this was not too difficult, for by now the ship had made a name for herself and she was considered a lucky vessel.

But the repairs and recruiting did take time, and it was not until the first of January 1814 that Stewart was finally able to get to sea. This cruise, however, was a bitter disappointment, the only important capture being the 14-gun British schooner *Pictou*. The only other British warship encountered was the frigate *Pique*, which the *Constitution* chased through the Mona Passage between Puerto Rico and Santo Domingo. The *Pique* was only a 36 and the British Admiralty, following the losses of the *Guerriere* and the *Java*, had issued orders to all her cruisers not to engage ships of superior force. The *Constitution* lost track of the *Pique* during the night. Apart from these incidents, Stewart seemed to be constantly overhauling ships and stopping them, only to discover that they were Americans. A few small prizes fell to the *Constitution* in the West Indies, but the only real excitement that came her way was when the *Constitution* herself was chased by two British frigates, the *Tenedos* and *Junon*, both 38's, with a combined fire power far greater than her own.

This event took place on April 3, when the *Constitution* was standing in for Portsmouth, New Hampshire, where she intended to end her cruise. At sunrise, however, the wind shifted to northeast, making approach difficult, and the *Constitution* was obliged to head around for Boston. But by eight o'clock the wind had shifted again to the north-northwest and it had almost fallen flat calm when the sails of two British frigates were sighted to east-southeast, apparently coming on rapidly before a fresh breeze.

Stewart might have been able to escape by running directly into Salem, but he had no pilot or anyone else aboard who was familiar with the waters between Baker's Island and the Misery, which he knew to be treacherous, and accordingly he held slowly, with almost no wind, upon the course which he knew had plenty of depth. Not until ten o'clock did the *Constitution* get the breeze from the southeast, which had thus far favored the enemy.

Now he could run for it. But the English were already within three miles, so Stewart sped for Marblehead. During the spirited chase, he ordered the provisions that remained, the spare parts, and some prize goods, thrown overboard. Then, since the British continued to gain, he pumped out all the remaining fresh water on board. But this brought the *Constitution* down too much by the stern, and finding the ship was only just barely holding her own, he emptied the spirits in her spirit room. This brought the ship back to sailing trim, and she was able then to run in safely to the shelter of Marblehead. It is, as Hollis remarks, a curious commentary on the old navy that a frigate should still have had enough whisky on board after a three-month cruise to make such a decided difference in her draft!

A few days later the *Constitution* slipped out undetected and ran safely down to Boston, only to be shut in that harbor by the British blockade for eight and a half months.

That was a trying season all around. Through the summer the British tightened the blockade, and Sir George Collier in the newly built frigate *Newcastle*, 50, which had been especially designed to cope with the heavier American frigates such as the *Constitution*, the *President* and the *United States*, was assigned to keep a particular watch upon Boston. For company he had the frigate *Acasta*, 40, and the brig-sloop *Arab*, 18. He stuck close to his post through the summer, the fall, and even into the early winter, with such tenacity and in such a threatening manner that the doughty merchants of Boston were frightened nearly out of their wits. The governor of Massachusetts even had the pusillanimity to suggest that the *Constitution* and the newly launched (but yet unarmed) ship of the line *Independence* be moved down the harbor below the forts—where they would be out of reach of cover by the batteries ashore—lest the British in trying to cut them out do some damage to Boston and Charlestown. This, of course, Bainbridge, who was senior officer present, refused to permit.

Not until mid-December did the British relax their vigilance. On the twelfth of that month the *Newcastle* appeared off the mouth of Boston Harbor, apparently to make sure that the *Constitution* was still there. Reassured of the Americans' presence Sir George then swung away and joined the *Acasta* in Cape Cod Bay. Stewart had been kept closely informed of the British ships' movements, and when a sudden norther swooped down on the seventeenth, forcing the Englishmen to stay were they were, he took a chance and ran for it, getting off safe to sea before the enemy was aware the *Constitution* was gone.

After clearing Cape Cod, the *Constitution* turned and bore away to the southeast. Eight days out, not far from the Bermudas, she overhauled and took the small British merchantman *Lord Nelson*. There is no doubt that Stewart meant to send her in as a prize, but first he sent one of his officers and a crew aboard to remove supplies that would be useful to the *Constitution*, and this officer, through some misunderstanding of his orders, proceeded to scuttle the vessel.

From the Bermudas the *Constitution* continued to sail eastward, past the Madeiras and through the Bay of Biscay. She then turned southward and cruised for several days within sight of the Rock of Lisbon, hoping to pick up an Indiaman, but such good fortune did not come her way. On the eighteenth of February, 1815, however, they sighted a large sail and started in chase without being able to identify the stranger, who headed for the Portuguese coast. Soon afterward another sail was sighted to leeward and since it seemed evident that the first ship would get into Lisbon before the *Constitution* could catch her, Stewart tacked and soon overhauled and took the British merchantman *Susan*, which he sent home under a prize crew.

The first ship proved to be the British 74-gun ship-of-the-line *Elizabeth*, which on arriving in Lisbon joined the British frigate *Tiber*, 38, under command of the same Captain Dacres who had been in command of the *Guerriere* at the time of her loss to the *Constitution*. Dacres was only too anxious for a return match with the *Constitution*. Learning from some merchantman at Lisbon that the American was at that time in those very waters, the *Tiber* and the *Elizabeth* in company put out in a fruitless search for her.

By now the *Constitution* was bearing southward toward Madeira in search of other prizes. February 20 dawned thick and cloudy with a light haze hanging low over the water so that distant objects could not be readily made out from deck level. About one in the afternoon the *Constitution* sighted a sail bearing about two points off the port bow. The *Constitution* immediately gave chase and soon brought a large ship into plain view through a break in the mist. At about the same time another sail was discovered a little to the westward of the first. Both were standing to the northward under starboard tacks and proved to be the British frigate *Cyane*, 32, Captain Gordon Thomas Falcon, and the ship-sloop *Levant*, 21, Captain George Douglas, sailing in company from Gibraltar for the West Indies.

At 4 A.M. the *Constitution* was nearly within range of the *Cyane* when the Englishman stood away to leeward—the American having the weather gauge—in order to bring her consort in closer for the fight that was obviously in the offing. Under full press of canvas the *Constitution* stood after her, and at 4:30 was actually about to open fire when her main royal, under the pressure of her cloud of canvas, broke off at the eyes of the topgallant rigging, and some time was lost in getting up a new spar and rigging it. However, even in her crippled state the *Constitution* had managed to hold her own with the *Cyane* in sailing, but the delay had given the two Englishmen time to join company and clear for battle.

By 5 A.M. the *Constitution* had again drawn near enough to risk a few shots from her bow chasers, but they fell short and soon afterward the two British ships were within hail of one another when they immediately hauled their starboard tacks and tried to get to windward of the American. Their apparent intent was to delay the action until after nightfall, when under cover of darkness they might hope to cripple the heavier ship. Indeed, it is unlikely the British ships would have engaged at all but for two valuable convoys that had sailed from Gibraltar about the same time as they. However, the British were unable to get to windward because of the *Constitution*'s speed, and accordingly they formed in line of battle, about half a cable's length—about two-hundred yards—apart and prepared to receive the American attack. At 6 P.M. the *Constitution* hauled up her courses and showed her colors, at which the Englishmen broke out their own ensigns, and though by this time night had fallen, the fog had rolled away, and they were able to make out one another plainly in the moonlight.

Soon after six the *Constitution* was close enough to open fire with the long guns of her port battery, and the British promptly responded with their starboard guns. For nearly twenty minutes a heavy artillery exchange between all three ships continued, the *Constitution* concentrating her fire upon the *Cyane*, but by 6:20 such thick clouds of smoke had gathered between them that it was impossible to maintain an accurate fire. Accordingly the *Constitution* ceased fire and, forging ahead swiftly, drew abeam of the *Levant*. The brief respite had given the *Constitution* time to reload, and as she drew abreast she loosed a torrent of grape, canister, and round shot into the smaller Englishman. Then, under cover of his own smoke, Stewart braced his sails aback and went astern enough to pour another heavy broadside into the *Cyane*. As the *Levant* then wore to come back to the assistance of the *Cyane* the *Constitution*'s sails were

again filled, and she shot ahead in time to fire two raking
broadsides into the stern of the *Levant* as she was turning. The
Cyane pluckily forged in between the two ships to take this fire,
and the *Levant* drew out of the fight with her braces gone and
the ship herself badly damaged.

At this point the *Cyane* attempted to run off before the
wind, but the *Constitution* wore around short and gave her a
raking fire over the stern. The Englishman quickly luffed up
and fired her port broadside, but Stewart brought the *Constitution* around within hailing distance on her port quarter
where he had her practically at pistol's point and wholly at his
mercy. Since his position was hopeless, Captain Falcon fired a
gun to leeward and hoisted a light in token of his surrender.
His ship had been hulled several times, five of his carronades
had broken loose, his main and mizzenmasts were wounded and
in danger of falling, and many of his men had been killed or
disabled. Stewart sent Lieutenant Hoffman aboard with a
guard of fifteen marines and a small crew, while the officers
were transferred to the *Constitution*. This took nearly an hour
and in the meantime the *Levant* drew off to patch up her own
damage.

It was 7:45 before Stewart was able to go in chase of her, but
Captain Douglas, unaware that the *Cyane* had surrendered,
had no intention of running away. At about 8 p.m. he was discovered standing for the *Constitution*, and forty minutes later
they passed within fifty yards of one another on opposite
courses. At once, and almost simultaneously, they both loosed
their broadsides, and the *Constitution* then headed around under her stern, raking her as he passed. Douglas now saw that
the *Cyane* had struck and he attempted to run, but it was too
late. In the last broadside his wheel had been shot away and his
lower masts badly wounded. After being chased for half an
hour longer he finally gave up and also surrendered.

So ended the last frigate action of the war. In fact there is
some question as to whether Stewart should have gone into it,
since he knew that peace had been declared. But the English-

men probably knew it as well as he. And none of them was aware, that the Treaty of Ghent had been signed on Christmas Eve 1814, some two months previously. Technically, as far as they were concerned, the war was still on. Moreover, the spirit of the times was such that had either Stewart or the British refused to engage, they probably would have been condemned at home as cowards. As it was, both Englishmen fought their ships stubbornly and well to the end, while Stewart's seamanship was probably the most brilliant of the war.

By dint of hard work the Americans managed to get all three ships into sailing order by the following morning, when it was decided to run on down to the Cape Verdes off the western tip of Africa where they could make more permanent repairs and prepare all three for the long homeward run across the Atlantic. They reached Porto Praya on the tenth of March where, to Captain Stewart's surprise, they found the brig *Susan* which he had taken outside Lisbon and he had assumed was on her way home. Now Stewart decided to use her to return all of his prisoners home to England. One hundred of the prisoners were put aboard to make her ready for sea, and the rest were put ashore the next day and preparations were made to transfer their effects. The work went slowly owing to a very thick, low lying fog which closed down over the water, obscuring the ships' hulls but leaving the air clear above the topgallant yards. It was not considered necessary to keep a lookout aloft, and for this Stewart came near to paying with the loss of his ship.

Stewart himself was shaving in his cabin, while the prisoners and crew were working on deck, when an English midshipman called in a low tone to his captain, who was also a prisoner, to look at the large ship in the offing. Lieutenant Shubrick, who was serving as first luff of the *Constitution*, just happened to overhear the remark and looked up too, in time to see the upper sails of a large ship—clearly a man-of-war—standing in toward the harbor. Almost immediately the tops of two others loomed up close behind her!

Stewart had no illusions as to the fate that awaited the *Constitution* if she were caught where she was. He knew the neutrality of Portugal would not prevent the British from entering the port and that the Portuguese governor would not lift a finger to restrain them. Furthermore, he knew only too well how delighted the British would be to capture the *Constitution*, which had been such a thorn in their sides, even as their last act of the war. Accordingly he cut his cables and ran for it, signaling to the *Cyane* and the *Levant* to follow his example immediately. Indeed, so precipitate was their departure that some of the English prisoners who had been left on shore ran to the Portuguese battery above and opened fire on the three ships as they left, probably more by way of giving warning to the incoming ships of the Americans' presence than from any hope of stopping them.

The *Constitution* and her prizes cleared the harbor close under the east point and hugged the north shore in an effort to get to sea to windward of the strangers, but their flight was discovered by the other ships' lookouts above the fog and a long, exciting chase began.

The newcomers proved to be the British frigates *Leander*, 50, Captain Sir George Collier; *Newcastle*, 50, Captain Lord George Stuart; and the *Acasta*, 40, Captain Kerr. They had been scouring the seas in search of the *Constitution* since Stewart had given the *Newcastle* and the *Acasta* the slip when he sailed from Boston.

And, indeed, it was a close thing, for the *Acasta* did succeed in weathering the *Cyane* and the *Levant* but was unable to gain on the *Constitution*. Seeing that he was drawing away from his prizes, Stewart signaled the *Cyane* to tack to the northwest, hoping to divide the enemy's force. Hoffman, in the *Cyane*, obeyed but to everyone's surprise none of the Englishmen followed her and she was soon able to run them out of sight and then stood away for New York, where she arrived on the tenth of April. Meantime the *Newcastle* had drawn near enough on the *Constitution*'s lee quarter to feel that she was within range and began firing by division. But the shots all fell harmlessly short, and Stewart now signaled to the *Levant* to make the same maneuver as the *Cyane*.

If the *Constitution*'s people had been surprised at the British reaction to the *Cyane*'s departure, they were doubly amazed now when all three of the pursuing vessels apparently believing they could not catch the *Constitution*, swung away after the little *Levant*, leaving the big fish alone to pursue his leisurely way westward across the Atlantic to Puerto Rico, where Stewart left his prisoners, and thence northward for New York, where he, too, arrived safely on the fifteenth of May, 1815.

The little *Levant* was not so lucky. After bearing away from the *Constitution*'s wake she was so hotly pressed by the British that she was forced to put back into Porto Praya, where she took refuge under the guns of the fort in the hope that Portuguese neutrality would be respected. Just as Captain Stewart had suspected, however, the British opened fire on the *Levant* even though Lieutenant Ballard had hauled down his flag and signaled his surrender. Ballard ordered his men to lie down on the decks, so they came to no harm. Some of the British shot did damage in the town beyond, however, and Captain Collier had to make his official apologies to the governor for that as well as to indemnify the Portuguese.

17

R.H.I.P.

S O M E T I M E S in rambling through an old cemetery one comes upon a headstone whose epitaph is headed by the letters R.H.I.P. Translated literally from the Latin "Requiescat Hic In Pace," from which it is taken, this means "May he rest here in peace." Somehow this seems to have been considered more formal and dignified than the customary R.I.P., which translated means simply "May he rest in peace."

To navy folk, however, the letters more frequently have another, less reverent meaning. To a navy man they stand for "Rank Hath Its Privileges." In both senses the letters might well be applied to the United States frigate *Constitution*, better known today as "Old Ironsides," for today she lies, to all intents and purposes, entombed at her wharf in the Boston Naval Shipyard, in Charlestown, Massachusetts. And she certainly "hath" her rank and privileges. Several times it has been proposed in Congress that she be retired and broken up. But each time such a popular outcry against such a move has been raised that not even Secretary McNamara, who has made the most sweeping changes in this nation's naval setup since Roosevelt I, has not dared to lay a finger on her! Today she has become virtually a national shrine to the American people.

Looking back today it is hard to realize that it is now 150 years since "Old Ironsides" fought her last battle, and yet this is true—a century and a half, plus a few months, have passed since her action with the *Cyane* and the *Levant*. She is changed, no doubt: new timbers, new fittings, new rigging, chains, cables—even the addition of certain modern facilities to meet the changes of time. Indeed, there are some who say that she cannot rightly be said to be the same ship, since hardly a stick of the original vessel remains. Yet this was true even of her younger days, when she was in active service and fighting her country's battles on the sea. We have seen how often she had to be overhauled even then; how frequently she had to be rerigged, how often rotted timbers had to be replaced; how even her wheel was replaced by one taken from a captured ship. The same is true of houses. There is many a one standing today in good repair that claims to date from a century or more before even the famous frigate's keel was laid down. But if we stop and think, these too have had rotten wood replaced and storm damage repaired and certain modern improvements made.

The claim that the *Constitution* no longer exists is sheer sophistry. She has never been retired from the list, although she may have been retired to inactive service. She has never been broken up or discarded or sold. She has never been replaced by other ships who perpetuate her name as were the *Enterprise*, the *Wasp*, the *Hornet*, the *Essex*, the *Bonhomme Richard*—even the *Constellation*, which still remains afloat even though as much altered by repair and replacement as the *Constitution* has been. No other ship has ever been named "*Constitution*," and so long as she remains afloat she is as authentic a remnant of our past as the House of Seven Gables, the Wayside Inn, Mount Vernon, Monticello, or a thousand other historic places. As for Williamsburg, Sturbridge Village, and the like—Hmmmph! They are replicas!

Yet the fact remains indisputable: The *Constitution* was in her heyday during her early 'teens. Her most memorable battle—that with the *Guerriere*—was fought during her fourteenth year. At the time of the final battle of her career she was not yet turned eighteen! This is scarcely surprising when we consider the doldrums that seemed to swallow up the navy dur-

ing the near half-century between the end of the War of 1812
and the beginning of the Civil War; or when we remember that
these were the years of change from sail to steam. Yet it was to
be many years before she was even retired to the inactive list. It
was to be many more before she would be turned out to pasture
altogether.

By the time she reached home in May 1815, following her
fight with the *Cyane* and the *Levant* and her subsequent flight
from Sir George Collier's squadron, the War of 1812 was fully
ended and there seemed no further need for her services for the
immediate moment. Accordingly she went up to Boston and
into the navy yard for extensive repairs, as was usual after a
long cruise. She was still being worked upon when, before the
year was over, Commodores Decatur and Bainbridge left for
the Mediterranean with two squadrons to put an end, once and
for all, to the shoddy trickery of the Barbary states—
especially Algiers—which had taken advantage of our preoccupation with the British to resume their old practices.

Because she was laid up under repairs the *Constitution* took
no part in this expedition. For six years then she appears to
have remained more or less idle, for we hear nothing of her
activities, though it is hardly likely that such a well-known ship
would lie idle at her dock in Boston throughout such a period.
More likely she spent the interval in cruising in home waters,
showing herself at various ports along the coast, in training
cruises and perhaps acting from time to time as a receiving
ship, taking in new recruits who were to be assigned to other
vessels and breaking them in to the ways of the navy.

At any rate it is not until May 1821 that her name comes
once again into the news. In that month she sailed for the
Mediterranean station from Boston with a new crew under the
command of Captain Jacob Jones, who had been a midshipman
aboard the *Philadelphia* when she was captured before Tripoli.
She went out to Gibraltar in the remarkably fast time of
twenty-one days, and based at Port Mahon, at Minorca, in the
Balearic Islands. From there she visited at a number of ports

throughout the Mediterranean, from Gibraltar to Smyrna, but apparently she did not look in at Tripoli, the scene of her baptism of fire, and when we remember that Captain Jones had spent some twenty months of his life as a prisoner there we can understand why she did not.

In 1823 she returned to Boston to refit and take on a new crew, but she did not sail again until the following spring when, under the command of Captain Thomas Macdonough, she went out once more to the Mediterranean, where she joined the squadron commanded by Commodore John Rodgers. This time she spent four years on the station, Captain Macdonough being relieved by Captain Patterson for reasons of health. This tour of duty was spent largely in the eastern Mediterranean, where the Turks, aided by the Egyptians, were attempting to beat the Greeks, who had rebelled, back into submission. The Greek cause won the support of liberals throughout the world at that time and many prominent men, most notably Lord Byron, who died in Greece, volunteered their aid. Among those who were most active in this movement was Dr. Samuel Gridley Howe, who is probably better known to most Americans as the husband of Julia Ward Howe. Young Howe went out to Greece as surgeon in the Greek navy shortly after his graduation from Harvard Medical School. He saw practically no sea service at all, but he did see that the Greek people, ground between the contending armies, were suffering far more than the combatants. Indeed, they were on the verge of starvation, and he returned home and campaigned for donations of supplies of medicines and food.

The American response was immediate and generous. Howe was able to build a hospital and see that many of the poor Greek refugees were fed and clothed and cared for. But, of course, he could not care for them all, and one leader of the disorganized Greek rebels who had received no aid attempted to seize several shiploads of the supplies for distribution among his troops. Fortunately, the *Constitution* sailed into the picture and Howe appealed to Captain Patterson for help in recover-

ing the stolen supplies and seeing to the proper distribution.
Patterson responded promptly, bringing the ship in close to
shore and sending a note to the old chieftan, Colocotroni,
threatening to send a landing party ashore unless the goods
were restored. This had the desired effect, and Colocotroni returned the stolen food and clothing to Howe with loud protestations of regret. After that the *Constitution* remained for several days in the area, and Dr. Howe was able to distribute his
relief without further interference.

Although it was scarcely as spectacular an event as a sea
fight, it was the sort of thing that the *Constitution* was in the
Mediterranean for: to display the flag and show that she was
prepared to support our citizens in their lawful rights and ven-
tures, be they philanthropic, as was Howe's, or commercial, as
were most of her encounters. In any case this seems to have
been as close to a brush as she came during her stay on that station, for everywhere else that she went she was received with
warm welcome and much curiosity.

In July 1828 the *Constitution* returned to Boston, where she
lay idle for some time. In 1830 occurred that first outburst of
public protest that was to save her for posterity. During the
year 1829 she was "surveyed" by a naval board and pronounced generally unseaworthy. Apparently her frames were
generally sound enough, but much of the planking of her sides
and decks needed to be replaced and prices had so risen since
she had been first launched that it was estimated that it would
cost more to put her back into shape than it had to build her in
the first place. Accordingly the secretary of the navy, at the rec-
ommendation of the Board of Naval Commissioners, ordered
her to be sold or broken up.

There was no fanfare about it. No headlines announced the
decision, only a brief note in the news items hidden deep on the
inner pages of the daily papers. Probably she would have gone
proudly but quietly to her end at that time if the notice had not
happened to attract the attention of a young student at Harvard's Dana School of Law (it was only after he finished law

school that he took up medicine) named Oliver Wendell
Holmes. So indignant was the young man at this threatened
end of the fine old ship that he sat down that very morning and
dashed off what has since become his best known poem:

Ay, tear her tattered ensign down!
Long has it waved on high,
And many an eye has danced to see
That banner in the sky;
Beneath it rung the battle shout,
And burst the cannon's roar;-
The meteor of the ocean air
Shall sweep the clouds no more.

Her deck, once red with heroes' blood,
Where knelt the vanquished foe,
When winds were hurrying o'er the flood,
And waves were white below,
No more shall feel the victor's tread,
Or know the conquered knee;-
The harpies of the shore shall pluck
The eagle of the sea!

Oh better that her shattered hulk
Should sink beneath the wave;
Her thunders shook the mighty deep,
And there should be her grave;
Nail to the mast her holy flag,
Set every threadbare sail,
And give her to the God of Storms,
The lightning and the gale!

Holmes meant the verses more as a sort of letter-to-the-
editor; a protest, to be sure, but he never dreamed it might
amount to more. It was published in the *Boston Advertiser* and
seemed instantly to stir the public's imagination. Other papers
in other cities reprinted it and the outcry rose to a growling
roar of public rage. The secretary of the navy hastily rescind-

ed the order, and at the next session Congress voted the necessary funds to rebuild the veteran warship practically without
alterations. On June 24, 1833, she entered the new dry dock
which had just been completed at the Boston Navy Yard, the
first vessel to use it.

They made quite a ceremony of the event, too. Commodore
Hull, her most famous wartime commander, took command of
her for the occasion and directed her docking in the presence of
Vice-President Martin Van Buren. Curiously enough it was not
until this moment that anyone had had a chance to make a full
examination of the damage that had been done to her keel at
the time of her launching. Some work had been done on it before the War of 1812, but then the workmen had been unable
to reach every part of those members. Now her keel was found
to be about two and a half feet out of line, a condition which
undoubtedly accounted for her swinging off course at the time
of the chase by the *Belvidera* and her consorts. Now the condition was fully corrected, and she came off the ways again to all
intents and purposes a new ship.

But now she was more than ever in the public eye, and her
next adventure was much less pleasant all around, even though
it all began as a prank. Following her rebuilding the *Constitution* was in need of a new figurehead. Her first, a figure of Hercules, had been shot away before Tripoli. This had been replaced by a figure of Neptune, and when this had rotted
through it, in turn, was replaced by a plain carved billet which,
if it resembled anything at all, looked most like a winged sea
dragon going backward. This was badly weathered and should
have been replaced while she was in drydock. But it had not
been done and now Captain Jesse Elliott, the new commandant
at the Boston yard, asked permission to replace it.

Now Captain Elliott was a Jacksonian Democrat, and it was
his intention to replace the billet with a standing figure of
President Andrew Jackson. It was his plan to keep the whole
thing a deep, dark secret and spring it on the people of Boston

at the unveiling, when the carving was actually finished and set in place.

What he did not realize, however, being a newcomer to the city, was that most of the businessmen and merchants and bankers and such of Boston—indeed of all New England generally—were anti-Jackson Whigs, the inheritors of the traditions of the Federalists and progenitors of today's strong Republican bloc in that area. Perhaps he had been fooled because he had arrived to take command of the yard just at the time of Jackson's visit to the city, and all that he had seen was that there had been a large and enthusiastic turnout to greet the President. Doubtless he really believed that the good people of Boston would be pleased by the gesture.

But Bostonians take their politics as seriously as do people in any other part of the nation, and when the news leaked out—as such news has a way of doing—the storm of indignation, protest, and vituperation that burst forth from all sides must have been startling and astonishing indeed to Captain Elliott. However, he was a stubborn, perhaps even a somewhat tactless, man, and when he was threatened with a coat of tar and feathers he only set his jaw more firmly and bade Mr. Beecher, the man commissioned to do the carving, to finish the job.

There was no grand ceremony when the figurehead was done and fitted in place. There had been threats of a second "Boston Tea Party" to tear the thing down and throw it in the sea. Captain Elliott took considerable pains to see to it that no such thing happened. He had the *Constitution* moored between two ships of the line, of which the United States now had several, and to make doubly sure he set a marine guard on constant duty in the bows to keep a day and night watch over the precious image.

But in spite of all his precautions the thing was done. It happened that one of Boston's more prominent shipowners remarked one day, to one of his captains who was in port awaiting a ship, that he would give a hundred dollars to see that fig-

ure's head cut off. He said it jokingly, never dreaming that
anything more would come of it. But Sam Dewey was never a
man to take a dare and let it pass. On the night of July 2,
1834, Boston was beset by an all-night series of thunderstorms.
That night Dewey shoved out from the Boston side of the
Charles River and rowed across to the navy yard alone. He
shipped his oars silently as he approached the outermost ship
of the line and used his hands to fend off and work his little
skiff around under her bows. There he came upon the *Constitution* lying snug between her guardians in the teaming rain and
almost continuous thunder. Silently Dewey worked his way in
under her bowsprit. Then with a coiled rope over his shoulder,
two gimlets in his pocket and a bucksaw in the crook of his
elbow, he climbed quietly into her fore chains and thence
worked his way out under the bowsprit. Since the rain was coming down in bucketfuls there was not much danger of his being
discovered. The marine guards had availed themselves of the
nearest cover, and in any case Dewey moved under cover of the
frequent claps of thunder. Once in position, he screwed the
gimlets into the ears, secured the rope to the gimlets in such a
way that the head could be lowered away to the water silently,
and then fell to work with the saw.

It was not easy work, for he had to stay perfectly still between the claps and rumbles of the thunder, the noise of which
drowned out the sound of the saw. Besides, the wood was hard
and did not cut as easily as pulpwood. Moreover, his first cut
struck a bolt and he had to make another, sheering away part
of the chin as he did so. But he stayed with it and some time
after midnight he succeeded in cutting it through and lowering
the severed head to his boat below.

By this time the little cockleshell was half full of rainwater,
so that the trip back to Boston must have been the most hazardous part of the undertaking. But Dewey made it. As soon as
he was ashore he dumped the head into an old gunny sack and
carried it off to his mother's house without meeting a soul.

There he hid it in a sea chest, and the next day presented himself to Mr. Lincoln to collect his hundred dollars.

Whether or not the merchant ever paid up is not part of the record. It is part of the record, however, that the next day the whole town was in an uproar—especially Captain Elliott! The latter was furious. He draped a five-striped flag over the stump of the figurehead to denote the disloyalty of New England, and early in 1835 sailed the ship around to New York. There he summoned Beecher from Boston and had him fit a new head to the stump.

So despite the indignation of Boston the *Constitution* got her Jackson figurehead in the end. She wore it proudly for forty years, after which it was again replaced and the figure of the former President sent to Annapolis, where it may still be seen on exhibition at the Naval Academy.

Meantime the authorities searched high and low for the original head but did not find it until Dewey himself surrendered it, some months after the decapitation, to the secretary of the navy. The fact that he was not even punished for his prank more than hints at political influence, and one cannot help but wonder if his employers did not suffer an attack of conscience and make a deal with the government in exchange for the return of the piece. Certainly they were in a better position than Dewey to accomplish such an end.

In 1835 American relations with France were somewhat strained and our ambassador to Paris was recalled. On March 16 the *Constitution* was sent to France to pick him up and bring him home. The crossing appears to have been a stormy one, for Captain Elliott reported that despite her recent repairs the ship labored very hard, parted some of her chain plates and pitched one of her 24-pounders out through a forecastle port. Nevertheless she arrived April 10 at Le Havre, where she picked up the minister, Mr. Edward Livingston, and his family, returning to New York early in May by way of Plymouth, England, and arrived in New York on June 22.

She was then ordered to the Mediterranean once more as the flagship of Commodore Elliott, and the squadron got away by the nineteenth of August. She remained on the Mediterranean station until 1838, when she returned to the United States, arriving in Hampton Roads on August 1. She moved over to the Norfolk Navy Yard the following day, and at once more than two hundred of her crew, whose times were up long since and who had not found her a "happy ship" under Commodore Elliott, demanded their immediate release from the service. Commodore Elliott himself was plagued with a number of charges and lawsuits, one of the strangest being that he had "encumbered the berth deck with jackasses for the improvement of the breed in the United States."

The *Constitution*'s next duty was on what was then known as the "South Pacific" station, which meant the west coast of South America would be her principal cruising ground. She was under the command of Captain Daniel Turner and served as the flagship for Commodore Alexander Claxton on that station. She sailed from New York on May 20, 1839, and remained in the Pacific for two years, until Commodore Claxton died on board. Turner succeeded to the command and returned to Norfolk in the fall of 1841. Coming around the Horn she again met with very heavy weather, and Captain Turner, on his arrival in Norfolk reported, that at that time "she labored beyond everything I had ever witnessed, and gave me a lively idea of what sailors understand by 'working like a basket.' "

In 1842–43 she served with the home fleet in Atlantic waters, and for a time was the flagship of Commodore Charles Stewart, who had commanded her during her last wartime cruise, and in 1844 she set out from Hampton Roads, under the command of Captain John ("Mad Jack") Percival, on what was to be the longest cruise of her career—around the world.

It was far from the swiftest voyage she ever made, however. First she ran south to Rio de Janeiro, where she dropped off the new American minister, Mr. Henry Wise. From there her course lay around the Cape of Good Hope to India, and thence to Burma and the Malay Peninsula. But at Singapore an un-welcome passenger came aboard—the plague—and some two hundred of her men were stricken. Fortunately most of them recovered, but she was delayed in port for five to six weeks.

The commander of the British squadron then based at Singapore was Commodore Henry Chads, formerly a lieuten-ant in the *Java* and a prisoner in the *Constitution* after their battle. He well remembered the kindness of his captors on that occasion, and now when the *Constitution* was crippled by sick-ness he repaid bygone favors by offering the full medical serv-ices of the British fleet on that station to help.

From Singapore they continued their leisurely cruise by way of Macao and Canton and Manila, and thence homeward by way of the Mexican coast and Cape Horn. She went out of commission in Boston on October 10, 1848, after a cruise that had covered 52,279 miles and taken some 495 days.

But there was life in the old girl yet. In 1849 she was flag-ship of the Mediterranean station for a brief period, returning in 1851 to New York where she was refitted and refurbished and sent out again to the Mediterranean. Between 1852 and 1855 she served in that part of the world, and also took part in suppressing the slave trade on the coast of West Africa, at which time she was based at her old stamping grounds in the Cape Verdes.

But her cruising days were numbered, for by that time steam and the screw propeller were rapidly taking over the seas from sail, and in 1855 she returned to Portsmouth, N.H., never to be used in really active service again.

In 1860 she was moored in the Severn River, off Annapolis, attached to the Naval Academy, but when the troubles with the South began it was considered best to move her out of harm's way. There was a good deal of threatening talk and the situa-tion became so grim that the effort was made to tow her out, but first the *Constitution* and then the tug went aground in the shallow river mouth. For a brief period it was feared that she

would be attacked there and burned by the Confederates, but
she was rescued from her precarious situation by the arrival of
troops from Massachusetts and New York, another tug was
brought in to help from Havre de Grace, and through their
combined efforts she was pulled into deep water then towed to
New York, where she lay out the Civil War in the Brooklyn
Navy Yard. Shortly before the end of the war the Naval Academy was moved to Newport, Rhode Island, and the *Constitution* was towed there to serve as a training ship. When peace
was finally restored, the academy returned to Annapolis and a
tug was sent to tow the frigate back to Chesapeake Bay. But
by this time the careful, loving hands of old time sailors and
young, eager cadets had put her back into prime condition, and
she soon outran her tow under her own canvas and finished the
rest of the voyage unassisted.

Not until 1877 did she reappear in the public eye. In that
year she was put back into commission, under command of
Captain O. C. Badger, and in January 1878 sailed for Le
Havre with a cargo of goods for exhibition at the universal
exposition in Paris. The voyage out was uneventful save for a
few leaks sprung in the passage, and she waited at Le Havre
some nine months until the exposition closed and she was able to
restow the articles she had carried over for the American portion of the exhibition.

Her homeward voyage was not so fortunate, however. First,
after crossing the English Channel, an unknown current set
her aground off Ballard's Point, near Swanage. The British
were helpful in the emergency, offering every assistance to get
her off, but it took the combined efforts of five tugs and a battle-
ship to get her afloat. After that she was laid up at the Royal
Naval Dockyard, at Portsmouth, undergoing repairs for several weeks before she was able to get away once more on January 30, 1879. Fourteen days later, when they were in mid-
ocean, her rudder head was wrenched off in a howling gale, and
she had no choice but to run off before the wind and hope for
the best.

The storm carried her all the way back to Lisbon, and once again she had to go into a government dock for repairs. This time it took much longer, and it was not until the middle of April that she finally got away for home, arriving in New York on the twenty-fourth of May.

For some two years thereafter she served as a training ship for apprentice boys, operating in southern waters during the winter and out of New York in the summer. But in 1881 she went finally out of commission at the Brooklyn Navy Yard—or the New York Naval Shipyard, as it was officially called. In 1883 she was towed up to Portsmouth, where she was used for several years as a receiving ship.

On the occasion of her hundredth anniversary, however, she was towed back to Boston and moored in the Charlestown Navy Yard, little more than a stone's throw from the place where she had been launched. There the governor, the mayor, the assistant secretary of the navy and the entire North Atlantic fleet gathered to do her honor on her birthday.

And there she still lies today, retired at last but secure in the knowledge that a grateful nation will look out for her with tender care. There have been several suggestions that she be towed for exhibition to this or that fair or exposition, the latest being that she be towed around to New York for the edification of sightseers in 1964. But all of these proposals have been vetoed as too dangerous for such a valuable and venerable relic. Accordingly she has been left to lie near her birthplace, where she may be visited—for a fee—by all who are willing to come to her.

R.H.I.P.—May she rest here in peace! And while we are about it, let us not forget also that "Rank Hath Its Privileges!" Surely she has earned both.

GLOSSARY OF
NAUTICAL TERMS AND
SHIPBOARD DEFINITIONS

ABACK: The trim of a ship's sails when so set that the wind, acting against them, forces the vessel astern.

ABAFT: Behind. For instance, the mainmast is abaft the foremast and the mizzen is abaft both. Anything toward the stern from the point of reference.

ABEAM: Ninety degrees from dead ahead; i.e., at a right angle to the ship's course. Cf. BEAM.

ABOARD: In or on the ship.

ABOUT: Change direction. "To come about" means to turn to the opposite tack in a wind-driven vessel.

ABREAST: Abeam of. Vessels sailing on opposite or the same courses, when squarely aligned at right angles to their courses, are abreast of one another. A sailor might say that a couple walking arm in arm were also "abreast of one another."

ADMIRAL: A naval rank not legally or officially recognized in the U.S. Navy until 1862, though prior to that time it was sometimes applied, with "commodore," as a courtesy title to "flag" officers—captain was the highest official rank attainable prior to that date—in command of fleets or squadrons or major shore installations. The word is derived from the Arabic *Amir-el-Bahr*; roughly, "commander of the seas." In the British navy the rank dates from 1297.

ADRIFT: Floating; not moored or under way.

AFT: At or toward the stern or back of the ship.

AGAINST THE SUN: Counterclockwise; from right to left.

ALEE: Away from the wind; to leeward (q.v.).

ALL-IN-THE-WIND: The moment when all sails begin flapping and shaking by being too close to the wind, i.e., when the vessel is sailed directly or almost directly into the wind. So long as a ship's sails are filled she will move ahead, but when she reaches that point where the wind will no longer catch against her sails and they begin to flutter, she has "come all-in-the-wind" and will either "come about" on a new course, yaw (see below) back to her original course, or lie in danger of being "taken aback."

ALL STANDING: (1) To bring to a sudden stop, as when the *Philadelphia* ran "all standing" on the reefs off Tripoli; (2) to turn in with all one's clothes on, as was often necessary aboard wind-driven ships; (3) to be completely equipped and ready for sea—as every frigate's captain hoped to be able to report his ship before sailing.

ALOFT: Above the upper deck; generally sails, masts, and rigging. Also a lookout stationed in the masthead or riflemen—generally marines—in the fighting tops in time of battle.

ALONGSIDE: Side to side; ship to dock; ship to ship.

AMIDSHIPS: The middle of a vessel crosswise.

ANCHOR: From an old Greek word meaning "hook." Hence a hooked instrument which, when attached to a cable and hooked on bottom, is designed to hold a vessel in a given position. ANCHOR LIGHTS: Riding lights legally required to be shown by all vessels at anchor. ANCHOR WATCH: A guard maintained on deck at night while the vessel is at anchor to look out for surprise attack or guard against vandalism, pilfering, stowaways, etc. "ANCHOR'S AWEIGH": The verbal report of the officer in charge of the anchor detail as soon as the "hook" is broken free of the bottom when the ship is about to sail.

APEAK: In a vertical line; an anchor hove in so that the chain hangs straight up and down.

ASTERN: Directly behind. Anything behind the ship is said to be "astern." The direction of a vessel when she goes backward.

ATHWART: Across. ATHWART-HAWSE: Across another vessel's cable or stem, a perilous position if the other ship is under way since it is a collision course. ATHWARTSHIPS: Across the middle of the vessel; at right angles to its fore-and-aft line.

AVAST: An order to stop, e.g., " 'Vast heaving!" is an order to stop hauling.

AWASH: Level with the water, e.g., the lee rail in a running sea, an overcrowed lifeboat more than half full of water, a dead body in the offshore surf.

AWEIGH: Off the bottom—primarily an anchor just lifted from its holding. (See sup.)

"AYE, AYE, SIR!": Traditional nautical response to the order of a superior officer indicating that his command has been heard and understood.

BACK: Of the wind when it shifts to counterclockwise; changing against the sun, left to right. When it turns with the sun—right to left—it is said to "veer."

BACKSTAY: A rope, line, or cable bracing a mast from a point aft.

BALLAST: Heavy weights, usually rock, placed low in the bottom of a vessel to give her stability, especially when unloaded.

BANK: An extensive shoal, usually well offshore, frequently coming close enough to the surface to be dangerous to large vessels but sometimes offering fine fishing for smaller craft; e.g., the Grand Bank of Newfoundland, George's Banks, whence Boston and New England get much of their cod and Spanish and Portugese fishermen most of their sardines.

BARE POLES: Stripped of sails and often yards. A sailing ship in hurricane or similar force weather may find it necessary to take in all sail and strip her yards. She is then said to be running under bare poles.

BARGE: A large ship's boat set aside for the use of the ship's officers.

BARK (or BARQUE): A three-masted sailing ship, square-rigged on the fore and main and fore-and-aft rigged on the mizzenmast. An especially popular type Down East (from Portsmouth, N.H., to the Bay of Fundy) because of its handiness with large hulls. BARKENTINE: A variation of the above, square-rigged on the foremast and fore-and-aft on the main and mizzen.

BARNACLE: A small shellfish which attaches itself to wooden pilings and often to ships' bottoms in such large clusters that the vessels' speed and sailing qualities are seriously impaired. When they become too thick it is necessary to careen the vessel and scrape her bottom. They cannot live in fresh water, hence Captain Hull took the *Constitution* up into the mouth of the Sus-quehanna, above Havre de Grace, to get rid of them.

BATTEN: A wooden wedge used to tighten ropes and canvas against an expected storm; e.g., "Batten down the hatches" means "prepare for weather."

BEAM: Width of a vessel at her broadest point, usually amidships. BEAM ENDS: Said of a vessel when she is hove down or listed to such a degree that her deck beams are nearly vertical. BEAM SEA: A sea running at right angles to a vessel's course. BEAM WIND: A wind at right angles to the ship's course. BROAD ON THE BEAM: A bearing of 90 degrees from the ship's course.

BEAR: To go or steer in a given direction. BEAR DOWN: Approach from windward. BEAR UP: Put the helm up and let the ship run off to leeward. BEAR IN: Approach the shore or other object. BEAR OFF: Steer away from shore or other object.

BEARING: The direction of an object from the vessel.

BEAT TO QUARTERS: To send the crew to battle stations by drum-beat.

BEAT TO WINDWARD: To make progress against the wind when sail-ing on the wind or close hauled; to make progress against the wind by a series of zigzag tacks.

BELOW: Beneath the main deck.

BERTH DECK: A lower full deck, about at the waterline, generally used for berthing purposes, not as a gun deck.

BINNACLE: The hooded, internally-lighted stand, usually of brass, in which the compass is hung. It is so placed that it is visible to the steersman at all times. BINNACLE LIST: A list posted in a man-of-war daily by the medical officer giving the names of those excused from duty on account of sickness.

BITTER END: The last bit of a rope or cable or the last link in an anchor chain. BITTER ENDER: A harsh captain, a martinet.

BOARDING HOOK (or PIKE): A long-handled, spearlike weapon, used as a grappling hook for boarding or as a spear for repelling boarders.

BOATSWAIN (or BO'S'N): The chief non-commissioned officer on a ship; best described as the ship's foreman through whom all orders pass to the crew.

BOW: The front of the ship; forward.

BOWSPRIT: A spar extending forward from the bow securing stays and rigging for the headsails.

BRIG: A two-masted sailing vessel, square-rigged on the fore and mainmasts. Also the ship's prison.

BRIGANTINE: A two-masted sailing vessel, square-rigged on the fore and fore-and-aft rigged on the main. In the *Constitution*'s time a brigantine was also square-rigged aft above the mainsail; i.e., the mainsail alone was fore-and-aft rigged.

BROADSIDE: The side of a vessel above water; of a man-of-war the full weight of all the guns on one side of the ship; a salvo of all guns on a side.

BULKHEAD: Walls or partitions separating internal sections of the ship.

BULWARKS: The wooden extension of the ship's sides above the upper deck.

BY THE BOARD: Overboard.

BY THE RUN: Let go altogether, as a rope allowed to run out of its own weight.

BY THE WIND: To sail close to the wind keeping the sails always filled.

CABLE: A rope or chain of great strength, generally referring to the anchor chain.

CABLE'S LENGTH: 100 fathoms or 600 feet.

CALL AWAY: To summon a boat's crew by boatswain's pipe or bugle to man and ready their boat for off-ship duty. CALL AWAY BOARDERS: To send a designated portion of the crew on board an enemy ship.

CALM: A wind of less than one knot. FLAT CALM: No wind at all. BECALMED: The situation of a ship in a flat calm, unable to move except by rowing, towing, or kedging.

CAREEN: To haul a vessel over on her beam-ends by means of ropes and tackles so as to clean her bottom. The operation was carried out only in water barely deep enough to float the ship at high tide and preferably over a sandy bottom.

CARRONADE: A short cannon, much lighter than the long guns of the same caliber. They were not accurate at long range, but were better than long guns for close fighting since they could throw much heavier shot.

CHAINS: Where the shrouds were secured to the sides. The platform thus formed gave footing for the leadman when taking soundings.

CHARLEY NOBLE: The galley smoke pipe. "To shoot Charley Noble" meant to fire a shot up the pipe to shake the soot loose.

CLOSE HAULED: To sail close to the wind; same as FULL AND BY, ON THE WIND, or BY THE WIND.

COCKBILL: To hang an anchor up and down, clear of the water; to incline the yards vertically—a sign of mourning.

COMMANDER: Originally "master-commandant," a rank which it replaced in 1838.

COMMODORE: Originally a courtesy title given to the senior captain of a squadron or fleet. It was officially recognized by the U.S. Navy in 1838 as a rank between captain and rear admiral. It has been discontinued from time to time, usually between wars, and was last reactivated during World War II.

DAVY JONES: Mythical assistant to King Neptune, lord of the sea. DAVY JONES' LOCKER: The bottom of the ocean.

DEAD RECKONING: Steering "by guess and by God"; a course run without sights or bearings.

DEADRISE: The vertical distance between the keel of a vessel and the turn of the bilge.

DEEP SEA LEAD: A lead weighing 50 pounds used at 120 fathoms or more; pronounced "dipsey."

DEEP SIX: Throw overboard.

DERELICT: An abandoned vessel.

DEVIL: The longest deck seam. THE DEVIL TO PAY: To "pay" a seam means to caulk or plug a ship's seams with cotton or hemp and pitch, hence the saying, "The devil to pay and only half a bucket of pitch!"

DOLDRUMS: A belt on either side of the equator in which little or no wind usually blows. Thus a ship becalmed is said to be "in the doldrums."

DOLPHIN: A fish which often runs ahead of a ship for hours as if playing tag with it. DOLPHIN STRIKER: An iron protruding downward from the bowsprit and serving as a brace for that spar.

DOUSE: Take in or lower a sail; also put out a light or throw water upon.

DOWNHAUL: A rope from the head of a headsail through a block at the foot of the stay used for pulling down the sail.

DUFF: A pudding of flour and water, a major item in seamen's rations in sailing ship times. When raisins were added it was called "plum duff."

EASE HER: An order to put the helm alee; to luff into the wind or sea.

EXEC: The executive officer; the second in command of ships of the U.S. Navy.

FAKE: A single turn of rope when a rope is coiled down. FAKE DOWN: To coil down a rope so that it is clear for running.

FALLING OFF: Paying off before the wind.

FANTAIL: That part of the stern of a ship extending aft of the sternpost; the after section of the main deck.

FATHOM: Six feet.

FID: A supporting bar; a crosspiece to hold the topmast in place.

FILL: To brace the yards so that the wind strikes the after surface and "fills" them.

FISH: A long piece of timber used to strengthen a mast or spar when it has been sprung or damaged. TO FISH: To repair a weakened spar with such a timber.

FIRST LIEUTENANT: Chief officer of a man-of-war after the captain, often referred to in sailing ships as the "first luff."

FRIGATE: A three-masted ship of war carrying its guns (20–50) on two decks. Square-rigged.

FOOTROPE: A rope secured under a spar, bowsprit, or boom for the seamen to stand on while working sail.

FORE AND AFT: In line with the keel.

FORECASTLE (usually FO'C'SLE): The upper deck forward of the foremast.

FORECASTLE DECK: A partial deck over the bow above the main deck.

FOREFOOT: The heel of the stem where it connects with the keel.

FOREPEAK: That part of the vessel below decks at the stem.

FORESAIL: The lowest sail on the foremast.

FREEBOARD: The distance from the waterline to the main deck or gunwale.

FRESH BREEZE: Wind force 17 to 21 knots. FRESH GALE: 34 to 40 knots.

FRESHEN THE NIP: To shift a rope so as to take the wear in another place.

FULL AND BY: Sailing close hauled, with all sails full and as close to the wind as possible.

FULL SPREAD: With all sails set.

GAFF: The spar to which the head of a fore-and-aft sail is secured.

GAIN THE WIND: To get to windward of another sailing vessel.

GALE: Wind force 28 to 55 knots.

GALLEY: The ship's kitchen.

GANGWAY: An opening in the bulwarks or rail to give access to the ship.

GAUGE: A position toward or away from the wind or sun with reference to another vessel; hence, the WEATHER GAUGE was the favored position in a battle between sailing ships.

GENERAL QUARTERS: Battle stations.

GIMBALS: A pair of rings, one within the other, with axes at right angles supporting the compass, lamps, etc. in a horizontal plane in all weather.

GRAPE (or GRAPE-SHOT): A bag full of musket balls tied roughly in the shape of a cone and of the weight and diameter of a cannon ball of the caliber of gun used. These burst when fired and spread like shotgun shot and were especially deadly at close range.

GROG: Rum and water. In the sailing navy every seaman was issued a daily ration of grog.

GUN DECK: The deck on which the main battery of guns was mounted, between the main and the berth decks.

GUNSHOT: Within range; usually a mile to a mile and a half.

GUNWALE (often GUNNEL): The upper edge of a vessel or a boat's side.

HALF DECK: A partial deck above the lowest complete deck and below the main deck; in some ships called the ORLOP DECK.

HALYARDS: Lines used for hoisting gaffs, sails, signals, etc.

HANDSPIKE: A small wooden bar similar to a capstan or anchor bar used for prying.

HARD ALEE: To put the tiller all the way down.

HARD AWEATHER: To put the tiller all the way up.

HARD OVER: An order to put the wheel or tiller as far over to the side designated as possible.

HARD UP: An order to put the tiller as far to windward as possible.

HARD DOWN: Order to put the tiller as far to leeward as possible

HAUL: To pull. Also a change of wind clockwise.

HAULED UP: Changing course closer to the wind.

HAUL TO WINDWARD: To bring a vessel to the wind when sailing free; also called HAULING HER WIND.

HEAD: The ship's latrine.

HEAD ROOM: Floor to ceiling height below decks. In the *Constitution, Constellation,* and other frigates this was barely enough to permit a short man to stand erect on the gun deck. Fore and aft and below decks it was frequently five feet or less.

HEADWAY: Moving ahead.

HEAVE DOWN: To list a vessel over in order to inspect, repair, or clean a vessel's bottom. An operation short of careening. HEAVE IN: To haul in. HEAVE SHORT: To heave in on the anchor chain until the vessel is riding nearly over her anchor. HEAVE TAUT: To heave in until the line has a strain upon it. HEAVE THE LEAD: To take soundings. HEAVE THE LOG: To measure the speed of a ship by means of the chip log. HEAVE TO: To bring a vessel's head to the wind or sea and hold her there by use of the sails or engines.

HELM: The wheel or tiller by which the vessel is steered from the deck.

HULL DOWN: A vessel sighted at such a distance that only her spars and upper works are visible while her hull remains hidden beneath the horizon.

HURRICANE: Wind force of more than 65 knots.

IN IRONS: The situation of a vessel having missed stays and when she refuses to fall off from the wind.

INSHORE: Toward the shore.

IN STAYS: Headed into the wind with all sails shaking.

IN THE WIND: So close to the wind as to have the wind spilled from the sails.

IRISH PENNANT: An untidy loose end of a rope.

JIB: A headsail set on a stay forward of the foremast. JIB BOOM: A spar rigged out beyond the bowsprit and through the bowsprit cap.

JIGGER: The small mast set at the stern of a yawl-rigged vessel.

JUMP SHIP: To leave the ship without authority.

JURY MAST: A temporary mast rigged to the stump of a mast carried away in battle or heavy weather. JURY RIG: A makeshift rig. JURY RUDDER: A makeshift rudder.

KEDGE: A small anchor used for kedging, by alternately carrying ahead in the ship's boat, dropping, and hauling the ship up to it.

KEEL: The heavy timber or bar forming the backbone of the vessel and running her full length from the stem to the stern post at the bottom of the ship. KEELSON: The timber bolted on top of the keel and utilized for strengthening the ship's structure.

KETCH: A small sailing vessel rigged like a yawl but with the jigger mast forward of the rudder.

KNOT: A measure of speed, *not* distance; one nautical mile per hour.

LABOR: When a vessel works heavily in a seaway she is said to labor.

LADDER: Any stairway aboard ship.

LANDFALL: First sighting of land after a voyage beyond the horizon.

LAND HO: Hail from the lookout when land is sighted.

LANDLUBBER: Seaman's term for those who do not go to sea.

LANYARD: A rope or cord made fast to any article to secure it in place.

LATEEN: A triangular fore and aft sail secured to a yard hoisted obliquely to the mast; a rig peculiar to the Mediterranean.

LEAD LINE: A line secured to a lead weight used to measure the depth of the water. LEADSMAN: The seaman who stands in the chains and heaves the lead.

LEAGUE: A measurement of distance favored when wind ships were in general use and equalling three nautical miles by British and American measure.

LEE, LEEWARD: Away from the wind. LEE SHORE: The land to leeward of the vessel.

LIE TO: Dead in the water; a vessel not at anchor but with no way on.

LIGHT AIRS: A force of wind 1 to 3 knots.

LIGHT BREEZE: Force 4 to 6 knots.

LOG: The record of a ship's activities and the weather. CHIP LOG: An instrument for measuring the vessel's speed.

MAIN DECK: The highest deck extending from stem to stern; in old ships the highest covered deck.

MARLINESPIKE: A pointed iron instrument used in working with rope or wire.

MAROON: To set a person ashore without means of returning.

MIZZEN: The third mast from forward of a vessel with more than two masts.

MODERATE BREEZE: Wind force 11 to 16 knots.

MODERATE GALE: Wind force 28 to 33 knots.

MOORING: Securing a ship to a dock or to a buoy, or anchoring with two anchors.

MUFFLED OARS: Oars silenced in pulling by wrapping with rags or canvas.

MUSTER: To assemble the crew. MUSTER ROLL: The crew's list.

NAUTICAL: Pertaining to ships or the sea. NAUTICAL MILE: 6,076 feet. (A statute, or land, mile is 5,280 feet.)

NAVIGATOR: The officer charged with the safe navigation of the vessel.

NEAP TIDE: A tide of minimum range, coming at the 1st and 3rd quarter of the moon.

NEPTUNE: God of the sea.

OFF-AND-ON: Standing toward the land and off again alternately, usually while waiting for a boat to come off or some other rendezvous.

OFFING: Seaward but still in sight of land.

OFFSHORE WIND: Wind blowing from the land.

OFF THE WIND: Sailing free.

OLD MAN: The captain.

ON SOUNDINGS: Within the 100-fathom curve.

ON THE BEAM: Same as abeam. ON THE BOW: Bearing of 0–45° from ahead. ON THE QUARTER: Bearing 135–180° from ahead (0–45° from astern).

ON THE WIND: Sailing close hauled.

ORLOP DECK: A lower or partial deck below the berth deck and on or above the protective deck on old vessels.

ORDINARY: The status of a man-of-war which is laid up at a navy yard and maintained with only such complement as is necessary to preserve her from deterioration. The current situation of the *Constitution* and the *Constellation*.

PAY: To fill the seams of a vessel with pitch.

PEAK HALYARDS: The lines hoisting the peak of a quadrilateral sail.

PIPE: The boatswain's whistle. PIPE TO: The boatswain's pipe call to an evolution. PIPE THE SIDE: To call the crew by pipe to man the gangway when an official enters or leaves the ship.

POLE MAST: A complete mast constructed from a single spar.

POOP: A partial deck at the stern over the main deck.

PORT: An opening in the ship's side, as a gun port; also the left-hand side of the vessel facing forward, in old ships usually called "larboard"; also a harbor, ship's destination or point of departure, or home; e.g., Port of New York, Port of London, etc.

PORT TACK: The tack on which the wind comes in over the port side.

PORTUGUESE MAN-OF-WAR; A jellyfish with a small, blue, sail-like projection above water and long, streaming tentacles beneath, often spreading as much as fifty feet, capable of giving a painful and sometimes near fatal sting, common in Florida and southern waters.

PRATIQUE: A limited quarantine; a permit by the port doctor for an incoming vessel, being clear of contagious disease, to have the liberty of the port.

PRIDE OF THE MORNING: A morning mist, often seen before a fine, bright day.

QUARTER: That portion of a vessel on either side of the stern and abaft the beam.

QUARTER BILL: A vessel's station bill listing the duties of the ship's crew in various given situations and emergencies.

RAKE: (1) The angle of a vessel's masts from the vertical; (2) to fire lengthwise of a target vessel's decks.

RANGE ALONGSIDE: To come close abeam of another vessel.

REACH: To sail with a beam wind.

REEF: (1) To reduce the area of a sail; (2) underwater ridge of rocks dangerous to navigation.

RIG: A general description of a vessel's upper works; to fit out aloft.

RIGGING: Ropes securing masts and sails.

ROUGH LOG: The ship's log as written up in pencil by the quartermaster and officer of the deck at the moment.

ROGUE'S YARN: Colored yarn woven in to identify rope.

RUDDER: A flat board or other structure fastened vertically astern by which the ship is steered.

RUNNING LIGHTS: Lights required by law carried by a vessel under way.

RUNNING RIGGING: That part of a ship's rigging which is movable, passing through blocks, etc., such as sheets, halyards, etc.

SAIL HO!: Lookout's hail to indicate a sail has been sighted.

SAILING FREE: Sailing other than close hauled, or into the wind.

SCHOONER: A fore-and-aft-rigged sailing vessel with two or more masts.

SCUPPER: An opening in the side of the ship to carry off water shipped in heavy weather.

SCUTTLE: (1) A small opening in a ship's deck leading to the deck below; (2) to sink a vessel by boring holes in her bottom or opening the sea cocks.

SCUTTLE BUTT: (1) In old ships a cask of fresh water lashed amidships or near the galley for the crew's use; (2) a shipboard rumor.

SEA ANCHOR: A drag thrown overboard and secured to keep a vessel's bow or stern to the wind.

SEA CHEST: A sailor's small trunk.

SEA COCK: A valve connected to the sea by which the vessel may be flooded.

SEA LAWYER: A seaman who is inclined to argue about his rights, especially against recognized authority.

SEA ROOM: Far enough from land to maneuver comfortably.

SECURE: (1) To make fast or safe; (2) to end a drill or exercise.

SET SAIL: Put to sea.

SHEET: The rope used to spread the clew of headsails and to control the boom.

SHIP: (1) A three-masted, square-rigged sailing vessel; (2) to enlist, to take on board. SHIP OF THE LINE: A man-of-war rating 74 or more guns.

SHIPSHAPE: Neat, seamanlike. SHIPSHAPE AND BRISTOL FASHION: In perfect order.

SLOOP: Single-masted sailing vessel with headsails carried on bowsprit and jib boom. SLOOP OF WAR: A three-masted vessel, square rigged, carrying 18 to 30 guns all on one deck.

SOUND: To measure the depth of the water with a lead.

SPEAK: To communicate with a vessel in sight.

SPLICE THE MAIN BRACE: To have a drink; officially to distribute an extra ration of grog to the crew in recognition of some duty well done or other occasion at the discretion of the commanding officer.

SPOON DRIFT: The spray and water driven from the top of the waves in a storm.

SPRING TIDE: A tide of maximum range coming at the new and full moons.

SQUALL: A sudden, violent gust of wind.

STANDING RIGGING: That part of a ship's rigging which is permanently secured and not movable.

STARBOARD: The right side of a vessel looking forward.

STARBOARD TACK: The tack on which the wind comes over the vessel's starboard side.

STATION BILL: The posted bill showing the stations of the crew at maneuvers and emergency drills.

STAYSAIL: A sail set upon a stay.

STEERAGE: The junior officers' quarters.

STEERAGE WAY: The slowest speed at which a vessel will steer.

STEM: The timber at the extreme forward part of a vessel, secured to the forward end of the keel and supporting the bow planks.

STERN: The after part of the ship.

STORM: Wind force 56–65 knots.

STORM CANVAS: Small, heavy sails used in heavy weather to replace the regular sails.

STRONG BREEZE: Wind force 22–27 knots.

STRONG GALE: 41–47 knots.

STUDDING SAILS (STUNS'LS): Light sails set beyond the outer leeches of the square sails in fair weather to take full advantage of the wind.

SUNDOWNER: A martinet; a crusty captain who insists on all hands being aboard by sundown unless otherwise excused.

SUN OVER THE FOREYARD: An expression used at first drink time; the time when the first grog ration was issued.

SUPERCARGO: A merchant ship's officer charged with the ship's business; a representative of the owners aboard—neither seaman nor landsman; not "fish, flesh, or good red herring."

SWALLOW THE ANCHOR: Go to sea.

TACK: (1) The lower forward corner of a fore-and-aft sail; (2) to sail close-hauled on the wind; (3) to change from one course to another by putting the helm down.

TAUNT: A vessel with lofty spars.

TAUT: With no slack; strict as to discipline.

THOLE PIN: Wooden or metal pins fitted into holes in the gunwales to serve as oarlocks.

TIDE: The rise and fall of the water level caused by the influence of the moon. TIDE RIP: Waves and eddies caused by the tide in shoal water; e.g., the current caused by a rising or falling tide at the narrow entrance to a bay or inlet

TILLER: A short piece of iron or wood fitting into the rudder head and by which the rudder is swung. TILLER ROPES: Ropes connecting the tiller to the helm.

TOMPION: A wooden plug placed in the muzzle of a gun to keep out the sea damp. Pronounced "tompkin."

TOP: The platform at the top of a mast, primarily to assist in repairing and securing the topmasts, but in battle serving as platforms for the marines or riflemen.

TOP HAMPER: The spars and rigging above decks.

TRADES: The practically steady winds found in the tropics and blowing toward the equator—NE in the Northern Hemisphere and SE in the Southern.

TRANSOM: Athwartships timbers bolted to the sternpost.

TUMBLE HOME: The amount the sides of a vessel come in from the perpendicular.

TURN TURTLE: Capsize.

UNDERTOW: A current offshore in surf.

UNDER WAY: Said of a vessel when not at anchor, made fast to the shore, or aground.

UNMOOR: To heave up one anchor and leave the other down so as to be ready to sail at a moment's notice.

UPPER WORKS: The parts of a vessel above the main deck.

VEER: To slack off and allow to run out; said of a change of direction of wind.

WAIST: The portion of the deck between the forecastle and the quarterdeck; amidships.

WAKE: A vessel's track in the water aft.

WARDROOM: Commissioned officers' quarters in a man-of-war.

WARP: To haul ahead by a line or an anchor.

WEAR: To change from one tack to another by putting the helm up.

WEATHER: To windward; the side from which the wind blows.

WEIGH: To lift the anchor off the bottom. This is a perennial source of argument—whether a vessel is said to be "under way" or "under weigh," i.e., moving ahead with steerage way or free of the bottom. Too many admirals have argued the semantic point for me to attempt to settle it here!

WESTERLIES: The prevailing winds of the temperate zone, especially steady in the Southern Hemisphere.

WHERE AWAY? A call in answer to a lookout's report of an object sighted.

WHITE SQUALL: A sudden squall accompanied by white spoondrift; especially impressive by moonlight.

WHOLE GALE: Force 48–55 knots.

WINDJAMMER: A sailing ship.

WINDWARD: Toward the wind.

WING AND WING: Sailing with booms on opposite sides.

WORK TO WINDWARD: Making up against the wind.

YARD: Horizontal spar to which square sails are set—in a square-rigged vessel.

YAW: To steer wildly or out of the line of the course, as with a heavy quartering sea which forces the stern to swing.

YAWL: A rig similar to a sloop rig but with a small fore-and-aft sail set on a short jigger mast aft.

BIBLIOGRAPHY

Albion, Robert G. *Forests and Sea Power; The Timber Problem of the Royal Navy, 1652–1862*. Cambridge, Mass.: Harvard University Press, 1926.

Allen, Gardner W. *A Naval History of the American Revolution*. 2 vols. Boston: Houghton Mifflin Company, 1913.

———. *Our Naval War with France*. Boston: Houghton Mifflin Company, 1909.

———. *Our Navy and the Barbary Corsairs*. Boston: Houghton Mifflin Company, 1905.

Almanac of Naval Facts. Annapolis: U.S. Naval Institute, 1964.

Ammen, Daniel. *The Old Navy and the New*. Philadelphia: 1891.

Barnes, James. *Naval Actions of the War of 1812*. New York: 1896.

Bluejackets' Manual. 10th ed. Annapolis: U.S. Naval Institute, 1964.

Brenton, E. P. *Naval History of Great Britain, 1783–1836*. 2 vols. London: 1837.

Brighton, J. G. *Memoirs of Admiral Broke*. London: 1866.

Bryant, Samuel W. *The Sea and the States*. New York: Thomas Y. Crowell Company, 1947.

Channing, Edward. *History of the United States*. 7 vols. New York: The Macmillan Company, 1905–25.

Chappelle, Howard I. *The History of the American Sailing Navy*. New York: W. W. Norton & Company, Inc., 1949.

———. *The History of American Sailing Ships*. New York: W. W. Norton & Company, Inc., 1935.

Cooper, James Fenimore. *History of the Navy of the United States of America.* Abridged in one volume, from the Octavo edition—continued to 1865. New York: 1856.

————. *Lives of Distinguished Naval Officers.* Philadelphia: 1846.

Durant, John and Alice. *Pictorial History of American Ships.* New York: A. S. Barnes & Co., Inc., 1953.

Emmons, G. E. *A Statistical History of the United States Navy.* Washington, D.C.: 1853.

Fiske, John. *The Critical Period in American History, 1783–1789.* Boston: 1898.

Footner, Hulbert. *Sailor of Fortune, the Life and Adventures of Commodore Barney USN.* New York: Harper and Brothers, 1940.

Forester, C. S. *The Age of Fighting Sail; The Story of the Naval War of 1812.* Garden City, N.Y.: Doubleday & Company, Inc., 1956.

French, Allen. *The First Year of the American Revolution.* Boston: Houghton Mifflin Company, 1934.

Grant, Bruce. *Isaac Hull, Captain of Old Ironsides; The Life and Fighting Times of Isaac Hull, and the U.S. Frigate Constitution.* New York: Pellegrini & Cudahy, 1947.

Graviere, J. de la. *Guerres maritimes.* 2 vols. Paris: 1881.

Harris, Thomas. *Life and Services of Commodore William Bainbridge USN.* Philadelphia: 1837.

Hollis, Ira N. *The Frigate Constitution.* Boston: 1900.

Ingersoll, Charles J. *Historical Sketch of the Second War Between the United States of America and Great Britain.* 2 vols. Philadelphia: 1845–49.

Irving, Washington. *A Biography of James Lawrence.* Philadelphia: 1813.

James, William. *The Naval History of Great Britain from the Declaration of War with France in 1793 to the Ascension of George IV.* 6 vols. London: 1837.

————. *A Full and Correct Account of the Chief Naval Occurrences of the Late War Between Great Britain and the United States of America.* London: 1817.

Jameson, John Franklin, ed. *Privateering and Piracy in the Colonial Period.* New York: The Macmillan Company, 1923.

Jones, C. C., Jr. *Life of Commodore Josiah P. Tatnall.* Savannah, Ga.: 1878.

Knight, Austin M. *Modern Seamanship.* 10th ed. New York: D. Van Nostrand Co., Inc., 1941.

Knox, Dudley W. *A History of the United States Navy.* New York: G. P. Putnam's Sons, 1936.

————, ed. *Naval Documents Related to the United States Wars with the Barbary Powers.* 7 vols. Washington, D.C.: Government Printing Office, 1939–45.

————. *Naval Documents Related to the Quasi-War with France.* 7 vols. Washington, D.C.: Government Printing Office, 1935–38.

Lane, Carl D. *The Boatman's Manual.* New York: W. W. Norton & Company, Inc., 1942.

Lane-Poole, Stanley. *The Barbary Corsairs.* New York: 1890.

Langer, William L., ed. *An Encyclopedia of World History.* Boston: Houghton Mifflin Company, 1948.

Lewis, Charles Lee. *The Romantic Decatur.* Philadelphia: University of Pennsylvania Press, 1937.

Lossing, Benson J. *Field Book of the Revolution.* 2 vols. New York: 1855.

————. *Field Book of the War of 1812.* New York: 1868.

Lovette, Leland P. *Naval Customs, Traditions and Usage.* Annapolis: U.S. Naval Institute, 1939.

Mackenzie, A. S. *Life of Commodore Oliver Hazard Perry.* 2 vols. New York: 1841.

————. *Life of Stephen Decatur.* Boston: 1846.

Maclay, Edgar Stanton. *A History of American Privateers.* New York: Daniel Appleton & Company, 1902.

————. *A History of the United States Navy from 1775 to 1898.* 2 vols. New York: Daniel Appleton & Company, 1902.

McMaster, John Bach. *A History of the People of the United States, from Revolution to Civil War.* 8 vols. New York: 1883.

Mahan, Alfred T. *The Influence of Sea Power upon History.* Boston: 1890.

————. *The Influence of Sea Power on the Wars of the French Revolution and Empire.* Boston: Little, Brown and Company, 1901.

————. *Sea Power in Its Relation to the War of 1812.* 2 vols. Boston: Little, Brown and Company, 1905.

Masefield, John. *Sea Life in Nelson's Time.* New York: The Macmillan Company, 1925.

Massachusetts Writers' Program. *Boston Looks Seaward: The Story of the Port, 1630–1940.* American Guide Series. Boston: 1941.

Miller, John C. *Crisis in Freedom.* Boston: Little, Brown and Company, 1951.

Morison, Samuel Eliot. *The Maritime History of Massachusetts, 1783–1860.* Boston: Houghton Mifflin Company, 1941.

Morison, S. E., and Commager, H. S. *The Growth of the American Republic.* 2 vols. 3rd ed. New York: Oxford University Press, Inc., 1942.

Morris, Charles. *Autobiography of Commodore Morris.* Annapolis: U.S. Naval Institute, 1880.

Morris, Richard B., ed. *Encyclopedia of American History.* New York: Harper and Brothers, 1953.

Nesser, Robert W. *Statistical and Chronological History of the United States Navy, 1775–1907.* New York: The Macmillan Company, 1909.

Paullin, C. O. *Commodore John Rodgers.* Cleveland: Arthur H. Clark Company, 1910.

———. *The Navy of the American Revolution.* Cleveland: Burrows Bros. Company, 1906.

Potter, E. B., and Fredland, J. R., eds. *The United States and World Sea Power.* Englewood Cliffs, N.J.: Prentice-Hall, Inc., 1955.

———, and Nimitz, C. W., eds. *Sea Power, A Naval History.* Englewood Cliffs, N.J.: Prentice-Hall, Inc. 1960.

Prentiss, Charles. *Life of the Late Gen. William Eaton.* Brookfield: 1813.

Roosevelt, Theodore. *The Naval War of 1812.* 2 vols. 7th ed. New York: 1898.

Routh, E. M. G. *Tangier: England's Lost Atlantic Outpost, 1661–1684.* London: 1912.

Rowe, William Hutchinson. *The Maritime History of Maine.* New York: W. W. Norton & Company, Inc., 1948.

Sabine, Lorenzo. *Life of Edward Preble.* Boston: 1847.

Sawyer, Edmund O., ed. *Our Sea Saga: The Wood Wind Ships.* San Francisco: privately printed, 1929.

Smith, Moses. *Naval Scenes of the Last War: Three Years on Board the Frigate Constitution, and The Adams; Including the Capture of The Guerriere, Etc.* Boston: 1846.

Spears, John R. *The History of Our Navy—1775–1898.* 5 vols. New York: 1899.

Sprout, Harold and Margaret. *The Rise of American Naval Power.* Princeton: Princeton University Press, 1939.

Statham, E. P. *Privateers and Privateering.* London: 1910.

Stevens, William O., and Wescott, Allen. *A History of Sea Power.* Garden City, N.Y.: Doubleday, Doran & Company, 1942.

Thomas, R. *The Glory of America; Comprising Memoirs of the Lives and Glorious Exploits of Some of the Distinguished Officers Engaged in the Late War with Great Britain.* New York: 1834.

Waldo, Samuel Putnam. *Biographical Sketches of Distinguished American Naval Heroes, &c, &c.* Hartford: 1823.

Who Was Who in America. Chicago: The A. N. Marquis Co., 1942.

Wilson, J. G., and Fiske, John, eds. *Appleton's Cyclopaedia of American Biography.* 6 vols. New York: 1900.

Wilson, Thomas. *The Biography of the Principal Military and Naval Heroes.* 2 vols. New York: 1817.

Winsor, Justin, ed. *The Memorial History of Boston.* 4 vols. Boston: 1881.

INDEX

Acasta, H.M.S., 238, 239, 244
Adams, John, 32, 74
Adams, U.S.S., 94, 96, 100, 107
Adeline (American merchant ship), 218
Adiona (British merchant ship), 218
Adriana (American merchant ship), 46
Adventure (British merchant ship), 19
Aeolus, H.M.S., 208–214
Africa, H.M.S., 208–214
Alexander the Great, 110
Algeciras, Spain, 109
Algiers, 3–4, 5, 8–9, 29–30, 75–84, 95, 115–116, 122, 164, 168, 248
Alicante, Spain, 84
Allen, William Henry, 173
Alliance (Continental frigate), 19
Alwyn, John, 226, 235
Amazon, H.M.S., 117, 121
Amelia (Hamburg packet ship), 56–57
American Revolution, 2, 12, 19–20, 98, 99, 112, 171, 194
Amory, William, 68, 71, 73
Anguilla Island, West Indies, 51, 52
Annapolis, Md., 191, 193–195, 204–205
   Naval Academy at, 183, 255, 257, 258
Antigua Island, West Indies, 51
Arab, H.M.S., 238
Argus, U.S.S., 111–112, 113, 114, 138, 139, 140–141, 152, 153, 156, 159, 161, 169, 177

armament, warship, 4–7
   American improvements in, 223
   of *Constitution*, 16–19, 33, 36, 187, 221
   for Tripoli action, 141
Arnold, Benedict, 20
Astor, John Jacob, 126
Avenger, H.M.S., 218

Badger, O. C., 258
Bahia, Brazil, 232–233, 236
Bainbridge, Joseph, 126, 145
Bainbridge, William, 52, 78–84, 92, 93, 104–105, 112, 117–123, 124, 125, 153, 159, 164, 166, 206, 216, 230–236, 237, 248
Balboa, Panama Canal Zone, 186
Balearic Islands, 248
Ballard, Lieutenant, 245
Ballard's Point, England, 258
Baltimore, Md., 8, 10, 32, 38
Baltimore, U.S.S., 46–49, 52, 61
Barbados Island, West Indies, 52
Barbary corsairs, 3–4, 9, 26, 75, 87, 95, 103–107, 118–120, 166
Barbary States, 3–4, 5, 8–9, 26, 29–30, 74–97, 100, 103–168, 248–249
   policy of tribute to, 4, 30, 76–79, 83, 148, 153, 164, 166–167
Bar Harbor, Maine, 186
Barlow, Joel, 194–195, 201
Barnegat, N.J., 207, 208

Barney, Joshua, 20
Barron, James, 93, 96, 150, 160–161, 165, 166, 170, 171–173, 180
Barron, Samuel, 93, 150–151, 152, 159–166
Barry, John, 19, 21, 38, 47, 50, 52, 56, 60, 94, 114
Barrymore, Midshipman, 180
Bastard, John, 208
Beale, Richard C., 22, 43–44
Beecher (carver of Jackson figure-head), 253, 255
Bellingham, Wash., 186
Belvidera, H.M.S., 204, 205, 208–214, 252
Bentley, Sam, 12
Berkeley, Vice-Admiral, 172
Bermuda, 239
Bingham, Arthur Batt, 193
Binney, Colonel, 217
Biscay, Bay of, 56, 65
Black Sea, 82
Bladensburg, Md., 180
Blake, Joshua, 140, 144
Bonhomme Richard (Continental frig-ate), 12, 20–21, 247
Bonne Citoyenne, H.M.S., 232–233
Boss, Edward, 55
Boston, Mass., 47, 53–54, 93–94, 177–178, 182, 191, 214–217, 219, 230, 236–239, 250–255, 257
construction and launching of *Con-stitution* at, 1, 7–8, 10–18, 22–23, 32–37, 85
Boston, U.S.S., 96
Boston Advertiser, 251
Boston Navy Yard, Charlestown, 187, 188, 230, 237, 246, 248, 249, 252–255, 259
Bowen, Richard, 105
Brazil, 92, 231, 232–233, 236, 256
Brenton, Captain, 216
Broaders, Mrs., 22
Broke, Philip, Sir, 208
Brooklyn Navy Yard, *see* New York Navy Yard
Burma, 257

Burr, Aaron, 180
Bush, William, 226
Byron, George Gordon, Lord, 249
Byron, Richard, 204, 208, 213

Cabo Frio, Brazil, 231, 232
Cadiz, Spain, 100, 103, 109–111
Caldwell, James, 140, 151
Campbell, Hugh, 52, 96, 100, 160, 169, 174–175
Canada, 203, 204, 217–218
Canton, China, 257
Cape Cod, Mass., 214, 239
Cape Verde Islands, 243–245, 257
Cap François, 56, 59, 63, 72, 162
Caribbean Sea, *see* West Indies
Carmick, Daniel, 68, 71, 73
Carnatic, H.M.S., 48–49
Carrol, Lieutenant, 157
Carthaginians, 110
Castle Island, Boston Harbor, 18, 35, 36
Catalano, Salvatore, 127, 130
Cathcart, James, 75, 77, 95
Cayenne, French Guiana, 56, 57
Celia (American merchant ship), 104–105
Chads, Henry D., 235, 257
Champlain, Lake, 52, 126
Charles River, 1, 14, 254
Charleston, S.C., 27, 28, 214
Charlestown, Mass., *see* Boston Navy Yard
Chauncey, Isaac, 96, 152
Cherbourg, France, 194, 196–197, 201
Chesapeake, U.S.S., 61, 96, 126, 152, 170, 171–174, 175, 176, 193
Chesapeake Bay, 178, 258
China, 257
Civil War, 183, 184, 257–258
Claghorne, George, 8, 11, 13
Clark, Marine Lieutenant, 23
Clark, Robert, 155
Claxton, Alexander, 256
Clinton, George, 29
Collier, George, Sir, 238–239, 244, 245, 248

Collins, Isaac, 55
Colocotroni, 250
Columbus, Christopher, 110
commerce, see trade
Congress, United States, 53, 74–75, 150, 163, 168, 175, 176, 202, 236, 252
Navy established by, 3–5, 6, 8–9, 31–32
War of 1812 declaration by, 204–205
Congress, U.S.S., 151, 160, 162, 168
Constantinople, Turkey, 79, 82–84
Constellation, U.S.S., 10, 21, 30, 32, 38, 51, 53, 60, 96, 114, 159, 160, 162, 168, 176, 236, 247, 270
Constitution, U.S.S.:
armament of, 16–19, 33, 36, 187, 221
commanders of, 8, 52, 54–55, 93, 94, 97–98, 114, 160, 169, 177, 230–231, 236, 248–249, 256, 258
construction of, 4–5, 8, 10–11, 30, 32
dimensions of, 10–11, 15–16
figureheads of, 8, 182, 252–255
fire boat volunteers from, 155
launching of, 11–15, 85
manning of, 19–25, 33–34, 221, 231, 232, 237, 256
repairs for, 175, 176–179, 183, 185, 201–202, 207, 247, 252
round-the-world cruise of, 256–257
today's mooring place of, 187, 188, 246, 259
as a training ship, 183, 258, 259
trial voyages of, 33–40
in Tripoli battles, 86, 146–147, 154
Constitution Wharf, Boston, 8
Cooper, James Fenimore, 60–61
Cordis, John Blake, 22
corsairs, see Barbary corsairs
Cox, George, 160
Crescent (Algerine frigate), 76–77
crews, 19, 22–25, 34
British impressment of, 9, 30, 47–50, 172–174, 189, 190, 192, 203–204
discipline for, 174–175, 179, 191, 231, 232
enlistment periods of, 170, 175

crews (cont.)
recruiting of, 22–23, 191, 207, 237
training of, 39–41, 207, 248
Croyable (French privateer), 38, 122
Culebra Passage, 51
Curtis, Roger, Sir, 198–200
Cyane, H.M.S., 181, 240–245, 248

Dacres, James Richard, 208, 209–210, 222, 226, 227–229, 240
Dale, Richard, 20–21, 38, 93, 95–96, 104
Danielson, Midshipman, 180
Davis, Charles, 198–200
Deal, England, 197
Deane, Silas, 20
Deane (Continental frigate), 19
Decatur, James, 143, 147
Decatur, Stephen, Jr., 52, 60, 87, 111, 114, 122, 123–136, 139, 141, 142–144, 154, 155, 160, 168, 180, 199, 206, 248
Decatur, Stephen, Sr., 38, 51
Decatur (American privateer), 219
Delaware, U.S.S., 38, 51
Denmark, 121, 166
Dent, John H., 138, 139, 161
Derna, Tripoli, 163
Deux Amis (French privateer), 114
Dewey, Sam, 254–255
Diane (French privateer), 114
Diggio (Deguyo), 192
Diligence, U.S.S., 52
Doane, Nancy, 111
Dolphin (Continental cutter), 19
Dominica, West Indies, 50, 51
Donnegal, H.M.S., 102, 103
"Don't give up the ship!" 126
Dorsey, Midshipman, 151
Douglas, George, 240, 242
Downes, Isaac W., 155
Dragon (British merchant ship), 19
Drake Passage, 51
duels, 179–180

Eagle, U.S.S., 52
East Indies, 99
Eaton, William, 78, 80, 163

Egg Harbor, N.J., 38
Egypt, 249
Elizabeth, H.M.S., 240
Elliot (British merchant ship), 19
Elliott, Jesse, 252–256
Embargo Act, 176
England, see Great Britain
English Channel, 194, 196, 201, 258
Enterprise, U.S.S., 93, 95–96, 110, 114,
    121–122, 124, 126, 127, 138, 139,
    141, 161, 247
Essex, U.S.S., 93, 99–100, 160, 165, 168,
    169, 176, 177, 231, 247
Evans, Samuel, 161
Exchange Coffee House, Boston, 216
Experiment, U.S.S., 114

Falcon, Gordon Thomas, 240, 242
Falmouth, Maine, 99
Fauchet, Joseph, 29
Fernando de Noronha, Brazil, 231
Fitzgerald, John F., 185
food, navy, 100
Fox, Josiah, 8
France:
    American ships harassed by, 3, 9–10,
        30–31
    American trade banned with, 176,
        189
    and the Barbary states, 79, 82, 84,
        148, 151, 152–153
    Constitution's voyages to, 194–197,
        201, 255, 258
    and Great Britain, war between, 27–
        31, 37–38, 48, 69, 79, 101, 194, 196
    and Hispaniola, 58–59, 66
    naval strength of, 6, 33
    quasi-war with, 26, 32–33, 41–53, 56–
        74, 82, 114, 122, 147, 161–162, 171
    and Turkey, war between, 79, 82
Franklin, Benjamin, 20
Franklin, U.S.S., 168
French Guiana, 56, 57
French Revolution, 3, 27, 58–59
frigates, 5–6, 7
Fundy, Bay of, 217, 262

Gallatin, Albert, 206
Ganges, U.S.S., 38, 51
Garts (passenger on Niger), 45
Gates, Horatio, 20
General Greene, U.S.S., 51
General Monk, H.M.S., 20
Genêt, Edmond Charles, 27–29
George Washington, U.S.S., 52, 78–84,
    122
Ghent, Treaty of, 243
Gibraltar, 82, 95, 100, 104, 106, 107,
    108–109, 111, 113–116, 168, 170,
    174, 240, 241, 248–249
Golconda (American merchant ship),
    177
Good Hope, Cape of, 231, 257
Governor Jay, U.S.S., 51
Granary Building, Boston, 8
Grant, Bruce, 18
Gray, William, 217
Grayhound, H.M.S., 48
Great Britain, 59, 79, 102–103, 114,
    117, 148, 191–201, 257, 258
    and American trade, 3, 9, 30–31, 171,
        176, 189–190, 203
    attitude toward Americans of, 3, 47–
        50, 61–65, 108–109, 111–112, 136,
        194
    and France, war between, 27–31, 37–
        38, 48, 69, 79, 101, 194, 196
    impressment of sailors by, 9, 30, 47–
        50, 172–174, 189, 190, 192, 203–204
    naval strength of, 6, 7, 33, 171
    and War of 1812, 203–245
Great Lakes, 203
Greece, 249–250
Greeks, ancient, 110
Guadeloupe, West Indies, 50, 52, 56, 60
Guerriere, H.M.S., 90–91, 191–193, 202,
    208–214, 216, 219–229, 236, 240, 247
Gulliver, Louis J., 186
gunboats:
    and Jeffersonian policy, 168–169,
        175, 176
    for Tripoli battle, 139, 141–146
guns, see armament, warship

Haiti, 56–59
Halifax, Nova Scotia, 208, 217, 218
Hamet Karamanli, 163–164
Hamilcar, 110
Hamilton, Alexander, 28, 180
Hamilton, Paul, 176, 178, 179, 180, 205–206
Hamilton, Philip, 180
Hamilton, Robert W., 55
Hampton Roads, 46, 172, 174, 177, 178, 189, 195, 256
Hannibal, 110
Hanover, Mass., 8
Haraden, Nathaniel ("Jumping Billy"), 55, 202, 207
Harris, James, 155
Harrison, William, 155
Hartt, Edmund, 8
Hartt's Naval Yard, Boston, 8
Hassan Bashaw (Algerine brig), 76
Havana, Cuba, 46, 49
Havanna, H.M.S., 198–200
Havre de Grace, Md., 161, 258
Heerman, Dr., 127
Henley, Midshipman, 145
Hispaniola, 58
Hoffman, Lieutenant, 227, 242, 244
Holland, 6, 27, 51, 52, 194, 197
Holland, Thomas, 198–200
Hollis, Ira N., 238
Holmes, Oliver Wendell, 91, 183, 250–251
Horn, Cape, 231, 256, 257
Hornet, U.S.S., 161, 169, 231, 232–233, 247
Howe, Julia Ward, 249
Howe, Samuel Gridley, 249–250
Hull, Isaac, 18, 21, 22, 52, 55, 63–65, 67–73, 90, 93, 94, 104, 110, 114, 138, 139, 140–141, 152, 161, 177–180, 189, 191, 192, 194–202, 205–231, 252, 262–263
Humphreys, Captain, 173
Humphreys, Joshua, 7

Ibrahim Lubarez, 104–105

impressment, 9, 30, 47–50, 172–174, 189, 190, 192, 203–204
Independence, Fort, 35
Independence, U.S.S., 239
Indian Ocean, 99
Insurgente (French frigate), 53, 56, 122
Intrepid, U.S.S., 114, 125–135, 154–159
Ireland, 203
isolation policy, 168–169, 175–176
Israel, Joseph, 155
Italy, 121–123, 125–126, 137–139, 160, 164, 168

Jackson, Andrew, 182, 252–255
Jackson, Henry, 8
James, Reuben, 87, 144
Java, H.M.S., 92, 233–236, 237, 257
Jay, John, 31
Jefferson, Thomas, 74, 77–78, 168, 174, 175–176, 206
Jersey (British prison ship), 20
John Adams, U.S.S., 96, 107, 152, 159, 162, 168, 176
Jones, Jacob, 52, 248–249
Jones, John Paul, 12, 52, 98
Junon, H.M.S., 237

kedging, 212–213
Keith, William, 155
Kennedy, John F., 185
Kerr, Captain, 244
King George (British merchant ship), 19
Knox, Henry, 5, 7
Kosciusko, Thaddeus, 201

Lafayette, Marquis de, 201
Lambert, Henry, 234–235
Lawrence, James, 126, 231, 232
Leander, H.M.S., 244
Lear, Tobias, 100, 103, 115–116, 164–166
Lee, Arthur, 20
Lee, Benjamin, 22
Leeward Islands, 50, 51, 52

Leghorn, Italy, 113, 168
Le Havre, France, 255, 258
Lelah Eisha (Algerine schooner), 76
Leopard, H.M.S., 61, 172–174, 193
Levant, H.M.S., 181, 240–245, 248
Lexington (Continental frigate), 19, 20
Lincoln (Boston shipowner), 253, 255
Lisbon, Portugal, 239–240, 259
Little Belt, H.M.S., 193–194
Lively (British merchant ship), 19
Livingston, Edward, 255
Livingston, Robert R., 96
London, England, 198, 199
Long Island, 19–20
Lord Nelson (British merchant ship), 239
Loring, Captain, 48–49
Louisa Bridger (British privateer), 114
Louis XVI, King of France, 27
Lynnhaven Bay, 172

Macao, 257
McCormick, Hugh, 155
Macdonough, Thomas, 52, 126, 143, 206, 249
McHenry, James, 18
McNamara, Robert S., 246
McNiell, Daniel, 52, 96
Madeira Islands, 181, 239, 240
Madison, James, 29, 176, 205, 206
Maidstone, H.M.S., 48, 103
Maimounia (Moorish cruiser), 103–104
Malay Peninsula, 257
Malta, 113, 116, 121, 124, 138, 140, 152, 159, 165, 168
Manila, Philippines, 257
Marblehead, Mass., 238
marines, 21, 23, 24, 75
  official establishment of Marine Corps, 23
  Tripoli action by, 163
Martinique, West Indies, 50
Massachusetts (*see also* Boston), 2, 18, 22, 99, 239
Mastico (Tripolitan ketch), 124–125

Masy (American merchant ship), 45
Mediterranean Sea, 3–4, 26, 29–30, 74–97, 103–175, 248–250, 256, 257
  naval forces in, 160–161
  peace settlement in, 164–168
Melampus, H.M.S., 172
merchantmen, *see* trade
Merrimack, U.S.S., 52, 53
Meshouda (Tripolitan cruiser), 104
Messina, Italy, 168
midshipmen, 24, 112, 179–180, 189
Minorca Island, 248
Mirboka (Barbary corsair), 104–107
Montezuma, U.S.S., 51
Morgan, Charles M., 179, 180
Morgan, John T., 8
Morocco, 3–4, 75, 103–107, 108
Morris, Charles, 127–128, 198–199, 201, 207, 212, 216, 225, 226–227
Morris, Richard V., 96–97, 107, 108, 162
Moselle, H.M.S., 189
Murad Rais, 95
Murray, Alexander, 56, 96

Nantucket, Mass., 204, 208, 214
Naples, Italy, 138–139, 168
Napoleon Bonaparte, 79, 84, 194, 201
nautical terms, glossary of, 260–275
Nautilus, U.S.S., 114, 137, 141, 155, 156–157, 161, 169
  as British captive, 209–214
Naval Academy, United States, 183, 184, 255, 257, 258
Naval History (Cooper), 61
navies:
  in American Revolution, 2–3
  classes of vessels in, 5–7
  European, 6–7, 33, 169
Navy, British:
  deserters from, 49–50, 172, 200
  strength of, 6, 7, 33, 171
Navy, Continental, 2–3, 19–20, 98
Navy, French, strength of, 6, 33
Navy, United States:
  British attitudes toward, 47–50, 61

Navy, United States (*cont.*)
establishment of, 4–5, 6–9, 26–27, 31–32
"father of," 98–99
Jeffersonian policy for, 168–169, 175–176, 206
size of, 50–51, 74–75
Navy Department, United States, 5, 7, 17, 21, 24, 32, 45–46, 54, 176, 202
Nelson, Horatio, Lord, 136
Netherlands, *see* Holland
Newcastle, H.M.S., 238–239, 244
New England, 2, 22–23, 215, 253, 255
Newfoundland, 203, 217–218
New Jersey, 207, 208
Newport, R.I., 40, 41, 184, 191, 258
New York, N.Y., 7, 186, 191, 205–206, 208, 214, 216, 219, 255, 259
New York, U.S.S., 52, 96, 107
New York Navy Yard, Brooklyn, 175–177, 180, 257, 258, 259
Nicholson, Samuel, Jr., 46
Nicholson, Samuel, Sr., 8, 11–12, 18, 19, 21–22, 23, 25, 34–39, 42–47, 50, 53–54, 55, 94, 97
Niger (British privateer), 44–46
Nissen, Nicholas, 121, 166
Nonintercourse Act, 176, 177, 189
Nootka Sound, 127
Norfolk, Va., 8, 45–46, 56, 174, 236, 256
Norfolk, U.S.S., 52
North Africa, *see* Barbary States
North Carolina, 42
Nova Scotia, 203, 217–218

O'Bannon, Presley N., 163
O'Brien, Richard, 4, 77, 78, 79–82, 84, 95
Oceana (Spanish ship), 190
officers, 19–25, 34
age of, 113, 114–115
duels by, 179–180
rank definitions, 260, 265, 266
Ohio River, 203
"Old Ironsides," nickname of, 52, 91, 223

"Old Ironsides" (James Fenimore Cooper), 60–61
"Old Ironsides" (Oliver Wendell Holmes), 91, 183, 251
Old Mill Prison, 20
Outer Banks, N.C., 42

Pacific Ocean, 231–232, 256–257
Panama Canal Zone, 186
Paris, France, 74, 201, 258
Paris, Treaty of (1783), 20
Patterson, Captain, 249–250
Peace Establishment Act, 74–75
Pechell, Samuel John, 192
Penner, Peter, 155
Percival, John ("Mad Jack"), 256
Petit-Thouars, George du, 44–45
Philadelphia, Pa., 7, 10, 14, 27, 32, 38, 46, 76, 97
Philadelphia, U.S.S., 86, 93, 95, 104–106, 112, 117–121, 122–123, 125–136, 150, 154, 160, 166, 199, 248, 261
Phillips, Captain, 46–50
Phoebe, H.M.S., 231
Phoenicians, 109
Pickering, U.S.S., 52, 99
Pictou, H.M.S., 237
Pigot (British schooner), 19
Pinckney, C. C., 31
Pinckney, U.S.S., 51
Pique, H.M.S., 237
piracy (*see also* Barbary corsairs), 3–4, 109
Porter, David, 206, 231–232
Portland, Maine, 99
Porto Plata, Santo Domingo, 59, 65–73
Porto Praya, Cape Verde Islands, 243, 245
Portsmouth, Dominica, 50
Portsmouth, England, 198–201, 258
Portsmouth, N.H., 8, 15, 76, 183, 185, 257, 259, 262
Portsmouth, U.S.S., 52
Portsmouth Gazette, 76–77
Portugal, 6–7, 56, 233, 239–240, 244, 245

Preble, Edward, 21–22, 52, 97–126, 134–142, 147, 150–160, 161
President, U.S.S., 93, 96, 159, 160, 166, 176, 177, 189, 191, 192–193, 204, 238
Prince Edward Island, 203
Prince Rupert's Bay, 50, 51, 52, 60
Princeton, Battle of, 20
prisoners:
   in Barbary States, 4, 77, 83–84, 120, 121, 122, 124, 136–137, 153, 164, 166
   of the French, 3, 31, 122
privateers (*see also* Barbary corsairs), 3–4, 28, 44, 60, 65–73, 137–138, 189
prize money, distribution of, 57
Puerto Rico, 51
Punic War, 110
Putnam's Monthly, 60

Quebec, 203, 217
Queen, H.M.S., 48

Raleigh (Continental warship), 19
Read, George C., 156, 205, 227–228
Redick, Midshipman, 180
Republicans, 253
Retaliation, U.S.S., 122
Revanche du Cerf (French privateer), 189
Revere, Paul, 8
Richmond, U.S.S., 52
Ridgely, Midshipman, 157
Rigaud, André, 59
Rio de Janeiro, Brazil, 256
Robinson, Thomas, 161
Rodgers, John, 52, 96, 97, 106, 107, 108, 151, 160, 161–162, 164–169, 177, 179, 191, 192–193, 204, 205, 207–208, 210, 216, 249
Rodgers, Richard, 179, 180
Romans, 110, 148
Roosevelt, Theodore, 246
Rose, Martin, 45
Rose (American merchant ship), 177
Roseau, Dominica, 50
Russell, Charles C., 21, 22
Russell, Jonathan, 194, 197
Ryswick, Treaty of, 58

sailors, *see* crews
Saint Bartholomew Island, West Indies, 51–52
Saint Eustatius Island, West Indies, 52
Saint Kitts Island, West Indies, 51
Saint Martin Island, West Indies, 51
Salem, Mass., 99
Sally (American privateer), 68–73
Salvador, Brazil, *see* Bahia
Sandwich (French privateer), 65–73
Sandy Hook, N.J., 179, 190, 192, 207
Sanford, Thomas, 68–69
Santo Domingo, 56–73, 162
São Fernhão do Noronha, Brazil, 231
Sardinia, 116–117
Sawyer, Vice-Admiral, 208
Scammell, U.S.S., 52
Schuyler, Midshipman, 180
Scipio, 110
Scourge, U.S.S., 138, 139, 141
Serapis, H.M.S., 12, 21
Sever, James, 15, 20, 21
Severn River, 257
Shakespeare, William, 203
Shannon, H.M.S., 126, 208–214
shipboard definitions, glossary of, 260–275
shipbuilders, 2, 7–8, 10–11, 14, 30
ships:
   harassment of, 2–4, 9, 30–31
   as payment to Algiers, 76–77
   war, types of, 5–7
ships of the line, 5, 6–7, 54
Shubrick, John, 225, 243
Sicily, 139
Simms, James, 155
Simpson, James, 104
Singapore, 257
Siren, U.S.S., 113, 114, 125, 126–131, 134, 137, 139–141, 145, 156, 157, 161, 169
Skillings brothers, 8
Skoldebrand (Algerine schooner), 76
slavery:
   in Barbary States, 4, 77, 83, 113, 125, 136
   and West African trade, 157

sloops of war, 6, 7
Smith, John, 112, 116, 117, 121, 139, 161
Smith, Robert, 176
Smyrna, Turkey, 249
Somers, Richard, 52, 114, 137, 145–146, 155, 156–159
Sonthonax (French governor), 59
South America, 52, 56, 231–236, 256
South Carolina, U.S.S., 51
South Pacific station, 256
Spain, 6, 27, 56, 58, 59, 66, 72–73, 100, 101, 103, 109–111, 166, 190
Spartan, H.M.S., 216
Spence, Midshipman, 151–152
Spencer (British merchant ship), 53
Spitfire (American merchant ship), 192
Sprogell, Sylvanus, 180
Stark, John, 20
State Department, United States, 45
Sterrett, Andrew, 93, 95–96
Stewart, Charles, 52, 113–114, 125, 126, 127, 134, 137, 139–140, 157, 161, 206, 236–245, 256
Stoddert, Benjamin, 32, 37–38, 56, 73
Strachan, Richard, Sir, 102
Stuart, George, Lord, 244
Suleiman Melli-Melli, 168
supernumeraries, 34
Supreme Court, United States, 57
Susan (British merchant ship), 240, 243
Sweden, 51
Syracuse, Italy, 116, 121–123, 125–126, 134, 137–138, 139, 160, 164, 168

Talbot, Silas, 19, 20, 21, 54–57, 60–73, 93
Talleyrand-Périgord, Charles Maurice de, 31
Tangier, Morocco, 104, 105, 106–107
Tenedos, H.M.S., 237
Texel, Holland, 194, 197
Thayer, Edmund, 8
Thorn, Jonathan, 126, 143
Thunderer, H.M.S., 48

Tiber, H.M.S., 240
Tingey, Commodore, 51
Tompline, Thomas, 155
Tonquin, the, 126–127
Toussaint L'Ouverture, Pierre Dominique, 58–60, 66
Townsend, Captain, 208
trade, 2–5, 31–32, 59–60, 75–76
    and British dominion of seas, 3, 30–31, 171, 176, 189–190, 203
    government restrictions on, 176, 177, 189
Transfer (Tripolitan brig), 130, 137–138
Trinidad, West Indies, 52
Tripoli, 4, 75, 77, 87, 93, 95–97, 104, 106, 111, 112–166, 248, 249
    American forces at, 141
    blockade proclamation for, 114–115
    Marine Corps landing in, 163
    as Mediterranean ruler, 148
    peace terms with, 164–166
Tripoli (Tripolitan polacre), 95–96
Trippe, John, 145, 189
Truxtun, Thomas, 21, 38, 51–52, 60, 161
Tunis, 4, 75, 78, 140–141, 163, 166–168
Turkey, 78–79, 82–84, 125, 249
Turner, Daniel, 256

United States:
    neutrality proclamations of, 3, 9, 28–29, 30–31
    War of 1812 declaration by, 204–205
    western frontiers of, 203
    world attitudes toward, 3–4, 112, 136, 150
United States, U.S.S., 10, 30, 32, 38, 50, 51, 52, 56, 60, 114, 176, 238
United States Navy, *see* Navy, United States

Van Buren, Martin, 252
Vengeance (French frigate), 161–162
    as American ship, 169
Vermont, 215
Vesta, H.M.S., 190

Virginia, U.S.S., 52
Virgin Islands, 51
Vixen, U.S.S., 106, 111, 112, 116, 117–119, 121, 124, 138, 139, 141, 156, 159, 161, 168, 169, 189
Volontaire (French frigate), 122

Wadsworth, Henry, 111–112, 155
Wallebogt Bay, 20
War Department, United States, 5, 17, 18, 32
War for Independence, *see* American Revolution
War of 1812, 29, 55, 88–92, 126, 175, 181, 203–245
 causes of, 203–204
 declaration of, 204–205
warships, *see* ships

Washington, D.C., 97, 202
Washington, George, 4, 19, 20, 29, 32, 33
Wasp, U.S.S., 247
Weehawken, N.J., 180
West Africa, slave trade of, 257
West Indies, 2, 3, 9, 47, 50–53, 56–74, 94, 122, 162, 237
whalers, 232
Whigs, 253
William (American merchant ship), 233
Williams, Jacob, 155
Windward Islands, 52
Wise, Henry, 256

yellow fever, 46
Yussuf Karamanli, 75, 153, 163–166
Yznardi, Josef, 110